The Death Penalty in the Caribbean

THE
DEATH PENALTY
IN THE
CARIBBEAN

Perspectives from the Police

Edited by
WENDELL C. WALLACE, PhD

Westphalia Press
An Imprint of the Policy Studies Organization
Washington, DC
2018

Westphalia Press
An imprint of Policy Studies Organization
1527 New Hampshire Ave., NW
Washington, D.C. 20036
info@ipsonet.org

ISBN-10: 1-63391-724-X
ISBN-13: 978-1-63391-724-8

Cover and interior design by Jeffrey Barnes
jbarnesbook.design

Daniel Gutierrez-Sandoval, Executive Director
PSO and Westphalia Press

Updated material and comments on this edition
can be found at the Westphalia Press website:
www.westphaliapress.org

"Poverty is no excuse for crime and self-deprivation but a surmountable hurdle in the journey to the top."
—Wendell C. Wallace

CONTENTS

FOREWORD

The death penalty for murder was abolished in Scotland, along with England and Wales, in 1965. It follows that the current generation of UK criminal trial judges, myself included, have no personal experience of a system in which death is either a mandatory or discretionary sentence for murder. I confess that, for my part, I am happy that that sentencing option is not available within the criminal justice system in which I work.

It is therefore of great interest to consider the perspectives contained in this book on the issue of the retention of the death penalty in English-speaking Caribbean jurisdictions. Judicial decision-making in the courts of the Caribbean and in the Privy Council has taken place in the context of national constitutions which do not prohibit the imposition of the death penalty for murder. In *Reyes v The Queen* [2002] 2 AC 235, which concerned the constitutionality of the mandatory death penalty in Belize, Lord Bingham of Cornhill observed: "The court has no licence to read its own predilections and moral values into the Constitution, but it is required to consider the substance of the fundamental right at issue and ensure contemporary protection of that right in the light of evolving standards of decency that mark the progress of a maturing society."

It is not difficult to discern a sub-text in this and other appellate court decisions that movement towards limits on the availability and imposition of the death penalty would be thought to be a desirable development. Yet the death penalty has not been abolished in any of the jurisdictions examined in this book, although it has become rare for it to be carried out. Conflicts of views as to its morality and, quite separately, its efficacy in discouraging serious crime, are not restricted to the judiciary.

The core element of this book discloses differences of view among the police leaders interviewed. Although most favour retention of the death penalty, not all do. Within the majority, there are a variety of reasons for advocating retention: these include the reduced likelihood of an erroneous execution, a need for deterrence, and a reflection of public opinion that it is the appropriate penalty for taking the life of another person.

The differences in the opinions expressed clearly demonstrate that the question "Should the death penalty for murder be retained?" is easier to ask than it is to answer. But the opinions of these respondents carry the weight of their experience: as such, this book is important reading for those involved in policymaking in any of the jurisdictions surveyed. It gives voice to a constituency whose views ought to be heard. Moreover, the book provides a valuable historical and comparative study of the death penalty in Caribbean jurisdictions, and an admirably clear discussion of the arguments for and against its abolition. All of the contributors deserve our thanks for a stimulating and comprehensive presentation of these difficult and controversial issues.

The Hon. Lord Tyre CBE
Judge of the Court of Session and the High Court of Justiciary, Scotland.

PREFACE

Caribbean police leaders perspectives on the death penalty provide an insight into the topic of the death penalty in the Caribbean as seen through the eyes of police practitioners who have decades of on-the-ground, experience-based knowledge in many aspects of policing. In fact, data for this book were obtained from personal interviews with eight police officer leaders throughout the Caribbean as well as a survey instrument aimed at gathering demographic antecedents. Crime, deterring crime, obstacles to effective policing, and crime prevention strategies are common issues facing the Anglophone Caribbean. However, debates surrounding the efficacy of the death penalty and its implementation and/or non-implementation are an inescapable feature of Caribbean jurisdictions.

The idea for the book was born out of three sources—my love for writing, my love for sharing knowledge, and the desire to use the insights gleaned from research to assist Caribbean policymakers with their decisions on retention/abolition of the death penalty, effective policing strategies as elucidated by local police leaders and to highlight challenges and barriers to effective policing in specific islands, but with the aim of highlighting collective Caribbean-wide problems. The idea for this product was furthered by discussions with numerous people who have continually impacted and refreshed by thought processes about policing in the Caribbean. I have benefitted from conversations with Sheridon "TM" Hill, Karen Lancaster-Ellis, Stephen Williams, Perry Stanislas, Collis Hazel, Andre Norton, and Anthony Rosales who all possess a great wealth of police experience and knowledge. Throughout this book, I have had unstinting support from my academic colleagues namely: Drs. Allan Patenaude, Christine Descartes, Keron King, Talia Esnard, and Katija Khan.

This genesis of this book was my stint at the Ministry of National Security as a part of the Trinidad and Tobago Police Service (TTPS). I was constantly bothered by the fact that in spite of the yeoman service rendered by police officers, they were hardly ever consulted or their views and opinions harnessed in a meaningful way. It was not until after I left my position in law enforcement in the Ministry of National Security in Trinidad and Tobago, and working in the private security field for a large state company, did I realize the critical value of understanding the "business" of policing and the true extent of how policing actually functioned. During my years in the private sector, I worked many long, arduous hours with a supervisor who ensured that security functions were reactive and that policing (private) was a facade to smooth over certain issues. Though frustrated, I set about gaining useful insights from these experiences, re-learning the art of policing and understanding the different cultural aspects of private policing that provided me with a somewhat unique perspective on policing, one which was key to the development and directing of several highly successful police-based training programmes.

The experiences mentioned supra also served to heighten my appreciation for police officers throughout the Caribbean and to raise my awareness regarding the extent of knowledge held by these capable, but oft much maligned, hardworking, conscious and selfless individuals. In the period after my brief stint with the private security industry and my eventual foray into academia, the underestimated role of the police came to the fore in a multiplicity of ways that are too numerous to mention in this forum. It is against this background that I sought the advice of police officers throughout the Caribbean in an effort to get insights into their views on the death penalty, crime prevention strategies, and barriers they confront in attempting to foster effective policing in the region. It was only then that I truly began to appreciate the depth of untapped knowledge held by police officers regarding the death penalty, barriers to and challenges faced in attempting effective policing in the Caribbean.

This book has three major objectives. The first objective is to give voice to the often voiceless police leaders in the Caribbean regarding their views on the death penalty. The second objective is to highlight the challenges and barriers to effective policing faced by these illustrious police officers in the region. And the third objective is to put forward the views of police leaders in the Caribbean regarding effective crime prevention strategies. All of the aforementioned studies were conducted on the premise of utilizing the worldview of the Caribbean-based police leaders to examine an important aspect of policing in the region. As a police officer colleague of mine stated to me during the brainstorming process of deciding the nature and scope of this book: "it is indeed refreshing to finally see that the voices of the voiceless police officers in the Caribbean are finally given light through a study using local police officers as proxies for this important study and importantly, conducted by a local researcher and not a tourist researcher on vacation."

This book is directed to students, government officials, policymakers, security professional, and individuals who are interested in the death penalty. Specifically for these readers, the book details the views of police leaders in the Caribbean on the socially bothersome topic of the death penalty as well as crime prevention strategies and barriers to effective policing in the region.

In conclusion, it was never my intention to research the stated topics and to publish this manuscript, however, due to my numerous observations on policing throughout the Caribbean as well as my research which indicated that police officers are hardly ever consulted and/or researched on the death penalty, I was literally forced, or maybe it was divine intervention that led me to author and to share this research with the world at large.

Dr. Wendell C. Wallace

ACKNOWLEDGMENTS

This book could not have been completed without the support and assistance of a number of individuals and agencies. First, I would like to recognize and thank the many hardworking, dedicated, loyal police professionals whose hard work, loyalty, dedication, and camaraderie over the past 20 years provided me with the critical support and knowledge necessary to design and author this book. My gratitude is extended to the Caribbean police leaders in the Anglophone Caribbean such as Clifford Chambers, Jason Forde, Michael Charles, Severin Moncherry, Trevor Modeste, Tyrone Griffith, Wendell Blanhum, and Wendel Robinson who gave unstintingly of their time, experiences, and knowledge and without them a major part of this book would not have been possible.

Second, I must extend my heartfelt gratitude to the authors of the book chapters who willingly accepted the challenge to become a part of this novel manuscript and who conducted their mandated tasks with aplomb and professional. Without this dedicated team of individuals, it would have been impossible to give voice to the views and opinions of the usually voiceless police officers. A special thank you is dedicated to Ainsworth Shakes, Atlee Rodney, Kelisha A. Francis, Karen Lancaster-Ellis, Kim Ramsay, Mellissa Ifill, Milissa Dupres, Portia Fraser, Steve Eugene Stewart, and Sheridon Hill.

Third, on a more personal note, I would like to recognize my family and close friends for their faith in my ability to complete this project and the support that they gave to make it happen. Especially to my parents Codrington and Ann Eastman-Wallace and my deceased grandparents Josey and Miriam Eastman, for starting me on the path that has brought me to this point, developing in me the determination to follow it, and providing me with the resources to do so; and to Maria Smith for encouraging me to take on this challenge, for enduring my frustrations and sharing my achievements as I worked to complete it, and for her wisdom and thoughtfulness throughout. Special thanks to my siblings Sandra, Roger (deceased but not forgotten), Dale, and Merville Wallace who assisted me in numerous ways and provided moral support throughout the duration of this project. I thank my uncles, aunts, children, nephews, nieces, cousins, and friends (Cecil, Ashton, Dariq, Elisha, Abigail, DeJuan, Malique, Janae, Toni-Lisa, Michelle, and Andy Wallace, Kurt, Brent, and Oswald Eastman, Onika and Asha Mars, Shaneika Joseph, Tyrelle Taylor, Tahj Adams, Antoinette Knights, Ayinka Nurse-Carrington, Michelle Nicholson, Brian Caesar, Cedric Neptune, Rachel D'Arceuil, Dr. Dianne Williams, Dr. Allan Patenaude, and Darlene Patenaude) for their unwavering support.

Fourth, I owe a debt of gratitude to the members of the Association of Caribbean Criminal Justice Practitioners (ACCJP) who gave suggestions and ideas on the formatting of the book. I also owe a huge debt of gratitude to the Hon. Lord Colin J. Tyre, Judge of the Court of Session and the High Court of Justiciary, Scotland, who invited me to his chambers in Edinburgh, Scotland when I was a mere student on vacation from my law studies at Northumbria University, Newcastle. Lord Tyre, thank you for authoring the foreword of this book. Finally, on behalf of the authors, thank you to Westphalia Press for accepting and publishing this book when others were hesitant to entertain the book idea.

Most of all, thank you God for the divine inspiration and strength which you gave to me to attempt and complete this book which hopefully would assist policymakers in the Caribbean to understand and appreciate the voices of our regional police leaders on the death penalty as well as the many underlying reasons for the continuous increase in crime and deviant activities in the region and to formulate policies for the alleviation of the problems. To every individual who assisted in the production of this book, even in the most miniscule manner, though your names may not be mentioned, thank you for your support and assistance.

Dr. Wendell C. Wallace

May 2018

CHAPTER I

The Importance of Caribbean Police Leaders' Perspectives on the Death Penalty

Wendell C. Wallace
The University of the West Indies, St. Augustine

"Research on policing should not be defined solely by academicians as police professionals can offer in-depth contextual and practitioner knowledge."

The death penalty is one of the most polarizing social issues under debate in the Caribbean today. However, most of the debates are undertaken either with little empirical evidence, devoid of the input of one of the major actors—the police, and/or, conducted generally by academicians. Nevertheless, police officers are the global society's frontline and the first line in the fight against crime. They have a close view of the deleterious effects of crime on a daily basis as well as have a personal stake in its reduction. Therefore, it is quite natural then to ask them: "What, in your opinion, works in the battle against crime?" However, as it relates to much crime control and intervention strategies, particularly the death penalty, police officers in the Anglophone Caribbean are hardly ever consulted on what in their view works best as tools of crime prevention.

The author argues that police officers should be researched with greater frequency on important policing matters such as the death penalty. This is premised on the notion that research on important aspects of policing should not be conducted solely by academic researchers to give voice to their perspectives, but that policing professionals with contextual understanding of crime, prevention strategies, and obstacles to policing, have much to offer and their voices should be heard on important discourses such as those which fall within the scope of this book. It is against this background that the author submits that research on policing should not be defined solely by academicians as policing professionals can offer much contextual and practitioner knowledge. Further, a strict academic pedagogical approach is insufficient and to measure and/or research critical policing issues with token input from police officers, particularly police leaders, would be to completely disregard the important work done by the police and to demean their knowledge base.

Due to the general increase in violent crimes across the Caribbean since the mid-1990s (Harriott, 2002), many residents, policymakers, local legislators, and affected family members have called for the implementation of the death penalty as the panacea to the burgeoning crime rates and to deter future criminal activities, more specifically, murder. These calls by residents and politicians alike are predicated on the notion that homicides and other serious crimes threaten the safety, sanctity, and moral fibre of Caribbean societies due to the increased brashness of criminals and the increasing heinous nature of murderous acts committed in the region.

These calls by regional politicians and residents are being made when globally the death penalty is seen as "cruel and inhumane punishment" (Amnesty International, 2012) and when more than three quarter of world governments have done away with it. In spite of this, calls for the implementation of the death penalty in the Caribbean are aplenty and are viewed as logical responses by some; however, the calls are also viewed as emotive responses to the crime situation by others. Instructively, these calls for the implementation of the death penalty as a crime control tool have divided the Caribbean populace as numerous scholars and researchers are diametrically opposed to its usage on wide-ranging grounds, while family members of victims are calling for the death penalty as a crime control tool. In sum, the end result is a barrage of positions both in favour of and against the use of the death penalty as a crime reduction tool in the Caribbean.

From a Caribbean perspective, there is a multiplicity of local and non-local literature on policing (Bowling, 2010; Deosaran, 2002; Harriott, 2002; Hill, 2012; Lancaster-Ellis, 2013; Mars, 2002; Stanislas, 2014, 2016; Wallace, 2013) and the death penalty (Burnham, 2005; Harrington, 2004; Hood & Seemungal, 2009; Hood, Seemungal, Mendes, & Fagan, 2009; Selwood & Fernandez, 2004; Tittemore, 2004). This literature encompasses social, criminological, and legal perspectives by academics, researchers, and lawyers; however, the views of police officers relating to the efficacy of the death penalty as a crime reduction strategy are hardly ever harnessed, measured in a meaningful way and simply do not seem to exist. This is surprising as, throughout the Caribbean, there are numerous senior and junior police officers with a wealth of experience and knowledge of local condition who retire from local police departments, often carrying with them a vast array of potentially helpful policing information as to "what works," "what doesn't work," and what are some promising initiatives in the context of reduction of serious crimes, especially murders.

This deafening silence from police leaders in the Anglophone Caribbean is either because they are not consulted on the issue of the workability of the death penalty as a tool of crime control or because they simply choose to remain silent, should be discontinued. The authors of this chapter argue that police officers in the Caribbean must now become an integral part of the discourse on crime and the efficacy of the death penalty as a crime reduction mechanism. With the aforementioned in mind, the current effort was conceptualized to garner the perspectives of police leaders in the Caribbean as it relates to the efficacy of the death penalty as a crime reduction tool as well as other crime prevention and reduction mechanisms.

Importantly, the contributors to this study are all scholars of either criminology and criminal justice or law and are therefore constrained to seek solutions and make judgments based on data and facts, not emotions, popular sentiments, gut feelings, superstition, or innate prejudices. The belief is that a wide cross-section of state actors must be consulted in the quest for solutions to crime and deviance in the region. We argue that this topic (crime and the death penalty) as well as the possible consequences for action or inaction, are too consequentially grave to entertain any form of academic inertia or partisan reporting.

With this in mind, the contributors to this chapter have sought to move away from facile analyses of the death penalty, which excluded police officers—who are often at the front and first line in the fight against crime. In so doing, police officers are now the focal point in this hermeneutic analysis on crime and the death penalty in the Caribbean. In sum, the chapter gives voice to the usually "voiceless police officers" who share their experiences and thoughts on the efficacy of the death penalty as a tool in the toolkit of criminal justice systems in the region.

BACKGROUND

Crime and violence are major developmental issues as well as a challenge for many Caribbean nations and policymakers across the region. The challenge of solving serious crime and violence including the high rate of murder has plagued Caribbean countries in recent times. This is evident as policymakers in the Caribbean continued to struggle to determine the nature, scope, and causes of the violence and to develop and implement an appropriate mixture of prevention, intervention, and suppression programmes. This is particularly poignant in relation to homicides and the usage of the death penalty as a form of sentencing for offenders convicted of murder in the Caribbean. While one study has shown that crime in the Caribbean is comparatively low and can be compared with industrialized countries such as Japan (UNDP, 2012), serious crime, especially murder, remains a critical issue for these countries. The nagging murder problem has reached epidemic proportions in many countries and is well documented for a myriad of reasons.

Instructively, the responses have been wide and varied including, but not limited to police reforms, hiring of foreign experts and police Chiefs, amendments to and passage of newer legislation, constant training, cross-country collaborations, creation of regional crime bodies (CARICOM Implementing Agency for Crime and Security (IMPACS) and the Regional Security System (RSS)) as well as the utilization of assistance from multilateral institutions and larger countries in the Western world.

In spite of these advances, serious crimes and murders remain a constant source of bother for Caribbean governments and police departments—and the death penalty, a contentious, touchy issue. The touch nature of the death penalty in the Caribbean is evident in the writing of Harrington (2004, p. 126) who points out, "the death penalty is a subject that, in the words of Justice Adrian Saunders of the Eastern Caribbean Court of Appeal, invariably elicits passionate comment." Continuing, Harrington (2004, p. 126) notes "Such comment is particularly so within the states that makes up the Commonwealth Caribbean, where rising rates of violent crime have led to strong public clamour for a swift and final response."

Indeed, the death penalty is the source of much controversy and numerous arguments abound in favour of, as well as against its implementation as contemporary Caribbean societies are grappling with increasing heinous crimes as well as seeking solutions to deal with them. The search for solutions is encapsulated by a statement emanating from the New York State Catholic Conference (1994) which surmised that "violent crime has reached unprecedented levels in our state and our nation. It tears at the social fabric and threatens the soul of our society. Many citizens of the

Caribbean are filled with fear, frustration, anger, and feelings of power-lessness. In the face of such emotion, many believe capital punishment to be an appropriate societal response."

The position of the New York State Catholic Conference (1994) is still relevant at the time of authoring the current effort as there have been con-tinuous, if not increased calls for the implementation of the death penalty as a crime reduction mechanism in the Caribbean. Further, throughout the Caribbean, there is popular support for the death penalty as a solution to the region's crime problem among politicians and the wider population (Amnesty International, 2012; Hood & Seemungal, 2006).

In fact, the increase in the number of murders and serious crimes in the region has bolstered renewed support for the death penalty across var-ious sectors of society in many countries (Carozza, 2003; Hood & See-mungal, 2011). Moreover, some countries have revisited the idea of fast tracking the implementation of the death penalty, considered abolishing appeals to international bodies, increasing the number of offences for which the death penalty can be applied and one country withdrew from the Inter-American Commission on Human Rights which preceded the execution of nine men over a 3-day period soon after. Politicians in var-ious countries openly expressed their support for the death penalty and one study in one country found the widespread support for capital pun-ishment in the Caribbean and the literature shows that there is popular support for the death penalty as a solution to crime in the region (Hood & Seemungal, 2011).

Throughout the English-speaking Caribbean, the mandatory death pen-alty remains the sole sentence for murder and a handful of other crimes. While the majority of countries in the Americas have either abolished or are taking steps to abolish capital punishment, the trend in the Caribbean is towards retention and efforts are being put to expedite the process to resume the death penalty. Notwithstanding the current reality, a number of decisions of the Inter-American Court on Human Rights and the Ju-dicial Committee of the Privy Council have failed to reduce the surge in serious crime in the Caribbean and have caused a range of governmental and law enforcement responses by officials in these countries.

Recent studies have shown that region's serious crime problem affects countries in different ways with murder being the challenging issue for a number of countries. While some countries have implemented various crime plans to deal with crime in general, there is a popular belief among politicians and the wider population in many Caribbean countries that the imposition of the death penalty is the panacea for solving the region's high rate of murder and serious crime despite the lack of supporting evidence.

RESEARCH CONTEXT—THE ANGLOPHONE CARIBBEAN

The Caribbean is comprised of a variety of countries (see Map 1) with differing social, economic, ethnic, and cultural identities. In spite of the differences, there are also many commonalities inclusive of, but not limited to crime, the criminal justice system, culture, history, and language. Some are small islands; however, there are also larger continent-bound states. Some of the countries are also independent island states; however, Guyana is located on the continental mainland close to the Caribbean Sea but has close cultural and historical ties with the Caribbean. Many of these countries have been independent nation states for over 40 years, some are still colonial dependents; some possess middle- to high-level incomes and some are the poorest states in the Western hemisphere. Others have extremely high rates of violent crime which position them among the highest in the world, while others are still generally idyllic with crime almost non-existent.

The Anglophone Caribbean refers to a set of English-speaking island states located in the Caribbean Sea consisting of the independent nations of Antigua and Barbuda ("Antigua"), the Commonwealth of the Bahamas ("Bahamas"), Barbados, Belize, the Commonwealth of Dominica ("Dominica"), Grenada, the Cooperative Republic of Guyana ("Guyana"), Jamaica, the Federation of St. Kitts and Nevis ("St. Kitts"), St. Lucia, St. Vincent and the Grenadines ("St. Vincent"), and the Republic of Trinidad and Tobago ("Trinidad and Tobago") (Fraser, 2006, p. 208). For the purpose of this study, the authors concentrated on Antigua and Barbuda, Barbados, Guyana, Jamaica, St. Lucia, St. Vincent and the Grenadines, and Trinidad and Tobago. The book is, therefore, a representation of the views from a wide range of member states of the regional Caribbean Community and Common Market (CARICOM).

Map 1: The Caribbean region

Source: https://en.wikipedia.org/wiki/Caribbean_Sea

POLICING IN THE ANGLOPHONE CARIBBEAN

Policing in the Anglophone Caribbean (hereafter the Caribbean) is generally modelled after a system which was developed in Great Britain, trialled in Northern Ireland and exported to regions where the British were once the colonial rulers (Palmer, 1988). Mawby (2003, p. 15–40) submits "the British eschewed the French approach of transposing their existing policing system, and created a new model appropriate for control of a subjugated population." This was developed from a model "first tried in another British colony, Ireland" (Palmer, 1988 as cited in Caribbean Human Development Report, 2012, p. 94; Mawby 2003, p. 15–40). This model (the British Colonial model of policing) presupposed a "lack of public consent and was used throughout British controlled Africa, Asia, and the Caribbean" (Mawby, 2003, p. 15–40). This type of policing is referred to as the British Colonial model or traditional policing. The criminal justice system (CJS) in the Caribbean is also generally modelled after that of Great Britain and still utilizes the adversarial Court model, the Jury System. The highly controversial death penalty that was adopted by most Anglophone Caribbean countries from their former colonial masters, Great Britain, still remains enshrined in their constitutions due to the "Savings Clause" (Birdsong, 2005; McDonald, 2015).

PREVIOUS RESEARCH ON THE DEATH PENALTY IN THE CARIBBEAN

The death penalty in the Caribbean has been widely discussed in the academic literature. These include Burnham (2005), Carozza (2003), and McKoy (2007b) on the unconstitutional nature of the death penalty, Frost (2014), McKoy (2007a, 2007b), García Ramírez (2010), Rediker (2013), and Tittemore (2004) on the mandatory death penalty, Carozza (2003) on the issue of capital punishment being cruel and unusual punishment, and Gifford (2009) and McKoy (2007a) on the Pratt and Morgan case and the effect of delays in the justice system in implementing the death penalty.

Burnham (2005) and García Ramírez (2010) also examined the controversial issue of the degrees in the commission of murder and the application of the death penalty in those circumstances, while the relationship between international law and domestic law on human rights issue of the death penalty in the Caribbean was researched by Amnesty International (2012), Carozza (2003), Helfer (2002), Mckoy (2007a, 2007b), and Tittemore (2004). Additionally, Burnham (2005), Helfer (2002), McKoy (2007), and Rediker (2013) all reviewed human rights and the right to life implications of the death penalty. Birdsong (2005) reviewed the effect of the savings clause in Caribbean constitutions on the application of the death penalty, and Eidson (2008), McKoy (2007a), and Rediker (2013) all examined the Caribbean Court of Justice and its potential role in carrying out the death penalty in light of the Privy Council's decision.

While some of the aforementioned studies were focused on the Caribbean in general, others have been country specific. As a result, the application of capital punishment in the Caribbean has been the subject of much scholarly review. For example, Gifford (2009) considered the death penalty across the English-speaking Caribbean, Antoine (2005), Birdsong (1999), and Broadbent (2004a, 2004b) looked at the death penalty in Barbados, while Frost (2014) looked at the death penalty in Barbados focusing on the decisions in Da Costa and Cadogan v Barbados. Carozza (2003) reviewed the death penalty in Belize; Gifford (2009) looked at the status of the death penalty in Jamaica, Concepcion (2000), Hood and Seemungal, (2006), Hood and Seemungal (2009), and Hood and Seemungal (2011) focused on the various aspects of the death penalty in Trinidad and Tobago and Berry and Robinson (2013) examined the death penalty in Jamaica.

Several of these studies have highlighted widespread support for the retention of the death penalty as a crime reduction tool in the Caribbean (Amnesty International, 2012; Hood & Seemungal, 2011; Rediker, 2013), while Amnesty International (2012), Greenberg and Agozino (2012), and Gifford (2009) found that the death penalty was not a useful deterrent to crime. Instructively, Greenberg and Agozino (2012) also found that there was no correlation between crime rates and the death penalty in the Caribbean (see Amnesty International, 2012 for support). In spite of the plethora of research on the death penalty in the Caribbean, the voices of police officers are silent in these discourses. In light of this, the researchers submit that this is a glaring omission in the literature that is addressed by the current effort.

THE STUDY

This study is premised on the notion that police officers; more-so, commissioned police officers (First Division officers) who are in the hierarchy of the Caribbean police organizations are policymakers for their organizations. These senior police officers also possess the potential to affect policymaking as they are often called upon by local legislators to assist in formulating policing policies for the wider populace. In spite of this, the views of these police leaders on crime reduction generally and specifically the efficacy of the death penalty in the Caribbean are hardly ever harnessed from an academic or non-personal perspective.

PURPOSE OF THE STUDY

This book has several purposes, including, but not limited to: (1) giving voice to the often voiceless police leaders in the Caribbean, on a topic that elicits passionate comments—the death penalty, (2) to provoke further discussion on the death penalty and to assist in the development of policies related to crime prevention and crime reduction using police officer views, (3) to accelerate meaningful discourse on the retention/abolition of the death penalty in the Caribbean, (4) to make a difference in the context of policing in the Caribbean, and (5) to act as the genesis of a collaborative approach to policing research between police officers and researchers so that there are improvements in service delivery to the Caribbean public.

METHODOLOGY

A mixed method approach (qualitative and quantitative) was utilized to achieve the study's goals. The study utilized structured interviews and standardized, self-administered questionnaires and the participants were garnered via the homogeneous purposive sampling method. A homogeneous purposive sample is one that is selected for having a shared characteristic or set of characteristics. Therefore, as the researchers were interested in understanding the significance of the death penalty to police leaders in the Caribbean, a sample of senior police officers was chosen. This is a homogeneous sample created on the basis of profession. Therefore, purposive sampling was selected to ensure that the "sample was tied to their objectives" (Palys, 2008, p. 697).

PARTICIPANTS AND PROCEDURES

At the time of conducting this research, the participants in the study were all senior police officers (police leaders) in their respective jurisdictions. Both the questionnaire and structured interview sheet were created by the researchers based on a previous model utilized by Dieter (1995). The questionnaire and structured interview sheet were sent to the researchers on the different islands with the same instructions as to the mode of conducting the research. This was done so as to ensure oneness of thought (Merrian & Huberman, 1984) in the research process. The researchers were instructed to select a senior police leader in their jurisdiction (either the police chief or someone who was in charge of a homicide unit or Criminal Investigations Department (CID) to administer the questionnaire and to conduct the interview with. The nature, aims, and objectives of the study were outlined, anonymity and confidentiality guaranteed, and consent received from the participants in writing before the instruments were administered.

A standardized questionnaire was utilized to gather data from the eight police leaders in the Caribbean. The questionnaire consisted of two sections. Section one gathered demographic data and section two collected data on the leader's views on the death penalty, crime prevention strategies, and challenges to effective policing in the region. The questionnaire contained a judicious mixture of open- and close-ended questions that were designed to elicit suggestions and recommendations for policing the Caribbean.

A structured interview sheet was also used to gather data from the police leaders, however, the respective researchers were asked to probe any areas that were not explicitly and/or sufficiently explained by the interviewees. The interviews sought to gather data on issues such as the police leader's careers, their personal policing philosophy on the death penalty, problems, and successes experienced, views on the criminal elements, the nature of the crime and general assessments of the criminal justice system in their respective jurisdictions. Importantly, the researchers were given some flexibility in their research approach; hence readers may observe structured approaches with minor divergences.

STRUCTURE OF THE BOOK

For the reader's benefit, the book is divided into 12 chapters, as well as my personal mantra which appears in every text that I author. The chapters in this book are arranged chronologically for easy reading. The book begins with the introductory chapter—"The Importance of Caribbean Police Leaders' Perspectives on the Death Penalty." This chapter sets the tone for the rest of the book as it presents an overview of the Caribbean, Caribbean policing, the methodology used during the conduct of the research and the rationale for the book. In chapter 2, Sheridon Hill and Kelisha A. Francis explicate on the history of the death penalty, while in chapter 3, Sheridon Hill presents an interesting and thought provoking piece titled "Untangling The Web: Rationalizing the Death Penalty Jurisprudence in the Caribbean." Chapter 4 is authored by Atlee P. Rodney and he expertly takes readers through his interview with the police leader in Antigua and Barbuda. This is followed by chapter 5 which examines policing in Barbados. This chapter is written by Kim Ramsey. The following chapter, chapter 6 is a brief, but well written piece by Portia Fraser as she interviews the police leader in her jurisdiction of Grenada.

Mellissa Ifill continues the discussion by succinctly placing the Co-operative Republic of Guyana into the discourse on police leaders and their views on the death penalty with her thought provoking interview of a police leader in that jurisdiction. The next piece, chapter 8, examines policing in Jamaica as written by Ainsworth Shakes, while chapter 9 takes readers on a journey to the beautiful island of St. Lucia as cogitated by Milissa Dupres-Roserie. Chapter 10 highlights the work of Steve E. Stewart as he explicates on policing by sharing the views of a police leader in St. Vincent and the Grenadines. Chapter 11 is expertly written by Karen Lancaster-Ellis on Trinidad and Tobago as she skilfully manoeuvers her way through the interview with demanding precision. Chapter 12 is a summary of the views of Caribbean police leaders on the death penalty, deterring crime, crime reduction strategies, and challenges faced in seeking to conduct effective policing in the region. Chapter 12 also reviews the material contained in the preceding chapters and offers finalized thoughts on the issues mentioned as viewed through the lens of Caribbean police leaders.

REFERENCES

Amnesty International. (2012). *Death penalty in the English-speaking Caribbean: A human rights issue.* United Kingdom: Amnesty International, International Secretariat.

Antoine, R. M. B. (2005). Waiting to exhale: Commonwealth Caribbean law and legal systems. *Nova Law Review, 29*(2), 141–169.

Berry, D., & Robinson, T. (Eds.). (2013). *Transitions in Caribbean law: Lawmaking constitutionalism and the confluence of national and international law.* Kingston, Jamaica: Ian Randle Publishers.

Birdsong, L. E. (1999). Is there a rush to the death penalty in the Caribbean: The Bahamas says no. *Temple International and Comparative Law Journal, 13*(2), 285–309.

Birdsong, L. E. (2005). The formation of the Caribbean court of justice: The sunset of British Colonial rule in the English speaking Caribbean. *The University of Miami Inter-American Law Review, 36,* 197–227.

Bowling, B. (2010). *Policing the Caribbean: Transnational security cooperation in practice.* Oxford: Oxford University Press.

Broadbent, G. (2004a). Trinidad and Tobago: Murder—constitutionality of constructive malice and mandatory death sentence, Khan v The State. *Journal of Criminal Law, 68*(4), 301–305.

Broadbent, G. (2004b). Barbados: Constitutionality of mandatory death penalty. *Journal of Criminal Law, 68*(6), 484–497.

Burnham, M. A. (2005). Indigenous constitutionalism and the death penalty: The case of the Commonwealth Caribbean. *I-CON, 3*(4), 582–616.

Carozza, P. G. (2003). My friend is a stranger: The death penalty and the global ius commune of human rights. *Texas Law Review, 81,* 1031–1089.

Concepcion, N. P. (2000). Legal implications of Trinidad & Tobago's withdrawal from the American convention on human rights. *American University International Law Review, 16*(3), 847–890.

Deosaran, R. (2002). Community policing in the Caribbean: Context, community and police capability. *Policing: An International Journal of Police Strategies & Management, 25*(1), 125–146.

Dieter, R. C. (1995). *On the front line: Law enforcement views on the death penalty.* United States of America: Death Penalty Information Center.

Eidson, W. (2008). The Caribbean court of justice: An institution whose time has come. *Chicago-Kent Journal of International and Comparative Law, 8,* 166–199.

Fraser, A. (2006). From forgotten through friction to the future: The evolving relationship of the Anglophone Caribbean and the Inter-American system of human rights. *Revista Instituto Interamericano de Derechos Humanos, 43,* 207–237.

Frost, S. (2014). DaCosta Cadogan v. Barbados. *Loyola of Los Angeles International and Comparative Law Review, 36*(1/6), 155–172.

García Ramírez, S. (2010). The Inter-American court of human rights and the death penalty. *Mexican Law Review, 3*(1), 99–127.

Gifford, A. (2009). Death penalty: Developments in Caribbean jurisprudence. *International Journal of Legal Information, 37*(2/7), 196–203.

Greenberg, D. F., & Agozino, B. (2012). Executions, imprisonment and crime in Trinidad and Tobago. *British Journal of Criminology, 52*(1), 113–140.

Harrington, J. (2004). The challenge to the mandatory death penalty in the Commonwealth Caribbean. *American Journal of International Law, 98*(1), 126–140.

Harriott, A. (2002). *Crime trends in the Caribbean and response.* Kingston, JA: The University of West Indies Press/UN Office of Drugs and Crime.

Helfer, L. R. (2002). Overlegalizing human rights: International relations theory and the Commonwealth Caribbean backlash against human rights regimes. *Columbia Law Review, 102,* 1832–1911.

Hill, S. M. (2012). Bridging the gap in data collection, research and analysis in crime control in the Caribbean. *United Against Crime, Association of Caribbean Commissioners of Police (ACCP), 9,* 41–43. Retrieved from https://issuu.com/accpolice/docs/eaccp_magazine.

Hood, R., & Seemungal, F. (2006). *A rare and arbitrary fate. Conviction for murder, the mandatory death penalty and the reality of homicide in Trinidad and Tobago.* A Statistical Study of Recorded Murders and Persons Indicted for Murder in 1998–2002.

Hood, R., & Seemungal, F. (2009). Experiences and perceptions of the mandatory death sentence for murder in Trinidad and Tobago: Judges, prosecutors and counsel. In R. Hood, F. Seemungal, D. Mendes and J. Fagan (Eds.), *A penalty without legitimacy: The mandatory death penalty in Trinidad and Tobago.* London: The Death Penalty Project, 1–30.

Hood, R., & Seemungal, F. (2011). Public opinion on the mandatory death penalty in Trinidad. A summary of the main findings of a survey. A report for the Death Penalty Project and the Rights Advocacy Project of the University of the West Indies Faculty of Law, 1–9.

Hood, R., Seemungal, F., Mendes, D., & Fagan, J. (2009). *A penalty without legitimacy. The mandatory death penalty in Trinidad and Tobago.* Papers Prepared for a Conference held in Port of Spain on March 7, 2009. Oxford: Holywell Press.

Lancaster-Ellis, K. (2013). Personal perspectives: Challenges for women in policing within the Caribbean. *Pakistan Journal of Criminology*, 5(1), 21–36.

Mars, J. R. (2002). *Deadly force, colonialism, and the rule of law: Police violence in Guyana*. Westport, CT: Greenwood Press.

Mawby, R. I. (2003). *Models of Policing*. In T. Newburn (Ed.), *Handbook of policing* (pp. 17–46). Cullompton: Willan.

McDonald, S. A. (2015). A true sense of independence: The abolishment of United Kingdom's influence towards the legal affairs of the Commonwealth Caribbean. *International Law Students Association Journal of International and Comparative Law*, 22(1), 133–154.

McKoy, D. V. (2007a). Identifying the Chi in Commonwealth Caribbean law: The contribution of the common law and human rights law to constitutional interpretation. Retrieved from https://ssrn.com/abstract=1021627.

McKoy, D. V. (2007b). Reshaping Commonwealth Caribbean jurisprudence: From Pratt and Morgan to Joseph and Boyce. Retrieved from https://ssrn.com/abstract=1021625.

Merrian, S. B., & Huberman, M. A. (1984). *Qualitative data analysis: Sourcebook of methods*. Beverly Hills: Sage Publications.

New York State Catholic Conference. (1994). Bishops statements—death is not the answer: A reaffirmation of opposition to capital punishment. Retrieved from http://legacy.bishopireton.org/faculty/GAVINW/HomepageGavin_files/Capital%20Punishment/NY%20Bishops%20--%20Death%20is%20Not%20the%20Answer.htm

Palmer, S. H. (1988). *Police and protest in England and Ireland*. Cambridge [Cambridgeshire]; New York: Cambridge University Press.

Palys, T. (2008). Purposive sampling. In L. M. Given (Ed.), *The sage encyclopedia of qualitative research methods*. (Vol. 2, pp. 697–698). Los Angeles: Sage.

Rediker, E. (2013). Courts of appeal and colonialism in the British Caribbean: A case for the Caribbean court of justice. *Michigan Journal of International Law*, 35(1/6), 213–251.

Selwood, D., & Fernandez, O. (2004). Capital punishment in the Caribbean. Evolving jurisprudence and the road to Abolition. Penal Reform International. Retrieved from http://www.abolition.fr/Upload/documents/selwoodfernandez.pdf

Stanislas, P. (2014). Transforming St. Lucian policing through recruit training in a context of high crime. In P. Stanislas (Ed.), *International perspectives on police education and training* (pp. 209–234). Abingdon: Routledge.

Stanislas, P. (2016). Challenges of late modernity, religion, homophobia and crime: Police and criminal justice reform in Jamaica and Uganda. In K. Sadique & P. Stanislas (Eds.), *Religion, faith and crime: Theories, identities and issues* (pp. 167–190). London: Palgrave Macmillan.

Tittemore, B. D. (2004). The mandatory death penalty in the Commonwealth Caribbean and the Inter-American human rights system: An evolution in the development and implementation of international human rights protections. *William & Mary Bill of Rights Journal, 13*(2), 445–520, Article 7.

UNDP Caribbean Human Development Report. (2012). *Human development and the shift to better citizen security.* United Nations. New York, NY, USA.

Wallace, W. C. (2013). *Community involved and planned policing (CIPP) model: An alternative to traditional policing in Trinidad and Tobago.* In M. de Guzman, A. M. Das & D. K. Das (Eds.), *The evolution of policing: Worldwide innovations and insights* (pp. 127–152). Boca Raton, FL: CRC Press/Taylor and Francis Group.

CHAPTER II

HISTORY OF THE DEATH PENALTY IN THE CARIBBEAN

Sheridon M. Hill and Kelisha A. Francis

The University of the West Indies, St. Augustine

INTRODUCTION

The functionalist perspective of crime argues that crime is an inevitable feature of every society (Durkheim, 2014). Too much crime leads to low order and control within society which is termed anomie, a state of normlessness (Durkheim, 2014). Therefore, in order to maintain a state of law and order, many crimes are punishable. Punishment ranges from the death penalty, imprisonment, paying fines and within recent times, community service. In this chapter, we explore the evolution of death penalty—one of the most controversial types of punishment for crimes, in the Commonwealth Caribbean.

The death penalty, which is also known as capital punishment, has been in existence from the genesis of time and has an arduous history which extends from the biblical era into contemporary times. The number of crimes that attract the death penalty, and, despite hanging being the sole method of execution in the Caribbean, there are many other methods of executions across the globe and numerous contradictions exist. However, as time elapsed, governments of varying countries have examined the harsh and cruel nature of the death penalty especially in light of a string of judicial decisions. In the case of the Caribbean, the judgments of the Judicial Committee of the Privy Council in the case of Pratt v Morgan (1993) UKPC 14 the Eastern Caribbean Court of Appeal in Spence and Hughes v The Queen, the Caribbean Court of Justice in AG and Others v Joseph Boyce and a couple of decisions by the various Appeal courts have severely restricted the applicability of the death penalty despite its popular appeal among politicians and the public at large in the region.

In a world that is geared towards protecting human rights and human life, many international organizations have joined together to abolish capital punishment. Additionally, the abolition of the death penalty is a prerequisite for membership into certain key multilateral institutions such as the European Union (Manners, 2002). In that regard, a number of countries including Australia and those in European continent, with the exception of Belarus, have abolished the death penalty. However, while these countries recognize human life as essential, many other countries retain this punishment. These countries are primarily located in Asian, African, and the American continents with the United States and the entire Commonwealth Caribbean among the most notable exceptions. In the case of the Commonwealth Caribbean, there is strong political support for the death penalty across the region from governments and wide cross-sections of society especially because of the high levels of murder and other types of serious crimes which do not appear to be decreasing.

However, over time a number of countries have abolished the death penalty beginning with San Marino in 1848 and more recently Suriname in the CARICOM Caribbean in 2015. There have been many changes to the form of execution over time based on the advocacy of international bodies such as Amnesty International, the Death Penalty Worldwide Project, Inter-American Commission on Human Rights (IACHR), United Nations (UN), and decisions from various bodies which restrict the applicability of the death penalty to a limited number of cases. However, despite this reality, Commonwealth Caribbean countries have retained the death penalty in the face assaults by the Judicial Committee of the Privy Council and a recent decision by the Caribbean Court of Justice. Against that background, this chapter focuses on the general history of the death penalty in the Caribbean region and discusses the following:

1. The origins of the death penalty.

2. The various methods of execution practised worldwide.

3. The offences which attract the death penalty and exemptions.

4. The retentionist approach of Caribbean countries.

5. The issues surrounding the death penalty in the Caribbean.

Official reliable data on executions in the Caribbean is difficult to access and this is a reflection of the data collection systems in developing countries in general and more specifically in the Caribbean region. Consequently, we use data from the Death Penalty Project Worldwide to abolish the death penalty which was accessed from its website regarding the last known executions in those countries and note that this data has been corroborated by several sources. In this chapter, Caribbean countries refer to the 15 full Member States of the CARICOM Community except for Montserrat. The chapter begins by briefly reviewing the origins of the death penalty in general. Next, we look at the various forms of execution followed an overview of the most popular offences which attract the death penalty around the world and in the Caribbean region. We then examine the countries that have abolished the death penalty, those that have retained it and some of the factors that have influenced Caribbean countries to retain the death penalty. We conclude with a brief overview of key issues surrounding the death penalty in the Caribbean.

THE ORIGINS OF THE DEATH PENALTY

In prehistoric societies there were no established laws for the death penalty, therefore many abided by the biblical law which states "an eye for an eye and a tooth for a tooth." However, the consequence of death occurred when persons committed crimes such as murder, rape, or treason and the methods varied. According to Galvin (2015), persons committing these reprehensible crimes were boiled to death and flayed until their skin was peeled off. It must be noted that imprisonment was not a common form of punishment. If a crime was committed and the death penalty was not prescribed for that crime, fines would be paid by offenders (Galvin, 2015).

The first death penalty law was established in 1772 B.C. under the Code of King Hammaurabi of Babylon, which codified the death penalty for 25 various crimes (Van de Mieroop, 2008). The Code of Hammaurabi mirrors Hebrew law (biblical law), which was highlighted in the foregoing paragraph. Galvin (2015) stated that various methods existed for different crimes committed. For example, burning would occur if mother and son indulged in incestuous relations; however, if one participated in adultery, impalement would be employed (Galvin, 2015).

If one takes a microscopic view of ancient Greek society it is noteworthy that their legal system was inaugurated over 2,600 years ago and the death penalty served as punishment for a plethora of crimes. Similarly, the Romans had an established legal system and practised capital punishment. According to Galvin (2015), one of their preferred methods of execution

was crucifixion. In medieval Europe, the death penalty was heavily practised. The Europeans thought that executing persons were cheaper than
imprisoning them (Banner, 2009).

The majority of the executions that occurred included many persons
from the lower class in society. Galvin (2015) argued that under the governance of King Henry VIII, ~70,000 persons were executed. Many of the
early methods of capital punishment were indeed cruel and harsh. Galvin
(2015) further argued that hanging in these times involved, hanging the
accused until unconscious. The accused would then be revived, and several parts of his body would be severed. The head would be the final body
part to be axed off, then chopped into pieces, and placed on public dis-
play. This was supposed to act as a deterrent also. Early methods of capital
punishment also included: crushing, falling (offenders were thrown from
a height), poisoning, strangulation, and asphyxia (Gatrell, 1996; Harding,
1996).

Even in this prehistoric epoch, there were those praising the "rightness"
of this type of punishment, as many opined that this was an appropriate
method of justice while minority groups argued the practise was barbar-
ic (Galvin, 2015). The death penalty originated as a form of justice and
to operate as a deterrent (Banner, 2009). However, there will always be
a debate on this phenomenon as societies will always be divided on its
continuance.

METHODS OF EXECUTION

Across the globe, there are many forms of execution from decapitation
or beheading to hanging—the sole method of execution in the Caribbean since its inception. However, none of these methods are deemed humane under international law. This section provides a brief examination
of these methods.

Decapitation or beheading—death by decapitation is a sentence associated
with Sharia law and carried out most conspicuously in Saudi Arabia, Iraq,
and Syria (Zech & Kelly, 2015). However, beheading with a sword or axe
has its place in history, as this was the preferred method in earlier times
(Hillman, 1993). This was employed as it was considered cheap, painless,
and a practical method (Berkowitz, 2006; Jones, 2005). Beheading was
widely used in Europe and Asia until the twentieth century but is still

practiced today in Islamic states such as Iraq, Iran, Syria, and Saudi Arabia (Bradley, 2015; Zech & Kelly, 2015). Beheadings are carried out for offences such as murder, rape, sodomy, drug trafficking, and other offences (Steiner, 2002). Whatever the conviction, the person is made to kneel before the executioner leaning forward with neck extended to receive a sword or an axe blade (Hillman, 1993). In some cases, the victim's head is placed on a chopping block making the executioner's duty easier.

Electrocution—the electric chair dates back to the 1880s when it was first used. This method of capital punishment was regarded as humane as opposed to hanging, which was the primary method of execution during this era. Dr. Alfred P. Southwick, a Dentist by profession was the mastermind behind this invention. He observed an intoxicated man shock himself to death and this appeared to be quick and painless. According to Bohm (2016) during this time, Alfred was selected as a committee member by the government to search for new methods of execution. Upon seeing the electrocution of the man, Southwick proposed the idea of the electric chair as he thought it would be painless (LeGraw & Grodin, 2002). He collaborated with one of the largest electric companies, and the chair was successfully created for execution (LeGraw & Grodin, 2002).

On June 4, 1888, the Electrical Execution Act was passed and contained a provision which stated that anyone sentenced to death after January 1, 1889 will be electrocuted instead of hanged. The first person electrocuted via this method was William Kemmler. He murdered his girlfriend and was sentenced to death via the chair at Auburn's Prison, New York. Kemmler lawyers argued that though this method was introduced as humane, it was indeed the opposite, inhumane, cruel, and harsh (Bohm, 2016). Eyewitnesses' report that Kemmler did not die immediately, and he had to be electrocuted multiple times (LeGraw & Grodin, 2002).

This process is very complicated in nature because prison officials work with much precision to ensure that there are no botched executions. The offender's body is shaved before being placed in the electric chair (Hillman, 1993). The offender is then buckled into this huge wooden chair, blindfolded, an electric cable is inserted on their shaved leg, a skull cap placed over their shaved head, and another cable is then connected to the cap (Hillman, 1993). An executioner controls a switch which sends electricity through the cables attached to electrocute the offender to death at various voltages (Denno, 2002). The United States remains the only country that continues to execute persons using the electric chair in the states of Alabama, Florida, South Carolina, Tennessee, and Virginia (Bedau, 1998).

Shooting by firing squad—the genesis of the firing squad, particularly in the United States, has its roots in Mormon belief (Gardner, 1979). The method reflects blood atonement that is a "murderer must have their blood shed in order to be forgiven by God for the heinous crime committed" (Gardner, 1979, p. 440).

This method of execution involves the prisoner to be seated on a chair which is placed between sandbags to prevent the bullets from ricocheting across the room (Denno, 2002). A target is placed over the prisoner's heart and shooters aim for this spot to ensure that the prisoner will die quickly. Five to 15 shooters (depending on the country) set up 20 feet from the chair with guns pointing through the wall aiming at their target. If the shots are successful the heart ruptures and the prisoner die from blood loss (Denno, 2002). In 2004, the state of Utah abandoned the use of firing squad and began execution by lethal injection, but this was short-lived as state officials reinstated the firing squad in March 2015 primarily because there were shortages of drugs available for execution by lethal injection (Toor, 2015).

Stoning—similar to beheading, stoning is mainly practised in Islamic States. Stoning is used to punish individuals who commit any crime that opposes Islamic law. Article 102 of the Islamic Penal Code of Iran states "the offender is buried and covered with soil (males up to their waists, females above their breasts" (Islamic Penal Code, 1991, p. 4). Sharia law specifies the size of stones to be used, to ensure that the execution does not occur too quickly or slowly. Article 104 of the Penal Code states "The stone shall not be so big as to kill the person by one or two strikes; neither shall it be so small that it cannot be called a stone" (Islamic Penal Code, 1991, p. 4). Some countries that practise stoning includes Afghanistan, Indonesia, Iraq, Iran, Nigeria, Pakistan, Saudi Arabia, Sudan, Somalia, United Arab Emirates and Yemen. It must be noted that some of these countries practise this unofficially while it is listed in the Penal Code for others.

Gas chamber—the gas chamber was primarily used in Nazi Germany where it was an apparatus for genocide during the Holocaust. However, before this period there were frequent experiments. In the United States, execution by gas chamber was introduced by the U.S. Army's Chemical Warfare Service during the First World War (Sloterdijk, 2009). Similar to the electric chair, the prisoner is strapped to a chair in a small chamber. The door of the chamber is sealed, and the gases are then released by an executioner who controls a lever which releases various gases (Rudolf, 2003). The gases primarily used in the chamber are hydrogen cyanide and carbon monoxide or carbon dioxide (Rudolf, 2003). Christianson (2010) argued that "during the period 1924 to 1999, the gas chamber claimed five hundred and ninety-four (594) lives, and was adopted by eleven (11) U.S. states until it was replaced by the lethal injection which was considered more humane" (Christianson, 2010, p. 2).

Lethal injection—the United States was the first country to use lethal injection as an execution in 1982 (Groner, 2002). It was considered cheaper and more humane than other forms of capital punishment such as hanging, electrocution, and the gas chamber (Denno, 2002). Although it was initially adopted by the state of Oklahoma, Texas was the first state to carry out an execution using this method, executing Charles Brooks Jr., in December 1982 (Denno, 2002). Lethal injection is the main method of execution in most states in the United States where capital punishment is practised (Bedau, 1998). Executions by lethal injection involve the administering of a cocktail containing a combination of three drugs in a specifically prescribed sequence and dosage. The three drugs are sodium thiopental, pancuronium bromide, and potassium chloride (Denno, 2007). Hillman (1993, p. 748) points out that "death results from anaesthetic overdose and respiratory and cardiac arrest while the condemned person is unconscious."

Hanging—hanging is one of the oldest yet most common forms of capital punishment. During the late seventeenth century, hanging was the most common form of execution in Europe (Scott, 2000). Up until the middle of the eighteenth century, all hangings were public because it was believed that this would act as a deterrent to criminal acts (Scott, 2000). Although public hangings were abolished, hangings continued behind prison walls and during the nineteenth century, there was much debate about abolishing the death penalty (Gatrell, 1996).

HANGING IN THE CARIBBEAN

Caribbean countries cannot deny their extensive and vivid history. They were invaded by European powers during the sixteenth century and were victims of colonialism and imperialism until their independence. Europe passionately fought for control over these islands because their soils were ideal for the production of crops, specifically sugar cane and cocoa. Slaves were brought to work on these plantations for the rapid production of these crops and for this reason this epoch is classified as the plantation economy. European ideals such as religion and laws plagued the region, thus justifying punishment and death for slaves. Though cruel and harsh, the colonial masters maintained that all punishments including capital punishment would preserve order in society (Brereton, 2013).

Although emancipation and independence occurred in the eighteenth and nineteenth centuries, many of these countries retained the Westminster system as they mimic the European system of development. According to Birdsong (2005), the mandatory death sentence was written into the constitution of each country as a part of their saving clause—a legal inheritance of the colonial power. Over time, the position in Barbados, Guyana, Trinidad and Tobago, Barbados, and Jamaica, the last few of the countries that retained the mandatory death penalty in their statutes, has changed following a string of judgments and changes in the statutes regarding the different categories of murder. In Barbados, Joseph and Boyce, Guyana passed the Criminal Offences (Amendment Act) No. 21 of 2010 abolishing mandatory death penalty and this was followed in the Bahamas which passed the Penal Code Amendment Act 2011 to make special provisions for murder in almost identical terms as Guyana, in the case of Trinidad and Tobago the decision in Nimrod Miguel v The State of Trinidad and Tobago (2011) UKPC 14 abolished mandatory death sentences and the Privy Council ruled that the death penalty is no longer mandatory.

OFFENCES WHICH ATTRACT THE DEATH SENTENCE

Drug trafficking and related offences (Asian countries): drug trafficking is one of the more recent offences for which the death penalty can be applied though in a limited number of countries around the world particularly in Asian countries most notably Singapore and the People's Republic of China. A 2012 study found that 33 countries had capital drug laws on the statute books. The list of countries include Bahrain, Bangladesh, Brunei Darussalam, Chad, Cuba, Egypt, Gaza OPT, Guyana, India, Indonesia, Iran, Iraq, Kuwait, Lao People's Democratic Republic, Libya, Malaysia, Myanmar, North Korea, Oman, Pakistan, Qatar, Saudi Arabia, Singapore, South Korea, South Sudan, Sri Lanka, Sudan, Syria, Taiwan, Thailand, United Arab Emirates, United States, Vietnam, and Yemen. The Corporate Republic of Guyana is the only Caribbean country that has the death penalty sentence for drug trafficking.

Military offence not resulting in death: in many countries death can be applied for breach of military offences such as desertion, assist the enemy in combat and assaulting or wilfully disobeying a superior. According to Hood and Hoyle (2015, p. 159) "at least 35 of the 39 of the retentionist countries retain the death penalty for offences against the military Code." Continuing, Hood and Hoyle (2015, p. 159) note that "Not only for killing civilians or captured enemy, but for mutiny desertion, insubordination, refusal to execute and order, abandoning a post, (especially a sentry) and cowardice in the face of an enemy." DRC, Egypt Equatorial Ethiopia, Guinea, Guatemala, India, and many other countries have numerous military-related offences for which the death penalty can be applied. The death penalty is still on the books for military offences in Barbados.

Murder/degrees and countries: in every country that retains the death penalty, regardless of their abolitionist or retentionist stance, murder—and its' various degrees depending on the jurisdiction—is commonly referred to as the most serious crime. This is reflected in the judgments of various regional and international courts as well as the treaties which permit the death penalty and those that promote abolition acknowledges that the death penalty specifically claim that it should only be carried out in the "most serious cases" or "the worst of the worst" as stated in the Privy Council. Even so, decisions of the Privy Council and Inter-American Court and Commission on Human Rights have expressly stated in cases where death results intentionally, the court must look at the circumstances under which the murder was committed (Article 4 of the American Convention, the Privy Council decision in The Queen v Spence and

Hughes affirming the Eastern Caribbean Court of Appeal decision in Spence and Hughes v The Queen).

Piracy: this is one of the lesser popular offences for which the death penalty is applied and has historic value. In few countries, the death penalty is applied to those convicted for the offence of piracy. Piracy remains on the statute books in a number of Caribbean countries and other countries around the world, including Botswana and Equatorial Guinea.

Spying/espionage: spying is one of the offences for which a person can face the death penalty in a number of countries in the Commonwealth Caribbean such as Barbados and other countries such as Egypt and Pakistan which practice Sharia law.

Terrorism: evidence suggests that a growing number of countries are using the death penalty to curb crime and terrorism. According to Amnesty International (2015, p. 3), "an alarming number of countries that used the death penalty in 2014 did so in response to the real or perceived threats to state security and public safety posed by terrorism, crime or internal instability." These countries were located in Asian and Europe and China and Pakistan feature prominently in Amnesty International's 2015 Report. However, Ethiopia and a number of other countries around the world including some Commonwealth Caribbean countries have the death penalty as the punishment for terrorism and related offences.

Treason: treason is punishable by death in a number of Caribbean countries. For example, Section 2 of the Treason Act, Chapter 11:03 of Trinidad and Tobago states:

> "A person owing allegiance to the state who, whether in Trinidad or elsewhere—
>
> a) Forms an intention to levy war against the State or to overthrow the government or the Constitution of Trinidad and Tobago by force and manifests such intention by any overt act,
>
> b) Adheres to the enemy of the State by giving them aid or comfort, is guilty of treason and is liable to suffer death by hanging."

Therefore, while acts of terrorism can be committed against any person or group of persons or against a country which the perpetrator is not a national of; an act of treason can only be committed must be against one's own country. Treason remains on the statute books of many countries including some in the Commonwealth Caribbean, such as Antigua and Barbuda, Barbados, Bahamas, Belize Dominica, Grenada, Guyana, St. Kitts and Nevis, St. Vincent and the Grenadines, and Trinidad and Tobago. Cosmoros, Cuba, Equatorial Guinea, Iraq, Nigeria, and Pakistan have a range of treason-related offences for which the death penalty can be imposed.

Offences resulting death: while the literature on the death penalty speaks of offences resulting in death, the reality is murder (and its varying degrees) is the main offence for which the death penalty is imposed around the world. For example, intentional death resulting from terrorism is murder, and any intentional death (in cases of homicide as opposed to suicide or pursuant to any statute) is still murder.

The most serious offences: while various regional and international instruments mandate that the death penalty only be applied to the most serious or the worst of the worst cases, many countries around the world, especially those in the Middle East and others that practice Sharia law apply the death penalty for a range of non-serious offence. In the Caribbean, many countries still carry the death penalty for a range of non-serious offences including treason, piracy, espionage, and military offences.

Other offences around the world: a number of countries, especially those in the Middle East and others that practice Sharia law, execute persons for a range of offences. These offences range from arson, abduction, apostasy, arms trafficking, and related offences, blasphemy, explosions, and acts that cause civil strife, economic crimes, castration, corruption and bribery, extortion, false accusation or testimony that leads to conviction and execution of an accused person, fornication by unmarried persons, adultery, extramarital and sexual relations among Muslim women and non-Muslim men. A complete list of most of the crimes that attract the death penalty and the countries that execute people for those crimes are listed in Table 2.1.

Table 2.1 *Other offences that attract the death penalty around the world*

Arson	PRC, Cosmoros, Guatemala, Guinea, Japan, Lebanon, Qatar, Saudi Arabia
Blasphemy	Iran, Pakistan, UAE
Explosions and acts to cause civil strife	Cosmoros, Guatemala, Japan
Economic crime	PRC, Cuba, Indonesia, Jordan, North Korea
Castration	Guinea
Causing: flood, buildings to collapse or causing death or other dangerous offences regardless of the offenders' intent	Guatemala, Guinea, Iraq, Japan, Pakistan, Somalia
Corruption/bribery	Cuba, PRC, Indonesia, Iran, Jordan, North Korea, Thailand, Vietnam
Extortion	Malaysia, Qatar
False accusation or testimony leading to conviction and execution of an accused	Oman, Sudan, Syria, UAE, United States, Yemen
Firearms trafficking and related offences	Malaysia
Fornication by unmarried persons, adultery, extramarital sexual relations among Muslim women and non-Muslim men, Sodomy (Sharia law)	Iran, Nigeria Qatar Saudi Arabia, Yemen (Sharia law)
Fraud	PRC, Iran, Cuba
Gang offences	PRC, Lebanon, Libya, Oman, Palestinian Authority, Sudan, Thailand
Economic crimes	PRC, Iran
Hijacking if suing a firearm	Cosmoros Indonesia, Pakistan
Hooliganism	Egypt, Libya, Palestinian Authority
Human trafficking, slavery, and sexual abuse	Kuwait, North Korea, Pakistan, Thailand
Kidnapping and related offences	PRC, Cosmoros, Equatorial Guinea, Guatemala, Guinea, India, Indonesia, Kuwait, Lebanon, Malaysia, North Korea, Pakistan, Qatar, Singapore, Taiwan, Thailand, Uganda, UAE, Yemen
Offences against the head of state and federal persons	Malaysia, Qatar
Poisoning	Cosmoros, Guinea
Rape (including gang rape) and sexual offences (some resulting death), relating to HIV/AIDs, prostitution	PRC, China, Egypt, Ethiopia, Iran, Iraq, Jordan, Kuwait, Lesotho, Nigeria, Pakistan, Qatar, Sudan, Thailand, Vietnam, Yemen
Rioting	PRC

Robbery not resulting death	PRC, DRC, Ethiopia, Equatorial Guinea, Indonesia, Iran, Lebanon, Libya, Malaysia, Nigeria, Qatar, Saudi Arabia, South Sudan, Sudan, Syria, Taiwan, Uganda, Vietnam, Yemen
Sabotage and impairment of social, economic, and military resources	PRC, Cosmoros, Cuba, Guinea, Lebanon
Sedition	Lebanon, Palestinian Authority
Superstition (and related crimes) heresy and witchcraft	DRC, Iran, Nigeria
Theft/larceny	North Korea
Torture	Kuwait, Qatar, Syria
Thuggery	Egypt
Use of explosive device	Guinea, UAE
War crimes	Ethiopia, India, Iraq, Zimbabwe

Source: Fieldwork (2018)

EXEMPTIONS FROM THE DEATH PENALTY

While most persons can suffer the death penalty for serious crimes in their respective countries, around the globe, various categories of persons are exempted from the death penalty. These categories include juveniles, elderly persons, mentally ill and mentally retarded persons, pregnant women, and women in general. However, these exemptions vary from country to country and among Commonwealth Caribbean countries—though to a very limited degree.

Juveniles: in many countries around the world, juveniles are exempted from the death penalty and this applies to every Commonwealth Caribbean country. However, there are unconfirmed sources which suggest scores of juveniles have been executed in countries around the globe particularly in Iran which practices Sharia law.

Elderly: similar to juveniles, persons who are beyond a certain age are not executed for various offences in many countries. However, countries that practice Sharia law do not exempt persons from execution based solely on age—the same way juveniles are executed in Iran and other similar countries. In the Commonwealth Caribbean, while elderly people are not exempted from execution in Dominica Grenada and Jamaica, based on

29

Article 4 of the American Convention, persons over 70 years shall not be executed. Therefore, following decisions in cases such as AG and Others and Joseph and Boyce, these international human rights obligations are binding on the member states.

Women/pregnant women: pregnant women are generally exempted from execution in most countries around the world. However, this simply means that women who are guilty of crimes which carry the death penalty will not be executed during their period of pregnancy but may be executed afterwards. However, it is interesting to note that in the Caribbean, Jamaica is the only country that does exempt pregnant women from execution.

Mentally ill: throughout the Commonwealth Caribbean, the Western Hemisphere and virtually every country in the world mentally ill persons are exempted from the death penalty. This exemption is based on the legal principle that mentally ill persons do not have control over their actions and crimes committed by such persons did not satisfy the legal threshold for the mens rea or mental state of mind required to complete the offence.

Mentally retarded/intellectual disability: the situation with mentally retarded persons is similar to mentally ill persons, however, there are variations in the law and as such, not all countries exempt mentally ill persons from the death penalty. Five Commonwealth Caribbean countries do not exempt this category of persons from the death penalty. These include Antigua, Guyana, Dominica, St. Kitts and St. Vincent and the Grenadines.

THE RETENTIONIST APPROACH OF CARIBBEAN COUNTRIES

Despite the mandatory death penalty for a variety of crimes on the statute books across the Caribbean, the death penalty is rarely implemented for a variety of reasons. The last execution was carried out on December 19, 2008, in St. Kitts and Nevis when Charles Elroy Laplace was hanged for the murder of his wife at 8.00 a.m. at the Her Majesty's State Prison in the national's capital Basseterre. On the other hand, Guyana has abstained from executions longer than any other Caribbean country since its last execution was carried 38 years ago in 1977 when Michael Archer and Peter Adams were hanged for murder in Georgetown. Following Guyana, the last time persons were hanged in the various territories were: Grenada (1978),

Barbados (1984), Belize (1985), Dominica (1986), Jamaica (1988), Antigua and Barbuda (1991), St. Lucia, and St Vincent and the Grenadines (1995), Trinidad and Tobago (1999), and the Bahamas (2000).

The largest number of persons to be executed at the same time occurred in Trinidad and Tobago when Nankisson Boodram also known as "Dole Chadee" and his eight accomplices were hanged in Port of Spain, over a 3 day period in June 1999 for the murder of the Baboolal family. Shortly afterwards Anthony Briggs was hanged in July 1999. However, the last hanging before Chadee and his gang occurred in 1994 when Glen Ashby was hanged under controversial circumstances 10 minutes before his lawyers received official notification from the Privy Council granting a stay of execution (Hassanali, 2011). Table 2.2 provides the details of the last known executions across the CARICOM Caribbean.

However, despite the lack of executions in the Caribbean, countries are considered retentionist based on a variety of factors. To begin with, most Caribbean governments are committed to resuming hangings (Amnesty International, 2012; Tittemore, 2004), they routinely convict people for murder, expressly stated that they strongly support the death penalty, have taken steps to resume hangings, and some have introduced new legislation that carries the death penalty. Amnesty International (2013) reports that persons continue to be sentenced to death across the Caribbean and by December 31, 2011, there were 31 persons on death row across the Caribbean.

In the not too distant past, six persons were sentenced to hanging in Trinidad and Tobago following their convictions for murder. In fact, persons continue to be sentenced to death across the region. From a purely political perspective, many Caribbean countries are determined to execute persons for serious crimes because they feel it will deter crime, appease the public, and demonstrate the political will to do something about crime. Amnesty International (2012) cites statements by senior politicians in St. Vincent and the Grenadines and St. Lucia that strongly support the death penalty.

Additionally, a number of Caribbean governments have taken steps to reverse the decisions of the Privy Council and some have not ratified the various Inter-American and United Nations human rights instruments. On the contrary, their actions are quite the opposite with Trinidad and

Tobago leading the way following its withdrawal and hanging of Glen Ashby (Tittemore, 2004). Jamaica and Guyana followed this trend.

Further actions taken by these Caribbean countries also include: (1) The Jamaican Charter of Fundamental Rights and Freedoms adopted in April 2011 contains provisions that appear intended to reverse the decisions of the 1993 landmark Privy Council case of Pratt and Morgan v Attorney General of Jamaica; (2) Countries vote against the UN General Assembly Resolutions entitled moratorium on the use of the death penalty; (3) Trinidad and Tobago, Guyana, and Jamaica have withdrawn from the Optional Protocol to the International Covenant on Civil and Political Rights (ICCPR) which allows individuals to exhaust all domestic appeals to appeal to the United Nations Human Rights Committee (Sellwood & Fernandez, 2004; Tittemore, 2004); (4) the governments of Trinidad and Tobago and Jamaica expressed desire to increase the number of sentences and executions (Amnesty International, 2012); and (5) actions by the government of Belize to amend its constitution to preclude constitutional challenges to the death penalty (Sellwood & Fernandez, 2004).

Table 2.2 *Last executions in the English-speaking Caribbean*

Country	Names of person/s	Dates of execution	Brief facts	Method and location of execution
Antigua and Barbuda	Tyrone Jordan	February 21, 1991	Murder	Hanged
Barbados	Noel Jordan Melville Inniss and Errol Farrell	November 10, 1984	Murder	Hanged
Bahamas	David Mitchell	January 1, 2000	Murders of two German tourists	Hanged
Belize	Kent Bowers	June 1985	Murder of Robert Codd	Hanged at Hattieville Prison
Dominica	Frederick Newton	August 8, 1986	Murder of a police constable during an attack on police headquarters in November 1981 aimed at releasing prisoners	Hanged

Grenada	Charles Ferguson	October 17, 1978	Murder	Hanged
Guyana	Michael Archer and Peter Adams	August 1977	Murder	Hanged
Jamaica	Nathan Foster and Standford Dinnal	February 12, 1988	Murder	Hanged
St. Kitts and Nevis	Charles Elroy Laplace	December 19, 2008	Murder of his wife	Hanged at 8.00 a.m. inside the state Prison Basseterre
St. Lucia	Joseph Solomon Vitalis	October 17, 1995	Murder	hanged in the prison
St. Vincent and the Grenadines	1. Douglas Hamlet 2. Franklin Thomas and 3. David Collins	February 13, 1995	Murder	Hanged
Trinidad and Tobago	Group 1. Dole Chadee Joey Ramiah and Ramkalawan Singh	June 4, 1999	Murder of a couple and their two children in 1994	Hanged at Port of Spain State Prison
	Group 2. Singh Ramsingh Russell Sankerali and Bhagwandeen Singh	June 5, 1999	Same as above	Same as above
	Group 3. Clive Thomas Robin Gopaul and Steven Eversley Anthony Briggs and Wenesclaus James	June 7, 1999	Same as above	Same as above
		July 28, 1999	Murder of taxi driver Siewdath Rankisoon on August 1992	Same as above Same as above

Source: Capital Punishment in the British Commonwealth
http://www.capitalpunishmentuk.org/common.html

ISSUES SURROUNDING THE DEATH PENALTY IN THE CARIBBEAN

When examining the death penalty in the Caribbean, there are several themes that continuously recur on this contentious issue. These include high crime rates, high murder rates, public opinion, and political support for the death penalty in the Caribbean. These issues are critically explored in this section.

High Crime Rates

One of the main reasons for the popular support of the death penalty in the Caribbean is the high level serious crime—especially murder—and the belief in the death penalty as an effective solution to the problem (Amnesty International 2012; Hood & Seemungal, 2006). High levels of serious crime and violence are a challenge in the Caribbean and in recent times, there has been a sharp rise in murders which have become more heinous and daring. The negative impact of the crime problem on these small, fragile, and vulnerable economies, many of which rely on tourism, is deep and wide (UNDP, 2012). Scholars agree on the acute vulnerability of the region based on its location between the drug producing countries in Latin America and the consuming countries in North America and Europe (Griffith, 2010; Klein, 2001; UNDP, 2012; UNODC, 2013). Against that background, a brief overview of the crime situation assists in underscoring the seriousness of the situation.

In the 2000s, Antigua and Barbuda, Bahamas, Belize, Dominica, Jamaica, St. Lucia, St. Kitts and Nevis, and Trinidad and Tobago saw record numbers of murders (Hill, 2013). One study found the region to be one of the most crime prone and violent regions in the world (Maertens & Anstey, 2007). Some of them include the murder of a British couple who were on vacation in Antigua and Barbuda, a daring robbery and murder of six people in Barbados, a grenade attack in Belmopan, Belize, consistent record number of murders in Bahamas, Trinidad and Tobago, the Lusignan and Bartica massacres in Guyana in 2007, murder rates of 1950s and 1960s in Jamaica, a surge in gang-related killings in St. Kitts and Nevis causing it to surpass Jamaica's murder rate and placing it among the top countries in the world and a prison escape and attack on a Magistrate in the Prime Minister's office are a few notable examples across the region.

High Murder Rates

Though one study found the Caribbean had a low level of crime in general, which is comparable to industrialized countries such as Japan (UNDP, 2012), murders and serious crime, in particular, remain a huge challenge for many Caribbean countries with some countries recording murder rates in excess of 30 per 100,000. Additionally, studies have shown that in recent times, the murder rates of many Caribbean countries have shown an upward trend, however, there has been a reversal in some countries (Jamaica, in particular) and some countries have remained fairly stable, though the rates are still considerably much higher than world standards.

From 2000 to 2009 the number of murders soared in the Caribbean with Jamaica, St. Kitts and Nevis, Belize, Antigua and Barbuda, Dominica, and St. Lucia registering record numbers of murders. A major study by the United Nations Office on Drugs and Crime (UNODC) and the World Bank found the Caribbean had the highest murder rate among several regions in the world at 30 murders per 100,000 people (Maertens & Anstey, 2007 as cited in Hill and Morris, 2017) and a later study found the Caribbean had the fourth highest murder rate behind central America (UNODC, 2011). Other studies have shown that the capitals in some of these countries have astronomically high murder rates: Belize (Gayle et al., 2010), Port of Spain (Maguire, Willis, Snipes, & Gantley et al., 2008), and Kingston (Gayle et al., 2010; Morris & Graycar, 2011).

Amid the growing body of research on crime rates in the Caribbean, two studies show that murders in the Caribbean rose from ~15 per 100,000 people in 2000 to 25 in 2009 (Hill, 2013; Seepersad, 2013). Hill (2013) found that Antigua and Barbuda, The Bahamas, Belize, Dominica, Jamaica, Trinidad and Tobago all reported record numbers of murders in this period. In Antigua and Barbuda, murders rose from 2 in 2000 to 19 in 2007. In the Bahamas, murders rose from 43 in 2001 to 94 in 2010. In Belize, murders rose from 47 in 2000 to 137 in 2010. In tranquil Dominica, murders rose from 2 in 2000 to 13 in 2009 and murders in Jamaica rose from 887 in 2000 to 1682 in 2009 (Hill, 2013). In Trinidad and Tobago, murders rose from 120 in 2000 to 547 in 2008. It was noted that murders in the Bahamas continue to rise with 149 in 2015.

Criminal Gangs

A number of studies have shown that gang violence is the most significant factor in the region's high level of murder (Hill, 2013; Katz, Maguire, & Choate, 2011; Maertens & Anstey, 2007; Maguire et al., 2008; UNDP, 2012; UNODC, 2010; UNODC, 2013). Hill (2013) found that the countries with the highest murder rates also had the highest percentage of gang-related murders (Jamaica, Belize, St. Kitts and Nevis, and Trinidad and Tobago) underscoring the point that criminal gangs are the main cause of the region's high level of murder. Katz et al. (2011) found gangs in the Caribbean were more violent than gangs in the United States, and some countries have passed anti-gang legislation to address the problem (Hill, 2013; Katz & Maguire, 2015). One study mapped the increase in violence in Trinidad to the location of major gangs (Maguire et al., 2008) and another highlighted the growing influence and impact of females in criminal gang activity (Wallace, 2013).

THE DETERRENT EFFECT OF THE DEATH PENALTY

It is noteworthy that while the Caribbean countries generally have a high level of violent crime including murders, the level varies across the region on murders and the various categories of violent crimes so the deterrent argument does not appear compelling. For example, Hill (2013) placed the countries in the region in four tiers based on the murder rates and Seepersad (2013) similarly found various categories of violent crimes based on the total number and rates of various categories of serious crimes including shootings and woundings, serious assaults, robberies, and sex crimes. Therefore, the deterrent effect of the death penalty appears to have varying effects on these countries because they each have laws containing the death penalty.

Moreover, if we take a global perspective on the deterrent effect of the death penalty some of the countries and regions in the world that have the lowest murder rate have abolished the death penalty. For example, the United Nations Office on Drugs and Crime Global Homicide Report (UNODC, 2013, p. 21) found that Europe (5.2%) and Oceania (0.3%) accounted for the lowest percentage of homicides by region. Interestingly, except Belarus, all European countries have abolished the death penalty. On the other hand, Guatemala, the lone country in Latin America that retained the death penalty has consistently been among the countries with the highest murder rates in the world. Using the death penalty as a deterrent to violent crime is a circuitous argument. For example, China and the United States are with murder rates that are below the global average but retain the death penalty, while El Salvador, Honduras, South Africa, and Venezuela have all abolished the death while these countries regularly feature among the top 10 countries in the world with the highest murder rates.

PUBLIC OPINION ON THE DEATH PENALTY

As stated previously, the death penalty has been a controversial topic over the years (McKoy, 2007). Although controversial in the Caribbean as there are many groups advocating for its abolishment (Amnesty International, Inter-American Court on Human Rights, and United Nations), retention of the death penalty has amassed significant public support. Public support stems from the rise in criminal activities throughout the various Caribbean countries and increasing crime and murder rates have created the perception that the death penalty would counteract these occurrences. Therefore, popular public opinion is retributive in nature because it perceives that justice will be served through this punishment and will act as a deterrent to serious crimes. However, despite wide public support for capital punishment, the view must balance the fact that the major cross-section of the public lacks the appropriate knowledge on the underpinnings of the death penalty (Amnesty International, 2012). It is crystal clear that the majority of support in the English-speaking Caribbean neglects keys factors such as the costs associated with the death penalty, the backlog of cases in the judicial systems, offenders' innocence, and its cruel and harsh nature. These will be discussed in order to give some insight into the details of the death penalty.

Costs

The prevailing public opinion is that it is cheaper to execute a prisoner instead of him serving a life sentence (Ellsworth & Gross, 1994; Harris, 1986). In Trinidad and Tobago, it is often echoed amongst many "hang dem, why must taxpayers' money feed dem in prison." This paints a picture of lack of knowledge about the overall cost of the death penalty. Death is the only sentence that is irrevocable, therefore capital cases are more time consuming and complex, therefore, the genesis of cost occurs before trial as lawyers and prosecutors must conduct thorough investigations "to prove aggravating circumstances in order to seek the death penalty" (Tabak & Lane, 1989, p. 133). Additionally, costs are also incurred when expert advice is requested. For example, psychiatrist, psychologists, and other social scientist expertise are needed to determine the mental health of offenders in these cases (Tabak & Lane, 1989).

Several studies have found that costs associated with executions are very high (Alacorn & Mitchell, 2011, 2012; Hance, Kay, Larson, & Lewis et al., 2013; McFarland, 2016; Roman, 2013). In the United States, the state of California spends billions of dollars to execute prisoners (Alacorn & Mitchell, 2011, 2012). Hance et al. (2013) presented findings revealed by Alacorn and Mitchell (2011) and one of the principal findings of the study was that over the last 30 years it cost ~US$308 million per execution. They also discovered that it cost $184 million more to execute prisoners compared to maintaining prisoners serving a life sentence.

In a recent research conducted by McFarland (2016), it was found that the cost of execution is higher. It is estimated that an additional $1 million (US) is spent on execution in most states as opposed to prisoners incarcerated. Roman (2013) argued that "total lifetime cost to Maryland taxpayers of murder cases where the death penalty is sought is US$186 million" (Roman, 2013, para. 7). If these are the costs incurred by developed countries, then it is logical to assume that costs will be high for developing countries. Additionally, in light of the economic downturn and accompanying scarcity of foreign exchange, it may be more prudent to utilize the limited resources on more important concerns than to execute individuals on death row.

Backlog of Cases

The Caribbean region struggles with a backlog of cases and the general public support of the death penalty perceives swift execution following conviction. However, this is not the case as the Privy Council decision in Pratt and Morgan underscored. Lack of resources in the English-speaking Caribbean countries is one of the main reasons for the backlog present in the judicial system and contributes to delays in execution. In 2016, Justice Vivienne Harris stated the lack of resources contributing to the backlog of cases in the Jamaican judicial system (Jamaican Observer, 2016).

Although there has been an increase in the crime rate in this country, the judge noted that "there are currently 35 judges in the Supreme Court and 7 in the Court of Appeal and these figures have remained fixed since Jamaica gained independence" (Jamaican Observer, 2016). Similarly, commenting on the backlog of cases in Barbados, the Chief Justice of Barbados, Sir Marston Gibson, stated that there were 2,100 civil cases filed in the High Court and there is a further 23,000 filed in the Magistrate Court (Barbados Today, 2013). Therefore, the backlog of cases cripples the judicial system as cases are pending since the early 1990s. Trinidad and Tobago is no different from these countries because of the lack of resources in its justice system. Lack of criminal defence attorneys and limited courts in the country are factors that continue to plague its justice system (Sant, Achong, & Wilson, 2016).

The backlog of cases in the judicial system contributes to the delays in implementing death sentences, and the process may take 5 or more years due to the inefficiencies in the court systems. In this regard, it must be critically noted that 5 or more years on death row is generally considered harsh and inhumane. One of the most important judgments of this era that depicts this argument is the decision in the Pratt and Morgan case. In this case, the Privy Council ruled that there was an unreasonable delay between the date of the death sentence and proposed date of execution as prisoners were held for over 5 years on death row and this was considered inhumane, degrading, and unconstitutional (Gifford, 2009). An offender on death row whose case is continuously delayed causes psychological distress because of the uncertainty of execution and it results in additional cost to taxpayers and the State (DeathPenalty.info.org).

Innocence

Research has found that the public is usually not concerned about offenders' innocence (Bobo & Johnson, 2004; Ellsworth & Gross, 1994). This should be a significant concern as the death penalty is irrevocable and there is the possibility of an innocent person being executed (Byron CJ and Saunders in Spence and Hughes v The Queen). Although there is no evidence that suggests that an innocent person has been executed in the Caribbean, there is evidence internationally that shows innocent persons were placed on death row. According to O'Malley (1999), Timothy Evans, an innocent person was executed in Britain and this was a driving force to abolish the death penalty in the UK. O'Malley (1999, p. 2) further stated that "in 1975, the government of Florida pardoned two African-American men, Freddie Lee Pitts and Wilbert Lee, who were twice tried and sentenced to death. They had spent 12 years waiting on death row for crimes committed by someone else."

Over the years there has been the rapid development of technology in the judicial system across the globe. The use of deoxyribonucleic acid (DNA) evidence in cases has proved on multiple occasions that innocent persons are often convicted of crimes (Baumgartner, De Boef, & Boydstun,

2008). DNA provides 99% reliability in many cases and over 300 persons were exonerated in the state of California alone after DNA testing was done (Hance et al., 2013). Due to the lack of DNA evidence in the ESC, the likelihood of executing the wrong person is higher.

Cruel, Harsh, and Unjust

Under international law, countries retain the right to impose the death penalty and this is catered for in the various treaties, convention, and protocols. These include the American Convention on Human Rights and the International Covenant on Civil and Political Rights which applies to all ESCs. Although all nations have not ended the use of this harsh sentence, it is the hope of the International Covenant on Civil and Political Rights (ICCPR) that all countries will ratify the Second Optional Protocol which requires all nations to abolish the death penalty. This sentiment was expressed by Tittemore (2004) regarding the American Convention on Human Rights. Additionally, Amnesty International is also adamant about ending this practise. The death penalty violates basic human rights such as the right to live and the right to live free from torture (UN General Assembly, 1948). Therefore, the Convention views execution as a breach of an individual's right to life, none of the methods used in capital cases are justifiable because all are torturous and can be deemed cruel and harsh.

Amnesty International notes that none of the methods used in these cases are painless. Often, botched executions occur, which causes more pain to the individual before they die. The general public is oblivious to these circumstances surrounding the death penalty in the Caribbean, but whole heartedly condemn Sharia law practised in Islamic states. However, according to Gifford (2009), there is no difference if the death penalty is constantly pursued as a solution for crime and criminal activities in the ESC.

Political Support

Government debates in the ESC to resume hangings and governments rages on and they regularly cite public support for the resumption of hanging because they believe this punishment should be imposed on those who commit the most serious offences. Politicians in these countries rarely examine the root causes of crime and believe in the retributive style of the death penalty as the panacea for decreasing crime rates in the Caribbean (Amnesty International, 2012; Hood & Seemungal, 2011).

It seems that politicians in the Caribbean change their views on the death penalty when they move from government to opposition. An example of this is the then Attorney General of Trinidad and Tobago who admitted that he was against the death penalty for many years until he became the Attorney General and "saw the law from a different side" (Hassanali, 2011). However, in 2011, then elected People's Partnership attempted to resume hangings but the opposition (People's National Movement) neglected to support the Bill proposed. In the case of Jamaica, the attempt to abolish appeals to the Privy Council, which was struck down as unconstitutional, was partly in response to the UK-based appeals court's judgment in death penalty cases and St. Vincent and the Grenadines Prime Minister, Dr. Ralph Gonsalves has publicly declared his government's support for the death penalty (Amnesty International, 2012).

The death penalty remains the law in the ESC countries that were colonialized by the British. However, the existing death penalty laws in the region were the same laws in Britain over 50 years ago which the British have amended thereby abolishing the death penalty since 1965 (Block & Hosteller, 1997). Although many changes have occurred in their judicial system, we in the Caribbean continue to grapple with these ancient retributive practices in the hope that they would bring about the desired changes in our societies.

Politicians in the ESC are passionate about citing public support and deterrence for the resumption of executions in the Caribbean (Amnesty International, 2012). However, there is an inadequate amount of studies throughout the region critically examining public support for the death penalty (Amnesty International, 2012). Although there is immense public support, this must be taken against the background of low public awareness of the adverse implications of various aspects of the death penalty. "The countries of the ESC have singularly failed to show political leadership in terms of drawing attention to the human rights issue inherent to any discussion of the death penalty" (Amnesty International, 2012, p. 30)

CONCLUSION

The death penalty continues to be a controversial issue in the Caribbean. Although it was the popular practice in many societies, times have changed and so has many of these countries' position on the death penalty. In this regard, it does not appear that the progress we have made is reflected in our laws. There is no denying that the death penalty is law in Caribbean countries, however, as we continue to evolve we must abandon the retributive approach and embrace a more restorative view of justice. Although many Caribbean countries lay claims to belief in and moving towards, restorative justice, our continuous embrace of the death penalty appears quite contradictory. Such a shift would never materialize if we fail to amend the existing constitutional laws and abolish this practice outright as Sir Fred Phillips has argued (Phillips, 2009). Therefore, governments and policymakers should be fearless to start the process of abolition in the Caribbean.

Additionally, it seems trivial for governments to continually cite public support and deterrence for retaining this cruel punishment. The public is ill-informed about the circuitous nature of the deterrent effect of the death penalty at both the regional and international levels. In the face of the vacuum of knowledge, there should be increased efforts to disseminate information on the issues surrounding the death penalty in the Caribbean. This would act as a catalyst to generate a different discourse between the State and the public about the fate of capital punishment in the Caribbean. After all, the region needs to complete the process that was set in motion by Lord Griffiths judgment in *Pratt and Morgan* and continued in a slew of judgments from the Organization of Eastern Caribbean States (OECS) countries in Spence and Hughes v The Queen and followed by the CCJ in AG and Others and Joseph and Boyce, and abolish the death penalty.

REFERENCES

Alacorn, A. L., & Mitchell, P. M. (2011). Executing the will of the voters?: A roadmap to mend or end the California legislature's multi-billion dollar death penalty debacle. *Loyola of Los Angeles Law Review, 44*(S41), 41–224.

Alacorn, A. L., & Mitchell, P. M. (2012). Costs of capital punishment in California: Will voters choose reform this November?. *Loyola of Los Angeles Law Review, 46*(S1), 1–36.

Amnesty International. (2012). *Death penalty in the English-speaking Caribbean: A human rights issue.* United Kingdom: Amnesty International, International Secretariat.

Amnesty International. (2013). *Death sentences and executions in 2012.* London, UK: Amnesty International Secretariat.

Amnesty International (2015). Death sentences and executions 2014. Amnesty International Ltd. London, United Kingdom.

Banner, S. (2009). *The death penalty: An American history.* Harvard University Press. London, United Kingdom.

Barbados Today. (2013, June 20). CJ worried about backlog of cases. Retrieved from https://dev.barbadostoday.bb/?p=64779.

Baumgartner, F. R., De Boef, S. L., & Boydstun, A. E. (2008). *The decline of the death penalty and the discovery of innocence.* New York: Cambridge University Press.

Bedau, H. A. (Ed.). (1998). *The death penalty in America: Current controversies.* New York: Oxford University Press.

Berkowitz, B. A. (2006). *Execution and invention: Death penalty discourse in early rabbinic and Christian cultures.* New York: Oxford University Press.

Birdsong, L. E. (2005). The formation of the Caribbean court of justice: The sunset of British Colonial rule in the English speaking Caribbean. *The University of Miami Inter-American Law Review, 36*(2/3), 197–227.

Block, B. P., & Hostettler, J. (1997). *Hanging in the balance: A history of the abolition of capital punishment in Britain.* Winchester: Waterside Press.

Bobo, L. D., & Johnson, D. (2004). A taste for punishment: Black and white Americans' views on the death penalty and the war on drugs. *Du Bois Review: Social Science Research on Race, 1*(1), 151–180.

Bohm, R. M. (2016). *Deathquest: An introduction to the theory and practice of capital punishment in the United States.* New York, NY: Taylor & Francis.

Bradley, J. R. (2015). *Saudi Arabia exposed: Inside a kingdom in crisis.* Hampshire, England: St. Martin's Griffin Press.

Brereton, B. (2013). The historical background to the culture of violence in Trinidad Tobago. *Caribbean Review of Gender Studies, 4*, 1–16.

Christianson, S. (2010). *The last gasp: The rise and fall of the American gas chamber.* Berkeley and Los Angeles: University of California Press.

Denno, D. W. (2002). When legislatures delegate death: The troubling paradox behind state uses of electrocution and lethal injection and what it says about us. *Ohio State Law Journal, 63*(1), 1–41

Denno, D. W. (2007). The lethal injection quandary: How medicine has dismantled the death penalty. *Fordham Law Review, 76*(1/3), 49–128.

Durkheim, E. (2014). *The rules of sociological method: And selected texts on sociology and its method* (Revised ed.). New York, NY: Simon and Schuster.

Ellsworth, P. C., & Gross, S. R. (1994). Hardening of the attitudes: Americans' views on the death penalty. *Journal of Social Issues, 50*(2), 19–52.

Galvin, A. (2015). *Old Sparky: The electric chair and the history of the death penalty.* Delaware, USA: Skyhorse Publishing, Inc.

Gardner, M. R. (1979). Illicit legislative motivation as a sufficient condition for unconstitutionality under the establishment clause-A case for consideration: The Utah firing squad. *Washington University Law Review, 1979*(2), 435–499.

Gatrell, V. A. C. (1996). *The hanging tree: Execution and the English people 1770–1868.* New York: Oxford University Press.

Gayle, H., Mortis, N., Vasquez, J., Mossiah, R. J., Hewlett, M., & Amaya, A. (2010). *Male social participation and violence in urban Belize: An examination of their experience with goals, guns, gangs, gender, god, and governance.* Belize City: Ministry of Education.

Gifford, A. (2009). The death penalty: Developments in Caribbean jurisprudence. *International Journal of Legal Information, 37*(2/7), 196–203.

Griffith, I. L. (2010). *Drugs and security in the Caribbean: Sovereignty under siege.* University Park, PA: Penn State Press.

Groner, J. I. (2002). Lethal injection: A stain on the face of medicine. *British Medical Journal, 325*, 1026–1028.

Hance, B. S., Kay, K. D., Larson, J., & Lewis, V. (2013). Death of the death penalty? An examination of California's capital punishment system. *Journal of Legal Issues and Cases in Business, 2,* 1–10.

Harding, R. M. (1996). The gallows to the gurney: Analyzing the (Un) constitutionality of the methods of execution. *Boston University Public Interest Law Journal, 6,* 153–178.

Harris, P. W. (1986). Over-simplification and error in public opinion surveys on capital punishment. *Justice Quarterly, 3*(4), 429–455.

Hassanali, S. (2011). Amnesty international takes T&T government to task. *Trinidad Guardian Newspaper.* Retrieved from http://www.guardian.co.tt/news/2011/02/20/amnesty-international-takes-tt-govt-task.

Hill, S. (2013). The rise of gang violence in the Caribbean. In R. Seepersad & A. M. Bissessar (Eds.), *Gangs in the Caribbean* (pp. 36–79). London: Cambridge Scholars Publishing.

Hill, S. M., & Morris, P. K. (2017). *Drug trafficking and gang violence in the Caribbean.* In M. Raymond Izarali (Ed.), *Crime, violence and security in the Caribbean* (pp. 52–57). New York and London: Routledge.

Hillman, H. (1993). The possible pain experienced during execution by different methods. *Perception, 22*(6), 745–753.

Hood, R., & Hoyle, C. (2015). *The death penalty: A worldwide perspective.* Oxford: OUP.

Hood, R. G., & Seemungal, F. (2006). *A rare and arbitrary fate: Conviction for the murder, the mandatory death penalty and the reality of homicide in Trinidad and Tobago.* Centre for Criminology, University of Oxford, UK.

Hood, R., & Seemungal, F. (2011). Public opinion on the mandatory death penalty in Trinidad. A summary of the main findings of a survey. A report for the Death Penalty Project and the Rights Advocacy Project of the University of the West Indies Faculty of Law, 1–9.

Islamic Penal Code of Iran. (1991). Retrieved from http://mehr.org/Islamic_Penal_Code_of_Iran.pdf.

Jamaican Observer. (2016). A plea for the Justice system. (October 19, 2016). Retrieved from http://www.jamaicaobserver.com/.

Jones, R. H. (2005). *Terrorist beheadings: Cultural and strategic implications*. Carlisle, PA: Strategic Studies Institute, U.S. Army War College.

Katz, C. M., Maguire, E., & Choate, D. (2011). A cross-national comparison of gangs in the United States and Trinidad and Tobago. *International Criminal Justice Review, 21*(3), 243–262.

Klein, A. (2001). Between the death penalty and decriminalization: New directions for drug control in the Commonwealth Caribbean. *New West Indian Guide, 75*(3–4), 193–227.

Katz, C. M. and Maguire, E. R. (2015). Diagnosing Gang Violence in the Caribbean. In A. Harriott and C. M. Katz (Eds.) Gangs in the Caribbean: Responses of State and Society (pp. 175-211). Kingston, Jamaica: University of the West Indies Press.

LeGraw, J. M., & Grodin, M. A. (2002). Health professionals and lethal injection execution in the United States. *Human Rights Quarterly, 24*(2), 382–423.

Maertens, F. & Anstey, C. (2007). Crime, violence, and development: Trends, costs, and policy options in the Caribbean. *United Nations Office on Drugs and Crime Latin America and the Caribbean region of the World Bank. United Nations: UN Latin America and the Caribbean Regional Office.*

Maguire, E. R., Willis, J. A., Snipes, J., & Gantley, M. (2008). Spatial concentrations of violence in Trinidad and Tobago. *Caribbean Journal of Criminology and Public Safety, 13*(1–2), 44–83.

Manners, I. (2002). Normative power Europe: A contradiction in terms?. *Journal of Common Market Studies, 40*(2), 235–258.

McFarland, T. (2016). The death penalty vs. life incarceration: A financial analysis. *Susquehanna University Political Review, 7*(4), 46–87.

Morris, P., & Graycar, A. (2011). Homicide through different lens. *British Journal of Criminology, 53*, 823–838.

O'Malley, B. S. (1999). The Gospel of life vs. The death penalty. Pastoral letter on capital punishment. *Origins-Washington, 28,* 717–719.

Phillips, F. (2009). *The death penalty and human rights.* Kingston, Jamaica: Ian Randle Publishers.

Roman, J. K. (2013). *Costs of the death penalty.* Testimony to the Judiciary Committee, Delaware Senate, March 20, 2013.

Rudolf, G. (2003). *The Rudolf Report. Expert report on chemical and technical aspects of the 'Gas Chambers' of Auschwitz.* Chicago, Illinois: Theses & Dissertations Press, Imprint of Castle Hill Publishers.

Sant, R., Achong, D., & Wilson, S. (2016, September 15). Slow pace of justice haunts legal system. *Trinidad Guardian.* Retrieved from http://www.guardian.co.tt/news/2016-09-15/slow-pace-justice-haunts-legal-system.

Scott, J. (2000). *England's troubles: Seventeenth-century English political instability in European context.* Cambridge, United Kingdom: Cambridge University Press.

Seepersad, R. (2013). Crime in the Caribbean. In R. Seepersad & A. M. Bissessar (Eds.), Gangs in the Caribbean (pp. 2–35). London: Cambridge Scholars Publishing.

Sellwood, D., & Fernandez, O. (2004). Capital punishment in the Caribbean: Evolving jurisprudence and the road to Abolition. Retrieved from http://www.abolition.fr./Upload/documents/Sellwood.Fernandez.pdf.

Sloterdijk, P. (2009). Airquakes [in]. *Environment and Planning D: Society and Space, 27*(1), 41–57.

Steiner, S. (2002). Sharia law. *The Guardian Newspaper.* Retrieved from https://www.guardian.co.uk/theissues/article/0,6512,777972,00.html.

Tabak, R. J., & Lane, J. M. (1989). Execution of injustice: A cost and lack-of-benefit analysis of the death penalty. *Loyola Los Angeles Law Review, 23,* 59–146.

Tittemore, B. D. (2004). Mandatory death penalty in the common-wealth Caribbean and the Inter-American human rights system: An evolution in the development and implementation of international human rights protections. *William & Mary Bill of Rights Journal*, 13(2/7), 445–520.

Toor, A. (2015, March 24). Utah reinstates death by firing squad Governor signs bill amid nationwide shortage of lethal injection drugs. *The Verge*. Retrieved from https://www.theverge.com/2015/3/24/8282275/utah-firing-squad-lethal-injection-death-penalty.

UNDP. (2012). *Caribbean human development report. Human Development and the Shift to Better Citizen Security*. New York, NY: United Nations Development Programme.

UN General Assembly. (1948). *Universal declaration of human rights*. UN General Assembly. http://www.un.org/en/universal-declaration-human-rights/.

UNODC. (2010). *Global homicide report 2010*. New York: United Nations Office on Drugs and Crime.

UNODC. (2013). *Global homicide report 2013*. New York: United Nations Office on Drugs and Crime.

Van de Mieroop, M. (2008). *King Hammurabi of Babylon: A biography*. Malden, MA, USA: John Wiley & Sons.

Wallace, W. C. (2013). *Girls and gangs in Trinidad: An exploratory study*. In R. Seepersad & A. M. Bissessar (Eds.), *Gangs in the Caribbean* (pp. 195–219). London: Cambridge Scholars Publishing.

Zech, S., & Kelly, Z. (2015). Off with their heads: The Islamic State and civilian beheadings. *Journal of Terrorism Research*, 6(2), 83–93.

CHAPTER III

Untangling the Web: Rationalizing the Death Penalty Jurisprudence in the Caribbean

Sheridon M. Hill
The University of the West Indies, St. Augustine

Abstract

In the recent past, the mandatory death penalty was the
sole sentence for murder and a handful of other crimes
in the English-speaking Caribbean. However, in recent
times, decisions of the Privy Council, Caribbean Court
of Justice, Eastern Caribbean Court of Appeal, and Inter-American Human Rights System have rendered the
death penalty a discretionary sentence throughout these
countries. Beginning with the decision in Pratt and Morgan v Attorney General of Jamaica [1994] 2 AC 1, the
Privy Council has handed down a number of judgments
which severely restricted the application of the death
penalty in the Caribbean. This trend has been followed
in the region in decisions of the Eastern Caribbean
Court of Appeal in Spence and Hughes and the Queen,
Criminal Appeal 20 of 1998 and 14 of 1997 at the Caribbean Court of Justice in AG and Others v Joseph
and Boyce [2006] CCJ 3 and in a number of advisory
opinions of the Inter-American Commission on Human
Rights and judgments of the Inter-American Court on
Human Rights. However, some decisions have differed
from earlier decisions and appear confusing based on
conflicting judgments and the right to retain the death
penalty in the constitutions, the Inter-American Human
Rights System and the International Covenant on Civil
and Political Rights (ICCPR). This chapter attempts to
rationalize the decisions of the various courts and bodies and establishes a trend in these decisions that stops
short of the outright abolition of the death penalty in
these countries.

Keywords: Death penalty, Jurisprudence, English-speaking Caribbean

"In this region, it hardly can be challenged that the question of the death penalty remains the most heavily contested human rights issue in the courts" (McKoy, 2007b, p. 11).

"Over the last two decades, new and challenging questions have been posed for determination by the courts. Judges, obliged to follow their consciences and their present understanding of the law, have been handing down decisions that underscore the view that they do not share a consistent approach to this area of the law. Nowhere is this more amply illustrated than in the judgments of our highest court, the Judicial Committee of the Privy Council. Important decisions on crucial issues of life or death are departed from or expressly reversed, with an unsettling frequency" [para. 175] (Saunders JA in Spence and Hughes v The Queen [2001] Criminal Appeal 20 of 1998 and 14 of 1997).

INTRODUCTION

Since Pratt and Morgan v Attorney General of Jamaica (1993) *UKPC*, the Judicial Committee of the Privy Council (JCPC) and other Appeal Courts in the English-speaking Caribbean have delivered several landmark and, at times, conflicting judgments on the death penalty. As noted Caribbean legal scholar Vasciannie (2008, p. 839) lamented, "Significantly, in some of these cases the Privy Council expressly departed from some of its earlier precedents and set aside decisions of the Jamaican Court of Appeal based on those precedents. Generally, this has given an uncertain texture to death penalty law in Jamaica, and indeed, in the wider Caribbean."

First, the decision in Pratt and Morgan in 1993 restricted the length of time condemned persons should stay on death row before their execution to 5 years. However, some aspects of this and other judgments of other appeal courts have appeared to extend the 5 years limitation. Later on, decisions of the Eastern Caribbean Court of Appeal (ECCA) in Spence and Hughes v The Queen Criminal Appeal 20 of 1998 and 14 of 1997 (Spence and Hughes) and the Caribbean Court of Justice (CCJ) in Attorney General of Barbados and Others v Joseph and Boyce (2006) CCJ 3, (Joseph and Boyce) both applied principles of international law in municipal law that appear contrary to the universally established principles of application. Then in a very strange series of events, the Privy Council's decisions in R v Reyes [2002] 2 WLR UKPC 11(Reyes), R v Hughes 2 WLR [2002] UKPC 12 (Hughes), and R v Fox 2 WLR [2002] UKPC 13 (Fox) ruled the mandatory death penalty unconstitutional, and shortly thereafter in an about turn, the London-based court overruled those earlier decisions by declaring that the death penalty was, in fact, lawful in the cases of Lennox Ricardo Boyce v The Queen [2004] 3 WLR 786 (hereafter Boyce), Charles Matthew v The State of Trinidad and Tobago [2004] 3 W.L.R. 812 (hereafter Matthew), and Lambert Watson v The Queen [2004] 3 W.L.R. (hereafter Watson).

These and other decisions have made the law on the death penalty appear as guess work underscoring the statement by Justice Saunders of the Caribbean Court of Justice while sitting in the ECCA in *Spence and Hughes*, which is quoted above. Additionally, the apparent uncertainty of the relationship between the recently established CCJ and the Privy Council, the two final appellate courts of the region, and the relevance of their judgments on each other, contribute to this dilemma. Against that background, this chapter seeks to clarify these issues.

This chapter begins with a review of the literature on the death penalty in the Caribbean. A brief background of the death penalty in the region and an overview of the death penalty laws and categories of persons who are exempted from the sentence are provided. Key decisions of the ECCA, the CCJ, and the Privy Council are then reviewed. This is followed by the Caribbean's role in the international human rights systems and the influence of international law. The chapter concludes by noting that despite the varying decisions of the appellate courts of the Caribbean, there is a consistent trend that has significantly eroded the death penalty beginning with *Pratt and Morgan* that stops short of the outright abolition of the death penalty in the English-speaking Caribbean.

SETTING THE SCENE: THE CARIBBEAN

The Caribbean region is a mix of English, Dutch, French, and Spanish speaking countries. While many of these countries are independent states, some are United Kingdom, United States, Dutch, and French Overseas Territories and Dependents. The countries vary in size, population, economic development (Hill & Morris, 2017), and several other factors including the fact that some countries are single islands; some are multiple island-states while others are land locked. The variation in the region is also reflected in the definitions of the Caribbean. For example, the Organization of Eastern Caribbean States (OECS), the Association of Caribbean States (ACS), the Caribbean Community (CARICOM), the Commonwealth, and English-speaking Caribbean (ESC) are among the more popular definitions. The literature is replete with scholarly works on the death penalty in the Commonwealth Caribbean (Amnesty International, 2012; Burnham, 2005a; Cross, 2014; Helfer, 2003; Novak, 2014; Tittemore, 2004). In this chapter, the Caribbean refers to the independent Commonwealth Caribbean countries of Antigua and Barbuda, Barbados, Bahamas, Belize, Dominica, Grenada, Guyana, Jamaica, St. Kitts and Nevis, St. Lucia, St. Vincent and the Grenadines, and Trinidad and Tobago.

The Caribbean is one of the most unique regions in the world (Maertens & Anstey, 2007) owing to its diversity and this includes the legal systems and Appeal courts. The two non-English-speaking CARICOM countries, Suriname (Dutch) and Haiti (French) have separate legal systems with Suriname adopting a Roman Civil Law system while Haiti has adopted a Napoleonic Civil Law Code. All other Commonwealth Caribbean countries have Common Law systems inherited from their former British colonial masters. The smaller OECS countries have a single Appeal Court while the larger countries of Barbados, the Bahamas, Belize, Guyana, Jamaica, and Trinidad and Tobago each has its own national Appeal Court. In that regard, it is noteworthy that prior to its membership in the CCJ, the Guyana Court of Appeal was the country's highest appellate court following the passage of the Judicial Committee of the Privy Council (Termination Act) 1970. The CCJ is currently the final appeal court for Barbados, Belize, Dominica, and Guyana while the Privy Council is the final appeals court for the remaining countries.

Since the early 1990s, the Caribbean has witnessed high levels of crime and violence and epidemic levels of murders. Several studies have attributed these phenomena to the drug trade (Griffith, 1997; Griffith & Munroe, 1997; Maertens & Anstey, 2007), rising gang violence (Hill, 2013; Katz, Maguire, & Choate, 2011; Maguire, Willis, Snipes, & Gantley, 2008) and easy access to illegal firearms and ammunition (Griffith, 1997; Maertens and Anstey, 2007; Montoute & Anyanwu, 2009). Moreover, the region's governments and law enforcement agencies seem helpless in responding to the wave of violence and this has led to the belief that application of the death penalty is the panacea for the region's crime and violence problems (Amnesty International, 2012).

As pressure continues to mount from Amnesty International and other abolitionist groups on Caribbean countries to abolish the death penalty, public and political support for the death penalty remains high (Amnesty International, 2012; Burnham, 2005a; Campbell, 2015; Helfer, 2002; Hood & Seemungal, 2006). In fact, the increase in the number of murders and serious crimes in the region has bolstered renewed support for the death penalty across various sectors of society in many countries (Burnham, 2005a; Campbell, 2015; Carozza, 2003; Hood & Seemungal, 2011). Moreover, some countries have revisited the idea of fast tracking the implementation of the death penalty (Helfer, 2002; Tittemore, 2004); Guyana, Trinidad and Tobago, and Jamaica considered abolishing appeals to international bodies (Helfer, 2002), Guyana increased the number of offences for which the death penalty can be applied (Klein, 2001) and Trinidad and Tobago withdrew from the Inter-American Commission on Human Rights shortly before execution of nine men over a 3-day period (Concepcion, 2000; Helfer, 2002; Tittemore, 2004).

The Caribbean's position on the death penalty is not unique as global experts note that "overwhelmingly, public opinion supports the death penalty, which is of importance because, many mesmerized by such polls, are reluctant to challenge them to undertake an authoritative evaluation" (Hodgkinson, Gyllentsen, & Peel, 2010, p. 11). Further, despite strong positions on both sides of the debate, the issue is not as clear as some may feel as a noted human rights scholar has noted, "It is often said that international law does not prohibit capital punishment. This is an unfortunate and imprecise statement, however, because several international treaties now outlaw the death penalty" (Schabas, 2003, p. 1).

THE LAW ON THE DEATH PENALTY

Death penalty laws in the Caribbean.

The death penalty remains fixed by law as the primary sentence for the crime of murder throughout the English-speaking Caribbean. However, the mandatory death sentence was struck down by the Eastern Caribbean Court of Appeal in *Spence and Hughes v The Queen* and was later affirmed by the Privy Council. In later decisions in cases from Belize, The Bahamas, Jamaica, and Trinidad and Tobago, the Privy Council also found the mandatory death sentence unconstitutional. The death sentence can be applied for various offences including drug-trafficking, espionage, genocide, military offences, terrorism, treason, and war crimes, while hanging is the sole method of execution.

While piracy and hijacking are mentioned in Guyana, in the Bahamas and Trinidad and Tobago, these offences were not found in their respective legislation. Additionally, while there is no general trend towards increasing the number of offences which can attract the death penalty, Guyana is the only country that carries the death penalty for drug offences. Table 3.1 contains the statutory provisions of the English-speaking Caribbean countries that retain the death penalty.

Savings Clause

According to Burnham (2005b, p. 250), "there are two types of savings clause in Caribbean constitutions." Continuing, Burnham (2005b, p. 250) contends that "the general savings clause purports to carry forward all laws from the old regime, while the special savings clause insulates from challenge penalties or punishments that were in existence at independence. Only the Constitution of Belize is free of any type of savings clause." It follows naturally, therefore, that the constitutional propriety and the nature of punishment are both saved by these clauses. The impact of the savings clause is cited in Hood and Seemungal (2006). Thus, the 2003 case of Balkisoon Roodal v The State of Trinidad and Tobago, which ruled the death penalty was an infringement of the right not to be subjected to cruel and harsh treatment or punishment was later overturned by the Privy Council in the Charles Matthews and in 2005 which held that, notwithstanding the death penalty was cruel and unusual punishment, it was protected by the savings clause in the Constitution of Trinidad and Tobago (Hood & Seemungal, 2006, p. 1). It has been argued that these

savings clauses add to the controversy regarding the death penalty jurisprudence in the Caribbean. According to Burnham (2005b, p. 249) in
the Privy Council cases of Boyce, Matthew and Watson, the court dealt
with the general savings clause in three territories and, in deeply divided
judgements, rendered three different outcomes.

Table 3.1 *The law on the death penalty in the Caribbean*

Country	Statute	Sections	Offences	Method and date of last execution
Antigua and Barbuda	Offences against the Person Act Treason Act Defense Act 2006 No. 10 of 2006	Sec 2, 3 Sec 7 Articles 37, 38, 44–46	1. Murder 2. Treason 3. Military offences not resulting in death	Hanging Last execution 1991 while some say 1989
Barbados	OAP Act 1984 Defense Act Defense Act Terrorism Act 2002 Terrorism Act 2002 Treason Act No. 1 of 1980	Article 2 Articles 35 and 36 Articles 42 and 43 Article 3(1)(c) Article 3(1)(c) Article 2,7	1. Murder 2. Espionage 3. Military offences 4. Terrorism (death) 5. Terrorism (no death) 6. Treason	Hanging 1984 last known hanging
Bahamas	1. 2011 Penal Code Amendment 2. Terrorism Act 3. Penal Code 4. Genocide Act	Sec 3(1) Sec 3(1) Article 389 Article 3(2)(a)	1. Murder 2. Offences resulting in death 3. Terrorism 4. Terrorism 5. Treason 6. War crimes and crime against humanity	Hanging 2000 David Mitchell for killing a few German tourists
Belize	Criminal Code Belize Defence Act Belize Defense Act Belize Genocide Act	 Article 30(1–3a) Article 67(3) Sec 2(1) 2(3)(a)	1. Murder 2. Military offences (not resulting in death) 3. Treason War crimes	Hanging 1985 executed for murder

Dominica	Offences against the Person No. 7 of 1873 Ch 10.01 L.R.0. 1991 Treason Act No. 2 of 1984	Article 2 Article 2	1. Murder 2. Treason	Hanging 1986
Grenada	Grenada Criminal Code Grenada Criminal Code	Article 230 amended by Art 36 of 1993 Article 322 amended by Art 36 of a993	1. Murder 2. Treason	Hanging 1978
Guyana	1. Criminal Law Offences Act & Laws of Guyana Chapter 1.01 2. Narcotic Drugs and Psychotropic Substances control Act of Guyana 3. Criminal law Act of Guyana 4. Criminal Law Offences 5. Criminal Law Offences	1. Sec 101, 102 2. Sec 6 3. Sec 101, 102 318(a) & (b) Sec 309A Sec 33(1), 34(1), 41(1), 76 (3) (a)	1. Murder 2. Drug trafficking resulting in death 3. Other offences resulting in death 4. Treason 5. Terrorism-related offences resulting in death 6. Military offences not resulting in death	Hanging 1997
Jamaica	Offences against the Person Act	Articles 2(1a–f) 3(1)(a) 3(1) (A)	Murder	Hanging 1988 Nathan Foster and Stanford Dinnal
S.K&N	Constitutional Order of 1983 Constitutional Order of 1983	Article 4(1) Article 4(1)	Murder Treason	Hanging 2008 last execution
St. Lucia	Criminal Code	Sec 85, 86(1) (a–f) 86 (1) (d) Sec 86(1)(f)	Murder Drug trafficking Terrorism	Hanging 1995 last execution

St. Vincent and the Grenadines			Aggravated murder Treason	Hanging 1995
Trinidad and Tobago	1. Offences against Person Act Chapter 11:08 2. Treason Act 3. Terrorism Act 4. Genocide Act	1. Sec 4 2. Article 2 3. Article 19(2)(b) 4. Article 3(1)(a)	1. Murder 2. Treason 3. Terrorism 4. War crime, crimes against humanity Genocide any other offence for which the law prescribes	Hanging 1999, 10 people were hanged in a 6 week period between June and July 1999. One person was hanged in 1994

Source: Fieldwork, 2017. Compiled using data extracted from http://www.
deathpenaltyworldwide.org/country-search-post.cfm?country=Guyana#f48-3.

Exemptions

Various categories of persons are exempted from the death penalty despite a conviction for murder and other offences which attracts capital punishment. While these categories of persons vary across the region, juveniles or persons who were 18 years of age at the time the murder was committed appears to be the only category that is exempted throughout the region. However, according to Tittemore (2004, p. 459–460) "in addition to persons under 18 years old, Article 4 of the American Convention on Human Rights also prohibit execution of persons over 70 years old and pregnant women." Therefore, despite the absence of these restrictions in the national laws of some countries, these categories would also be exempted in all countries based on rulings in Spence and Hughes v The Queen and AG and Others v Joseph and Boyce. However, persons who are mentally ill generally cannot be convicted of criminal offences because of their mental state and this may be a matter of evidence and not law. The St. Kitts and Nevis situation is an anomaly because it is a trite law that mental capacity is a prerequisite to a conviction for a criminal offence. It is arguable that someone who is mentally ill can be convicted of any crime in general and more specifically murder which requires a higher level of "mens rea" or the legally required guilty state of mind. Table 3.2 contains the list of exemptions across the English-speaking Caribbean.

Table 3.2 *Categories of person exempted from the death penalty in selected Caribbean countries*

Country	Under 18 years at the time of the crime	Elderly	Women	Mentally ill	Mentally retarded	Pregnant women
Antigua and Barbuda	Yes	No	No	Yes	No	Yes
Barbados	Yes	No	No	Yes	Yes	Yes
Bahamas	Yes	No	No	Yes	Yes	Yes
Belize	Yes	No	No	Yes	Yes	Yes
Dominica	Yes	Yes	No	Yes	No	Yes
Grenada	Yes	Yes	No	Yes	Yes	Yes
Guyana	Yes	No	No	Yes	No	Yes
Jamaica	Yes	Yes	Yes	Yes	Yes	Yes
St. Kitts and Nevis	Yes	No	No	No	No	No
St. Lucia	Yes	No	No	Yes	Yes	Yes
SVG	Yes	No	No	Yes	No	Yes
T & T	Yes	No	No	Yes	Yes	Yes

Source: Fieldwork, 2017.

Literature on the Death Penalty in the Caribbean

The death penalty in the Caribbean has been widely discussed in the literature. For example, several studies reviewed the unconstitutional nature of the death penalty (Burnham, 2005a; Carozza, 2003; Lehrfreund, 2011; McKoy, 2007a, 2007b), others have focused on the mandatory nature of the sentence (Frost, 2014; García Ramírez, 2010; McKoy, 2007a, 2007b; Rediker, 2013; Tittemore, 2004; Vasciannie, 2008). Several studies found that the death penalty was not a useful deterrent to crime (Amnesty International, 2012; Gifford, 2009; Greenberg & Agozino 2012) while Greenberg and Agozino (2012) also found there was no correlation between crime rates and the death penalty. One author reviewed the cruel and unusual nature of capital punishment (Carozza, 2003), while two studies focused on the decisions the Pratt and Morgan decision and the effect of delays in the justice system in implementing the death penalty (Gifford, 2009; McKoy, 2007a, 2007b). Several studies considered the human rights and right to life implications of the death penalty (Amnesty International, 2012; Burnham, 2005, 2005b; Helfer, 2002; McKoy, 2007a, 2007b; Rediker, 2013), others looked at the Caribbean Court of Justice and its potential role in carrying out the death penalty in light of the Privy Council's decision (Berry & Thompson, 2013; McKoy, 2007a; Rediker, 2013), while some authors reviewed the impact of Caribbean constitutions on the death penalty cases in the region (Burnham, 2005a; Helfer, 2002; Morrison, 2006).

Some studies have focused on the death penalty across the Caribbean in general while others have focused on specific countries. As a region, the application of capital punishment in the Caribbean has been the subject of much scholarly review. For example, Gifford (2009) considered the death penalty across the English-speaking Caribbean, other works considered the death penalty in Barbados (Antoine, 2005; Birdsong, 1999; Broadbent, 2004b; Cross, 2014) while Frost (2014) looked at the death penalty in Barbados focusing on the decisions in *Da Costa and Cadogan v Barbados*. Carozza (2003) reviewed the death penalty in Belize; Lofquist (2010) reviewed the historical account of the death penalty in the Bahamas while two studies (Gifford, 2009; Vasciannie, 2008) looked at the status of the death penalty in Jamaica and a few studies focused on various aspects of the death penalty in Trinidad and Tobago (Broadbent, 2004a; Concepcion, 2000; Hood & Seemungal, 2006, 2009, 2011) and Vasciannie (2008) in Jamaica.

Several studies have highlighted Caribbean people's widespread support for retention of the death penalty in the Caribbean (Amnesty International, 2012; Burnham, 2005a; Hood & Seemungal, 2011; Norris & Chadee, 2001; Rediker, 2013). Two considered scholars focused on the controversial issue of the degrees in the commission of murder and the application of the death penalty in those circumstances (Burnham, 2005a; García Ramírez, 2010) while the relationship between international law and domestic law on human rights issue of the death penalty was reviewed in Amnesty International (2012), Carozza (2003), Helfer (2002), Mckoy (2007a, 2007b), and Tittemore (2004). Other researchers have reviewed the effect of the savings clause in Caribbean constitutions on the application of the death penalty (Birdsong, 2005; Burnham, 2005b). The fairly recent establishment of the CCJ and its potential impact on the death penalty has received some attention in the literature (Berry, 2013; Burnham, 2005a; Byron & Daikolis, 2008; Eidson, 2008; Helfer, 2002; Ventose, 2013), while Rupnow (2013) reviewed some of the key issues involved in the death penalty across the region. A few studies have focused on the impact of international law and supervisory institutions on death penalty cases in the Caribbean (Carozza, 2003; Concepcion, 2000). This paper parts ways with the previous work by attempting to present the evolution of the jurisprudence on the death penalty in the Caribbean focusing on some of the key judgments and decisions of the ECCA, CCJ, Privy Council, and the Inter-American System.

THE EASTERN CARIBBEAN COURT OF APPEAL (ECCA)

Background

The Eastern Caribbean Court of Appeal is an Appeals Court for six independent countries (Antigua and Barbuda, Commonwealth of Dominica, Grenada, St. Kitts and Nevis, St. Lucia, St. Vincent and the Grenadines), and three overseas territories (Anguilla, British Virgin Islands, and Montserrat). The Court, which is based in Castries St. Lucia, was established in 1967, hears appeals from the nine member States and final appeals against decisions of this court are heard by the Caribbean Court of Justice only in the case of the Commonwealth of Dominica since 2015, and the Judicial Committee of the Privy Council for the remaining countries. As such, the court is not a final appeals court. However, consideration of the ECCA is given because (a) within recent times the court has delivered a number of judgments that limit the application of the death penalty and (b) it is important to note that three of the current judges of the CCJ, including current President, Sir Dennis Byron, have delivered leading judgments in those cases while they were sitting at the ECCA. While these two issues overlap because the judges presided over some of these cases, it is important to distinguish these issues because of the current position of these judges in the CCJ.

DEATH PENALTY JUDGMENTS

In Spence v The Queen, a 1998 appeal from the high Court of St. Vincent and the Grenadines and Hughes v The Queen, a 1997 appeal from the High Court of St. Lucia, the court merged the two matters because the issue and law were identical and the matters were referred to as Spence and Hughes v The Queen with judgment delivered in 2001. In those appeals, the ECCA ruled that the mandatory death penalty was unconstitutional in St. Lucia and St. Vincent and the Grenadines and represented the first successful challenge to the mandatory sentence and the decision that was upheld by the Privy Council. In Christopher Remy v The Queen, a distinction was drawn between capital and non-capital murder and in Trimmingham v The Queen (2005) which followed Spence and Hughes, the ECCA found that based on the primacy of the right to life and the approach that this emphasis requires, it will only be in the most extreme case of murder that the death penalty should be imposed (Barrow JA citing Saunders JA in Christopher Remy v The Queen) (para 23). These three decisions are among the leading cases restricting the death penalty in the OECS countries which represent a significant number of English-speaking Caribbean countries.

Case No. 1: Spence and Hughes v The Queen (2001)

This was the first challenge to the mandatory death sentence and was heard by then Chief Justice Sir Dennis Byron and Justices of Appeal Redhead and Saunders. CJ Byron and Saunders J gave the majority decision that the mandatory death sentence was unconstitutional. Redhead dissented principally because he felt that there must be certainty in the law and judges should not usurp the functions of parliamentarians who are elected to give effect to the wishes of the people as expressed in the Constitution and the various laws of the land [para. 166]. As such, he rejected the argument that the mandatory death penalty as expressed in Laws of St. Lucia was unconstitutional. However, Byron and Saunders took the opposite position which led to the landmark decision. Byron's decision was based on several issues including:

(a) The impact of international legal norms on the various laws and constitutions of region [para. 9] for which he found support in Lord Wilberforce's statement in *Minister of Home Affairs v Fisher* and highlighted in Tittemore (2004, p. 455).

(b) Whether the Savings Clause debars review of the mandatory death sentence. He relied on the *Pratt and Morgan* and *Greene Brown* as authority that it did not debar review.

(c) Whether the mandatory death sentence violates domestic law. He found that it did.

(d) The relevance of decisions of the Inter-American Human Rights System. On this point, Sir Dennis acknowledged that while it is a constitutional principle that if Parliament has legislated and the words of the statute are clear, the statute must be applied even if the words are in breach of international law. However, he found that as St. Lucia is a party to the Inter-American Convention on Human Rights and Universal Declaration on Human Rights, it is also well settled law that domestic provisions whether of the Constitution or statute law should as far as possible be interpreted so as to conform to the state's obligations under international law as articulated in Neville Lewis v The Attorney General of Jamaica [2001] 2 AC 50 [1999] 57 WIR 275 (Lewis v AG) and Matadeen v Pointu [1998]1 AC 98 (hereafter Matadeen).

(e) The arbitrariness of the mandatory death penalty. He found that the mandatory death penalty is a final decision that does not consider the circumstances of the accused.

(f) Remedies available to the court. He found that courts should consider alternative sentences in exceptional cases.

In agreeing with Byron, Saunders acknowledged the plethora of varying decisions on death penalty matters and focused his decision on three main issues: (1) the finality of the death penalty, (2) the lack of court's discretion when sentencing persons for murder, and (3) the varying degrees of and circumstances under which murder is committed. His analysis of, and conclusions on, these factors led him to the conclusion that the mandatory death penalty was illegal.

Case No. 2: Christopher Remy v The Queen (2003)

This appeal from the High Court of St. Lucia was heard before Justices of Appeal Saunders, Redhead, and Georges. Remy was convicted of murder and appealed against conviction and sentence. The majority judgment was delivered by Redhead with Georges concurring while Saunders delivered a dissenting view that the sentence should be quashed and remitted to the trial judge for a more appropriate sentenced to be passed [para. 15]. This is an interesting decision which applied a discretionary approach to the application of the death penalty. However, based on the facts of the case, Redhead and Georges found that it constituted the "worst of the worst cases" requiring the death penalty while Saunders differed. Redhead's reason for agreeing with the trial judge was based on the following statement the judge made at the trial stating:

> "I am of the view that this premeditated and planned attack on the deceased warrants severe punishment. This was a murder that had been carefully and deliberately planned. This was a murder where the victim was the father of a police officer, the said police officer having gone to the accused's home to execute a warrant of the family court of which the Appellant was upset and set out to revenge. His statement to several witnesses who testified was evident of what he planned to do with the police officer. He was bent on revenge. He could not wait until Monday where he was asked by the Commissioner to return. In my opinion, the deceased suffered the consequence of death because of the acts of his son, a police officer acting in the execution of his duties. The evidence is palpably clear that the police officer was the principal target and there is enough evidence that he resembled his father and he also drives his father's vehicle from time to time" [para 86].

However, Saunders cited the Indian case of *Bachan Sing v Punjab*, the South African case of *The State v Makyanwane* and his earlier decision in *R v Wilson Exhale* and found that Remy's actions did not fall within the rarest of cases or the most exceptional case where there is no reasonable prospect of reformation and the object of the sentence would not be properly achieved by another sentence, or the worst of the worst cases." This case underscores how judges using the same guidelines to apply the death penalty in a discretionary manner to the same facts can arrive at different outcomes.

Case No. 3: Daniel Dick Trimmingham v The Queen (2004)

This appeal from the High Court of St. Vincent and the Grenadines was heard by Acting CJ Brian Alleyne and JAs Barrow and Gordon. The unanimous judgment which imposed the death penalty was delivered by Barrow with Alleyne and Gordon concurring. The appellant Daniel "Dick" Trimmingham was convicted of murder and sentenced to death. The court found that the murder was gruesome and reviewed a number of issues dealt with by the trial judge including:

(a) the approach to sentencing for murder;

(b) the categories of murder including the "the most exceptional and extreme cases" [para. 24];

(c) the "worst of the worst cases" [para. 26];

(d) the object of sentencing [para. 27]; and

(e) "the factors the judge must consider in passing sentence" [para. 28–33].

Barrow JA found that notwithstanding the trial judge's error in the exercise of her discretion, it was the duty of the Appeal Court to conduct that exercise afresh and find the relevant factors before concluding that the imposition of the death penalty was a just decision [para. 34–36]. In arriving at his decision, Barrow reviewed the position in England prior to the abolition of the death penalty as contained in the *Homicide Act of 1957*, the Privy Council decision in *Evon Smith v The Queen* and endorsed the view expressed by Saunders JA in *Christopher Remy v The Queen*, that the death penalty should only be imposed in "the worst and most extreme cases" of murder [para. 23].

It is arguable that these three cases, starting with *Spence and Hughes*, have significantly contributed to the sea-change in the death penalty jurisprudence in the Eastern Caribbean countries and the wider Caribbean as the Privy Council affirmed the decision in *Spence and Hughes* on appeal. Further, the fact that Chief Justice Byron and Justice Saunders (currently the two most senior CCJ Judges) and Justice Barrow, the most recent appointment to the CCJ's bench, have previously ruled that the mandatory death penalty is illegal while sitting on the ECCA is some consolation to abolitionists and dilutes the perception of the CCJ as a future hanging court.

The Caribbean Court of Justice (CCJ)

The most recent legal development in the Caribbean is the Caribbean Court of Justice (CCJ) which is the highest Appellate Court for Barbados, Belize, Guyana and more recently, the Commonwealth of Dominica. The CCJ was established on February 14, 2001 with the signing of the agreement among 12 CARICOM States. Two additional states (Dominica and SVG) signed the agreement on February 15, 2003. The Right Honourable Mr. Justice Michael De La Bastide was sworn in as the first President of the Court and inauguration followed on April 16, 2004 at Queens Hall Port of Spain, Trinidad and Tobago, the seat of the court. The CCJ has an original jurisdiction for all Caribbean Single Market and Economy (CSME) and CARICOM matters and an appellate jurisdiction for the countries that have abolished appeals to the Privy Council and made the CCJ their final appeal court. The court has seven judges from within and outside the Caribbean region. An interesting feature of the CCJ is the fact that the majority of sitting judges of the CCJ emanates from the Caribbean and might be in favour of the death penalty, unlike the Privy Council. Among the current judges, five are from Caribbean territories (Chief Justice Byron is from St. Kitts and Nevis, Justices Adrian Saunders is Vincentian, Professor Winston Anderson is Jamaican, Maureen Rajnauth-Lee is from Trinidad and Tobago and Denys Barrow is from Belizean); while Justice Jacob Wit is Dutch and Justice David Hayton is British.

ESTABLISHING THE CCJ'S FOUNDATION

Following a number of decisions of the Privy Council that were critical of the law and practice regarding capital punishment in the Caribbean (Burnham, 2005a), the CCJ was widely viewed as an alternative to the Privy Council (Rediker, 2013) as several commentators anticipated a new and fresh Caribbean jurisprudence (Berry & Robinson, 2013; Burnham, 2005a, 2005b; McKoy, 2007a, 2007b; Rediker, 2013). Despite its limited membership and recent existence as the final Appellate Court and the perception that it would be a hanging court (Anthony, 2003; Birdsong, 2005; Eidson, 2008) the decision in *Joseph and Boyce* which held that the death penalty should only be applied in conformity with guidelines established by international law, left many Caribbean people "sorely disappointed" (McKoy, 2007a, 2007b, p. 6).

As Eidson (2013, p. 196) puts it, "this case is one of the more important that the Court has decided in that the idea that the Court will be one prone to handing out death sentences in attempts to gain popularity amongst the citizenry of the Caribbean has been eroded." The CCJ's decision in *Joseph and Boyce* limits the application of the death penalty and can be viewed from two perspectives: (1) the future implications for the death penalty based on its maiden judgment in *Joseph and Boyce (2006)* and (2) the number and ranking of the current CCJ judges who delivered judgments that restricted the application of death penalty in cases before the ECCA prior to their appointments to the bench of the CCJ. Its implications for the death penalty in the region are considered here.

Joseph Boyce and Others

Though the CCJ has presided over three death penalty cases it has only delivered judgment in the case of *Joseph and Boyce*. However, one judgment in two cases from Belize that have been consolidated is reserved and due to be delivered early in 2018 while two additional death penalty matters from Barbados that have also been consolidated, is expected to be heard in early 2018. In its inaugural death penalty judgment the court held, while the death penalty was lawful, it must be consistent with all the legal procedures established in a number of Privy Council cases and the sentence should only be applied in the most serious cases. The case also dealt with a number of issues surrounding the Pratt and Morgan decision and much broader issues of:

(a) The relationship between international and domestic law.

(b) The status of previous Privy Council decisions that have not been overruled by the CCJ.

(c) The CCJ's ability to overrule decisions of the Privy Council.

(d) The questioning of the 5-year limit as set down by the Privy Council.

(e) The reviewability of the prerogative of mercy following the Privy Council decision in Lewis v the Attorney General of Jamaica; and maybe most importantly.

(f) The case emphatically stated the role of the court, in particular, the issue of creating a Caribbean jurisprudence.

The case sets the tone for future cases coming before the CCJ and "this decision has given a very important indication of where the jurisprudence is heading" (McKoy, 2007a, p. 6). The case was heard by all seven judges of the CCJ, with the De La Bastide P and Saunders J delivering a

joint judgment while their colleagues agreed with their decision though
taking different routes to arrive at the same destination.

Regarding the reviewability of the prerogative of mercy, they agreed that
it is reviewable by the courts in line with the decisions of Lewis v AG,
Yassin v Attorney General of Guyana [1993] 4 LRC 1 and Laurino v Attorney General of Belize [1995] 3 Bz LR 77 (Laurino) departing from De
Freitas v Benny [1974] 26 WIR 523 (De Freitas v Benny) and Reckley v
Minister of Public Safety and Immigration [1996] 2 W.L.R. 281 (Reckley No. 1). They also agreed that rights created in signed and ratified but
unincorporated treaties must be respected regardless of the lack of incorporation into the domestic laws of Barbados or any other state in the region. According to Tittemore (2004), this decision follows the decision
in Thomas & Hilaire v Baptiste decided by the Inter-American Court on
Human Rights.

Berry (2013) argues that while this may seem troubling to many in the
Caribbean because of its incompatibility with the regional jurisprudence,
as the rules for applying international law in municipal courts are precise,
comprehensive, and comprehensible. With regards to the 5-year limit imposed by *Pratt and Morgan*, the court disagreed with the Privy Council's
rejection of relaxing the 5-year limit based on the time limit of 18 months
to exhaust all appeals to the international bodies which the state has no
control over. Possibly the most poignant statement contained in the judgment was made in the joint judgment of De La Bastide P and Saunders J:

> "The main purpose in establishing this court is to pro-
> mote the development of a Caribbean jurisprudence, a
> goal which Caribbean courts are best equipped to pur-
> sue. In the promotion of such jurisprudence, we shall
> naturally consider very carefully and respectfully the
> opinions of the final courts of other Commonwealth
> countries and particularly, the judgments of the JCPC
> which determine the law for those Caribbean states that
> accept the Judicial Committee as their final appellate
> court. In this connection we accept that decisions made
> by the JCPC while it was still the final Court of Appeal
> for Barbados, in appeals from other Caribbean countries,
> were binding in Barbados in the absence of any materi-
> al difference between the written law of the respective

countries from which the appeals came and the written law of Barbados. Furthermore, they continue to be binding in Barbados, notwithstanding the replacement of the JCPC, until and unless they are overruled by this court ..." (p. 18).

Previous Decisions by CCJ Judges

Among the current CCJ judges, the President, Sir Dennis Byron, the longest serving judge, Justice Adrian Saunders, and the most recent appointee, Justice Denys Barrow, have all given leading judgments in death penalty cases during the tenure on the bench of the ECCA. Brief overviews of some of their judgments are as follows:

(a) <u>Sir Dennis Byron</u>: In *Spence and Hughes*, Sir Dennis found the mandatory death penalty provided by the laws of St. Vincent and the Grenadines was unconstitutional because, inter alia, the impact of international norms of constitutional cannot be ignored.

In that case, he stated,

"The provisions of the Constitution that are relevant to this case are part of the fundamental rights and freedoms which have sought to entrench and guarantee that citizens enjoy rights and dignity associated with humanity. These rights fit into the universal pattern as evidenced by declarations and covenants to which nations around the world, including our own, have subscribed. The issue in this case, related as it is to the question of capital punishment, is part of a developing area of legal thought and jurisprudence on the value of human life" (2003, p. 1073). It is particularly interesting that Sir Dennis Byron sought refuge in international law principles that clearly conflicted with clear precise words of the domestic statute in order to hold the mandatory death sentence illegal—a rather ingenious attempt at judicial activism to reach a rather strange decision.

(b) <u>Justice Adrian Saunders</u>: In *Spence and Hughes* Saunders agreed with Sir Dennis. After reviewing decided cases from various jurisdictions across the Caribbean, the Commonwealth, including India, and the United States, he stated, "the court should give weight to the jurisprudence of the Inter-American Court" [para. 213]. "The mandatory death penalty in these two countries, as presently applied, robs those upon whom sentence is passed of any opportunity whatsoever to have the court consider mitigating circumstances even as an irrevocable punishment is meted out to them" [para. 215]. He concluded by stating, inter alia, "I agree with Sir Dennis Byron that the most appropriate response to a finding that the mandatory death sentence infringes section 5 would be a legislative one. Until there is such a response I would respectfully agree with the Order proposed by Sir Dennis and the sentiments expressed by him regarding the sentencing procedure to be observed in the future and the manner in which persons on death row should be treated" [para. 222].

c) *Justice Denys Barrow*: In the Trimmingham case, freshly minted CCJ Judge Barrow approved statements by Byron and Saunders which held that the mandatory death sentence was invalid and followed the decision in *Spence and Hughes* and Saunders JA dissenting judgment in Christopher Remy v The Queen stated,

"The foregoing cases establish that the first principle by which a sentencing Judge is to be guided in these cases is that there is a presumption in favour of an unqualified right to life. The second consideration is that the death penalty should be imposed only in the most exceptional and extreme cases of murder" [para. 16]

He further stated,

"It is a mandatory requirement in murder cases for a Judge to take into account the personal and individual circumstances of the convicted person. The Judge must also take into account the nature and gravity of the offence; the character and record of the convicted person; the factors that might have influenced the conduct that caused the murder; the design and execution of the offence, and the possibility of reform and social re-adaptation of the convicted person. The death sentence should only be imposed in those exceptional cases where there is no reasonable prospect of reform and the object of punishment would not be achieved by any other means. The sentencing Judge is fixed with a very onerous duty to pay due regard to all of these factors" [para. 17].

More recently, at a symposium held by the University of the West Indies to commemorate the 10th anniversary of the CCJ, on the eve of his election to the court's bench, Barrow in his opening remarks opined:

"The fundamental rights provisions in our various constitutions of the Commonwealth Caribbean being reflections of our overarching principles of international human rights have opened up our domestic law in a major way to the influences of international law. Decisions from the Caribbean Court of Justice (CCJ) show that Commonwealth Caribbean jurisprudence is now fully in step with developments in the wider world and not only draws upon, but contributes to these developments. International instruments such as the European Convention on Human Rights, especially since it has become part of English law to which we still reflectively turn for judicial decisions, have been heavily relied on in Caribbean cases involving human rights such as the protection of law, cruel and unusual treatment, the right to life, protection of property and more" (Barrow, 2016, p. 1).

These statements and judgments of these CCJ judges clearly indicate their restrictive approach to the death penalty which is consistent with the court's inaugural decision in Joseph and Boyce. In fact, Justice Saunders who concurred with CJ Byron in Spence and Hughes also gave the joint judgment with De La Bastide P in Joseph and Boyce. And while it is arguable that based on the current composition of the court, it does not seem inclined to stray from its earlier decision; the court has an excellent opportunity to give a clear indication of its position in the imminent judgment in the consolidated cases from Belize and upcoming appeal cases from Barbados.

It is noteworthy that the joint judgment of De La Bastide P and Saunders J in Joseph and Boyce clearly indicated the position of the judgments of the Privy Council regarding decisions in countries which have retained the London-based court as their final appellate court. In this regard, the CCJ indicated that it will attach a significant weight of the judgments of the London-based courts in matters being ventilated before the CCJ. Moreover, the CCJ stated that Privy Council decisions that predate the Caribbean court will stand until the CCJ overrules them. Therefore, the Privy Council will continue to play a significant role in the regional jurisprudence.

JUDICIAL COMMITTEE OF THE PRIVY COUNCIL

At the time of authoring this chapter, the Privy Council was the final appeal court for eight independent Commonwealth Caribbean countries. However, with Dominica's recent membership in the CCJ, the continuing raging debate among the remaining OECS countries for the remaining countries to collectively make the CCJ its final court and mounting pressure on the Trinidad and Tobago and Jamaica, the two largest countries, to make the CCJ their final appeals court, it is likely that the remaining Caribbean countries will soon sever ties with the London-based court. The case against the Privy Council has been well documented and prosecuted. Arguments against the high cost of litigation, the UK judges being out of step with the ethos and culture of the Caribbean, and many view the court as the last vestige of our colonial past. One of the leading advocates of this cause is former Chief Justice of Trinidad and Tobago, Privy Councillor and inaugural President of the CCJ, Michael De La Bastide.

The impact of the Privy Council's decisions on the death penalty beginning with Pratt and Morgan has altered the landscape of the death penalty in the Caribbean in titanic proportions. Various commentators have lamented the onerous responsibilities; some of these decisions have placed on Caribbean countries when attempting to implement the death penalty and their impact. This was highlighted in the CCJ case of Joseph and Boyce which prompted De La Bastide P and Saunders J to comment:

> "The decision caused disruption in national and regional justice systems. Its effect was that, in one fell swoop, all persons on death row for longer than five years were automatically entitled to have and had their sentences commuted to life imprisonment. In Jamaica, there were 105 such persons, in Trinidad and Tobago there 53, and in Barbados 9. Justice systems were required to make sharp adjustments to their routines. Some countries were compelled to place on indefinite hold hearings of all other appeals, both civil and criminal, in order to concentrate on those appeals that were in danger of running afoul of the Pratt and Morgan guidelines" [para. 46].

The decision in Pratt and Morgan made many people in the Caribbean feel the Privy Council's position on the death penalty is inconsistent with the laws of Caribbean countries and as such, the UK-based court is effectively overruling the constitutions of the region, which provide for the death penalty (Helfer, 2002; Simmons, 1999). According to Pollard (2004, cited in Eidson 2008, p. 198) "this was felt by the Caribbean Community as a usurpation of their rights to self-determination, which further indicated that the Privy Council does not reflect the general sensibilities, cultural values, and feelings of justice in the region." These sentiments have been echoed by several commentators (Eidson, 2008; McKoy, 2007a, 2007b; Tittemore, 2004). Shortly after Pratt and Morgan, the Privy Council in the matter of appellants (1) Neville Lewis (2) Patrick Taylor and Anthony McLeod, (3) Christopher Brown, and (4) Desmond Taylor and Steve Shaw v Attorney General (2000) WIR 275 UKPC 303 ruled that "the state must allow condemned inmates access to the international human rights process, which is outside the control of the state, and which may take more than five years" (McKoy, 2007b, p. 3). These obligations stretch the capacity of Caribbean countries that stops short of the outright abolition of the death penalty.

IMPLICATIONS OF THE PRATT AND MORGAN DECISION

The decision in Pratt and Morgan remains one of the most significant death penalty judgments in the Caribbean which effectively limits the sentence only to circumstances where the accused persons have been on death row for less than 5 years. However, a seemingly confusing aspect of this ruling is whether there is a blanket 5-year rule which precludes the imposition of the death penalty or whether the rule only applies in certain circumstances. For example, does the rule only apply if the prosecution contributes to the delay in carrying out the death penalty such as failure to inform the accused of his right to appeal or in processing the notice of appeal, similar to the facts in Pratt and Morgan case?

On January 15, 1979, Earl Pratt and Ivan Morgan were convicted of murder they were arrested for that was committed on November 6, 1977. On November 2, 1993, Lord Griffiths gave the decision on behalf of his seven other colleagues holding that the delay by the prosecution made the imposition of the death penalty unlawful. McKoy (2007a, 2007b, p. 10–13) sets out the procedural history in Pratt and Morgan

which I would not repeat but suffice it to say that a significant period
elapsed between the sentence and the issuance of the three warrants of
execution which included 2 years before the hearing of the appeal and
3 years delay in the judges giving reasons for their decision. However, Lord Griffiths also dealt with a number of issues, which this author
argues, places limits on the application of this principle. For example,
Lord Griffiths opened the door for extending the 5-year period when
he stated:

> "There is an instinctive revulsion against the prospect of
> hanging a man after he has been held under sentence of
> death for many years. What gives rise to this instinctive
> revulsion? The answer can only be our humanity; we re-
> gard it as an inhuman act to keep a man facing the agony
> of execution over a long extended period of time. But
> before their Lordships condemn the act of execution as
> "inhuman or degrading punishment or other treatment"
> within the meaning of section 17(1) there are a number
> of factors that have to be balanced in weighing the delay.
> If delay is due entirely to the fault of the accused such
> as an escape from custody or frivolous and time wasting
> resort to legal procedures which amount to an abuse of
> process the accused cannot be allowed to take advantage
> of that delay for to do so would be to permit the accused
> to use illegitimate means to escape the punishment in-
> flicted upon him in the interest of protecting society
> against crime."

He further stated:

> "A much more difficult question is whether the delay
> occasioned by the legitimate resort of the accused to all
> available appellate procedures should be taken into ac-
> count or whether it is only delay that can be attributed to
> the shortcomings of the State that should be taken into
> account."

These views were also echoed by Justices De La Bastide and Bernard et al.
in the CCJ case of Joseph and Boyce (Tittemore, 2004, p. 466).

DECISIONS SINCE PRATT AND MORGAN

Since the Pratt and Morgan decision, the Privy Council has made serious inroads that limit the application of the death penalty in a number of cases, however, the court has gone both left and right on many issues. Starting with Lewis v Attorney General of Jamaica the court held that the prerogative of mercy was reviewable by the courts overruling De Freitas and Benny. In Spence v The Queen, the court held that mandatory death sentences are unconstitutional in the Eastern Caribbean States. According to Burnham (2004) in a trilogy of cases, the UK court ruled that the mandatory death penalty is unconstitutional Reyes v The Queen, (Belize) 2002 R v Hughes and (St. Lucia) 2002 Fox v The Queen (St. Kitts and Nevis). In Balkisoon Roodal v State of Trinidad and Tobago (2003), the court ruled that the death penalty was an infringement of the right not to be subject to cruel and unusual treatment or punishment. In Charles Matthews v The State (Trinidad and Tobago) and Lennox Ricardo Boyce v The Queen (Barbados), the Privy Council found that the death penalty could be applied in these two countries because their savings clauses had not been amended. However, in Lambert Watson v The Queen, the court held that the mandatory imposition of the death penalty was unconstitutional in Jamaica as it was not saved by the Constitution.

In the OECS case of Trimmingham v The Queen (2009) UKPC 25, the court held that the death penalty should only be applied in the "worst of the worst" cases or the "rarest of the rare" and where there is no prospect of reform and the goals of the punishment cannot be accomplished by any other means. This principle was upheld in the Maxo Tido v The Queen. In Charles Matthews v The State of Trinidad and Tobago (2004) UK PC 33, the court held that the mandatory death penalty, though cruel and harsh punishment, is lawful because of the savings clause in the constitution. However, in Nimrod Miguel v The State of Trinidad and Tobago (2011) UKPC 14, the court held that the mandatory death penalty was unlawful and should be restricted to felony murders. More recently, in Hunte and Khan v The State of Trinidad and Tobago (2015) UKPC 33, the court held that the mere fact that a matter is before the Privy Council does not give it an automatic right to commute a lawfully passed sentence of death on the ground that it would be unconstitutional for that sentence to be carried out.

The cases above highlight the uncertainty of the Privy Council in death penalty cases. Moreover, a deeper analysis of the breakdown of the position of the judges in these cases reveals deep divisions on these issues. A cursory glance at the OECS level reveals that cases such as Spence and Hughes and Christopher Remy were decided by two to one majority, while at the Privy Council, decisions such as (1) *Lambert Watson*, (2) *Boyce*, and (3) *Matthews* were decided by five to four majorities. Additionally, many of the dissenting decisions in earlier cases such as *de Freitas v. Benny* [1976] A.C. 239 have matured into "ratio decidendi" in later cases. These results underscore, not only the division among jurists, but the manifest uncertainty of this area of law.

The Inter-American System on Human Rights

Background and The Caribbean's Unique Position

Caribbean countries are interwoven in the Inter-American System in the Western Hemisphere as all 14 independent CARICOM Member States are members of the Organization of American States (OAS). However, with the exception of Haiti, their membership in the regional organization has been much later than their Latin and North American counterparts, due largely to their dates of independence which began with Jamaica and Trinidad and Tobago in 1962. They have actively participated in the various organs of the Inter-American system and are a signatory to various treaties regarding human rights, torture, and the death penalty. However, "the subject matter of the Inter-American Human Rights System has since expanded to include numerous treaties and protocols and conventions addressing on human rights issues" (Tittemore, 2004, p. 9).

Organs: Inter-American Commission and Court on Human Rights

The two relevant organs of the Inter-American system regarding the death penalty are the Inter-American Court on Human Rights and the Inter-American Commission on Human Rights. Clare Roberts of Antigua and Barbuda, Sir Henry Forde and Peter Laurie of Barbados, John Donaldson of Trinidad and Tobago, and Patrick Lipton of Jamaica have served as Commissioners and Oliver Jackman of Barbados served the Commission and was the elected Judge of the Inter-American Court (Tittemore, 2004, p. 472) within recent times, Tracy Robinson of Jamaica (2014) and Professor Rose Marie Belle Antoine of Trinidad and Tobago (2015) served as Chair of the Commission, respectively.

Human Rights Regime

Regarding legal instruments, the Inter-American Convention on Human Rights, the Additional Protocol to the Convention on Human Rights in the Area of Economic Social and Cultural Rights (Protocol of San Salvador), the Additional Protocol to the Convention on Human Rights to Abolish the Death Penalty are the most relevant to capital punishment in the Caribbean.

While the Inter-American Commission on Human Rights was created in 1959 to monitor observance of recognized human rights, the Inter-American Court on Human Rights was created in 1979 following the coming into force of the American Convention. The Court has both a contentious and compulsory jurisdiction. According to Tittemore (2004, p. 455) "as defined under Article 62 of the American Convention, the Court's contentious and compulsory jurisdiction, which involves alleged violations of rights of persons under the Convention by states that are parties thereto, comprises all cases concerning the interpretation and application of the American Convention provisions in respect of those states that have accepted the Court's jurisdiction."

He also highlights that "the distinction between OAS Member States concerning their participation in the Inter-American human rights system are further defined by language-of the twenty-four states that are parties to the Convention, eighteen are Spanish-speaking, with Dominica and Barbados, Grenada and Jamaica being the only English-speaking parties" (Tittemore, 2004, p. 456). And while 18 Spanish-speaking states have accepted the contentious jurisdiction of the court, only Barbados has done so of the English-speaking parties (Tittemore, 2004, p. 456). Additionally, while Cuba and Guatemala are the only Spanish-speaking countries that retain the death penalty, apart from the United States all other English-speaking countries are from the Caribbean.

It is also important to note that the American Convention, similar to the International Covenant on Civil and Political Rights (ICCPR), does not prohibit the death penalty for states that retain capital punishment. However, Article 4 of the Convention places several limitations on its application which includes: (1) the right to life, protection of the law, and freedom from arbitrary deprivation of life, (2) for countries that have not abolished the death penalty it applies only to the most serious crimes, (3) the death penalty shall not be re-established in countries where it was abolished, (4) the death penalty shall not be imposed for political crimes, (5) persons under 18 years, over 70 years, and pregnant women shall not suffer the death penalty, and (6) persons condemned to death shall have the right to pardon, amnesty or commutation of death sentence and the death sentence shall not be imposed while such petition is pending. Additionally, Tittemore (2004, p. 460) cites Advisory Opinion OC-3/83 which places further limits on the application of the death regarding the following: "1) mandatory procedural requirements before imposing the death penalty, 2) the application of the death penalty to only to the most serious crimes, and 3) mandatory consideration of factors regarding the accused person that may preclude the death penalty."

The Caribbean's Record

The Caribbean's poor record in the Inter-American Human Rights System is well documented in several scholarly works and highlighted in Privy Council judgments (Concepcion, 2000; Fraser, 2004; García Ramírez, 2010; Helfer, 2002; Tittemore, 2004). One author and past member of the Inter-American Commission has provided a detailed account of the region's record in the Inter-American system (Tittemore, 2004), while another has viewed the relationship through three phases namely: "Phase 1: Forgotten, 1670–1980" (Fraser, 2005, p. 211), "Phase 2: Peripheral vision, 1980–1993" (p. 214), and "Phase 3: 1994–Present Engagement with confrontation" (Fraser, 2006, p. 211–219). It is this latter phase cited by Fraser (2006) which has attracted the most attention especially regarding the death penalty issue and Trinidad and Tobago's abysmal record underscored by the Tittemore (2004, p. 464) as the "Crisis in the 1990s" and the hanging of Anthony Briggs highlighted by Tittemore (2004, p. 464–485).

According to Tittemore (2004), the Pratt and Morgan decision led to two major developments. First, a large number of petitions were filed with the Commission resulting in drastic measures being undertaken to deal with the volume of requests. And second, Caribbean governments began pressing the Commission and the UNHRC to process. This led to innovative and drastic measures to respond to these requests in a timely manner. During this period, Trinidad and Tobago denounced the American Convention on May 26, 1998.

Scholars such as Burnham (2005), Helfer (2002), and Tittemore (2004) agree that the Privy Council's decision in Pratt and Morgan which was preceded by the UK case of Soering v The United Kingdom highlighting the "Death Row phenomenon" precipitated an avalanche of litigation on the death penalty in the Caribbean. In this regard, it is noteworthy that the ruling in Pratt and Morgan stated that "where the defendants pursue claims before the international bodies such as the United Nations Human Rights Committee and the Inter-American Human Rights Commission, the five year period suggested by the court included a period of eighteen months in which those claims must be determined" (Tittemore, 2004, p. 466). It follows, therefore, that the Pratt and Morgan decision would have been a significant factor in the volume of litigation before the Inter-American system decision.

Key Decisions of the Inter-American Commission and Court on Human Rights (IACHR)

In the wake of the *Pratt and Morgan* ruling a number of death penalty claims from the Commonwealth Caribbean were ventilated under the Inter-American system. Tittemore (2004, p. 477) found that these claims mainly consisted of the inconsistency of the mandatory death penalty with human rights standards, issues of pre-trail and post-conviction delay, conditions of detention, and the adequacy of legal representation. He contends that the majority of these claims were focused on the mandatory death penalty with the lion share of the case emanating from Trinidad and Tobago. This led to the Court's landmark decision in the consolidated case of Hilaire, Constantine & Benjamin, Case 11.816 Inter-Am Ct. H.R. (ser. C) No. 94. Tittemore (2004) found that these cases were decided based on the merits of the petitions including:

(a) The mandatory nature of the death penalty.

(b) Fairness in the application of the Prerogative of Mercy.

(c) The right to a fair trial within a reasonable time.

(d) Treatment and conditions of detention, the fairness of the petitioner's criminal proceedings.

(e) The unavailability of legal assistance to pursue constitutional motions before the domestic courts.

Tittemore (2004) also note that the cases came mainly from Trinidad and Tobago Constantine 11.787, Inter. Am. C.H.R. 128 (Unpublished

1999) (Constantine), Jamaica McKenzie 12.023, Inter. Am. C.H.R. 41 (1999) (McKenzie), Grenada Baptiste v Grenada, Case 11.743, Inter. Am. C.H.R. 38 (Baptiste), and The Bahamas Edwards, Case, 12.067, Inter. Am. C.H.R. 48 (2001) (Edwards).

Key findings of the Commission on these issues from the four jurisdictions can be summed in the following manner: the cases of McKenzie Baptiste and Edwards found (a) the mandatory death penalty contravened the provisions of the American Convention, resulting in arbitrary deprivation of life and failed to consider the individual circumstances of each case, (b) various aspects of the process to give effect to the Prerogative of Mercy (note) were incompatible with the Convention and Article XXIV of the Declaration, (c) inhumane treatment and prison conditions prior to trial and following convictions breached the provisions of the American Convention and the Declaration on Human Rights, and (d) failed to make effective legal remedy available to several persons to pursue constitutional motions. Additionally, McKenzie and Edwards also held that (a) the state did not try these men within a reasonable time and (b) the trials were not fair due to deficiencies in criminal proceedings, improper delays in permitting persons to contact their attorneys following arrest.

Following these findings by the Commission, a number of matters were referred to the court resulting in important decisions on a range of human rights issues. In the case of Trinidad and Tobago, which accepted the mandatory jurisdiction of the court and responsible for the vast majority of cases, especially the mandatory death penalty, the court's ruling in Thomas Hilaire, Constantine & Benjamin dealt with each issue discussed above. Moreover, based on Trinidad and Tobago's predisposition to executing persons on death row, the court issued provisional measures including asking the states to stay the execution and ensure that the petitioners were not executed before their complaints could be processed within the Inter-American Human Rights System (Tittemore, 2004, p. 482). However, based on Trinidad and Tobago's frustration with the process, the Privy Council's lifting of the stay of execution on Briggs on July 22, 1999, and, inter alia, its own interpretation of its obligations under the Convention, it executed Briggs 6 days later on July 28, 1999.

The court eventually gave its ruling in the case on June 21, 2001 which dealt with six principle issues (1) mandatory death penalty, (2) right to fair trail within a reasonable time, (3) detention conditions, (4) amnesty

pardon or commutation of sentence, (5) reparations, and (6) non-com-
pliance with provisional measures. In particular, the court found

(a) that state violated the right to life under Articles 4(1) and 4(2) in
    conjunction with Article 1(1) of the American Convention;

(b) the State's responsibility for violating the right to a fair trial within
    reasonable time under Articles 7(5) and 8(1) in conjunction with
    Articles 1(1) and 2 of the Convention to the detriment of 30 of the
    petitioners;

(c) pre- and post-trail detention took place in grossly overpopulated and
    unhygienic conditions that lacked sufficient ventilation and natural
    light;

(d) individual mercy petitions must be exercised through "fair and ade-
    quate procedures in conformity with Articles 4(6) of the Convention
    and in conjunction with relevant due process guarantees established
    in Article 8," the latter of which the court considered necessary to
    make the right under Article 4(6) effective;

(e) in response to the execution of Joey Ramiah which was the subject of
    the court's provisional measure, the court found Trinidad and Toba-
    go in breach of its provisional measure and arbitrarily deprived Ra-
    miah of his right to life in violation of Article 4 of the Convention
    and also found the act "aggravated" because it occurred despite the
    existence of provisional measures ordered by the court in his favour;
    and

(f) reparations were ordered by the court to Ramiah's family members
    for representation.

Other IACHR Cases and Decisions

Other notable cases from the Caribbean decided by the Inter-American
Court includes James v. Trinidad and Tobago, Order for provisional measures, Inter. Am. Ct. C.H.R. (Ser. E) Nos. 1–3 (1998), (James case) Da
Costa Cadogan v Barbados, Boyce et al. versus Barbados, Preliminary Ob-
jections, Merits, Reparations, and Costs, Judgment, Inter. Am. Ct. H.R.
(Ser. C) No. 169. The Inter-American Human Rights System has made significant contributions to the death penalty jurisprudence in the Caribbe-

an. For example, Tittemore (2004, p. 501) argues that "until the decision in Hilaire v Trinidad and Tobago, Case 11.816, Inter. Am. C.H.R. 66 (unpublished 1999) no other international human rights tribunal had evaluated the implications of mandatory sentencing for the implementation of the death penalty"—a defining moment in the region's jurisprudence.

The Inter-American Commission and Court on Human Rights continue to play a pivotal role in ensuring Caribbean countries adhere to international human rights norms and guidelines. In this regard, it is noteworthy that while the landmark decision in Pratt and Morgan dealt with undue and inordinate delay on death row, and the various aspects of the death penalty per se, *Hilaire* dealt with the mandatory nature of the death penalty and related issues including, inter alia, the right to life, conditions of incarceration both pre- and post-trial, mentioned above.

The Caribbean's Record on Human Rights Issues

The Inter-American Court on Human Rights decision in Hilaire brings the Caribbean's human rights record under scrutiny despite its membership and participation in the Inter-American System. It seems less than encouraging! To date, of the major human rights Conventions and Protocols, no Caribbean country has signed or acceded to the Protocol to Abolish the death penalty; Barbados, Dominica, Grenada, and Jamaica are the only states that are party to the Inter-American Convention on Human Rights and only Barbados has accepted the contentious jurisdiction of the Inter-American Court on Human Rights and Trinidad and Tobago withdrew from the American Convention. In that regard, a number of issues surrounding the death penalty including the sentence itself are related to the contentious human rights issues contained a plethora of global treaties and protocols. The region's track record on these treaties is highlighted in Table 3.3.

It is against this checkered human rights record of Caribbean countries that the following specific international human rights issues are noted.

ABOLITION OF THE DEATH PENALTY AS A HUMAN RIGHTS ISSUE

The Commonwealth Caribbean stands out as one of the few regions of the world that have slavishly adhered to this tradition. Most countries in

Table 3.3 *Ratification of international and regional human rights treaties relevant to the death penalty*

Country	Convention on Human Rights	(First) Optional Protocol to ICCPR	UN Convention against Torture	American Convention on Human Rights	Inter-American Convention to Punish Torture	Rome Statute of International Criminal Court
Antigua and Barbuda			x			x
Bahamas	x					
Barbados	x	x		x		x
Belize	x		x			x
Dominica	x			x		x
Grenada	x			x		x
Guyana	x	x	x			x
Haiti	x					x
Jamaica	x	withdrawn		x		
St. Kitts and Nevis						x
St. Lucia						x
SVG	x	x	x			x
T&T	x	withdrawn		withdrawn		x

Source: Amnesty International (December 15, 2012).

the Americas have abolished the death penalty (Venezuela in 1863, Costa Rica in 1882, Panama in 1903, Ecuador in 1906, Uruguay in 1907, Colombia in 1910, Mexico in 2005, and Argentina in 2008) and two CARICOM Caribbean countries (Haiti and more recently Suriname) and wider Caribbean (Dominican Republic) though many Caribbean countries still retain capital punishment.

To date, "only Barbados, Dominica, Grenada, and Jamaica have ratified the American Convention on Human Rights and only Barbados recog-

nizes the jurisdiction of the Inter-American Court on Human Rights"
(Amnesty International, 2012, p. 13). Trinidad and Tobago stands out
as the most delinquent country because despite being one of two countries to have accepted the compulsory jurisdiction of the Inter-American
Court on Human Rights, along with Barbados, it denunciation from the
American Convention on Human Rights makes it the only country that
has withdrawn from the Inter-American System.

The Mandatory Death Sentence in Murder Cases

According to Tittemore (2004, p. 466), the judgments in the trilogy of
cases in the Privy Council were issued "subsequent to the adoption of
a series of similar decisions by the human rights supervisory bodies of
the inter-American system, the Inter-American Court of Human Rights,
and the Inter-American Commission on Human Rights, which found the
mandatory death penalty in the Commonwealth Caribbean to be incompatible with the right to life, the right to humane treatment, and the right
to due process under regional human rights instruments." Moreover, in a
number of cases the Inter-American Court on Human Rights has ruled
out that the mandatory death penalty in murder cases is illegal.

Cruel and Harsh Punishment

According to Carozza (2003, p. 1071), the IACHR held that mandatory
death sentences also violate the right to humane treatment because they
are contrary to the underlying principles of the Convention as a whole
which are rights that are guaranteed as a derived from the dignity of the
human person and Article 5 in particular, that the rights guaranteed are
derived from the dignity of the human person; in other words, capital
punishment violates "the essential respect for the dignity of the individual, by depriving the accused of life without considering the particular
circumstances of that person's case."

The Right to Life

The issue of death penalty's infringement on the right to life was brought
about because of the decision of the IACHR which states that mandatory death sentences do not take into consideration the unique nature of
the peculiar circumstances of each crime and the arbitrary nature of the
mandatory imposition. This is supported by the provision of Article 4 of
the Inter-American Convention on Human Rights which states that "no

one shall be arbitrarily deprived of his life." In this regard, as murder can be committed in various ways, the failure to take into account the various mitigating circumstances offends this provision of the convention.

The Influence of International Law

As Caribbean countries are members of the OAS and UN, they are bound by the various hemispheric and global treaties, accompanying protocols on human rights and decisions of the Inter-American Commission on Human Rights. Since the *Pratt and Morgan* decision, the influence of international law has had a profound impact on the death penalty jurisprudence in the Caribbean or what the CCJ in *Joseph and Boyce* calls the confluence between national and international law. This move by the ECCA, CCJ, and Privy Council has caused much debate (Anderson, 2011; Barrow, 2016; Berry, 2013; Helfer, 2002; Phillips, 2009; Tittemore, 2004; Ventose, 2013), despite the limitation of the discourse to the Privy Council and CCJ.

The source of much of this international law debate lies in the fact that Commonwealth Caribbean countries follow the dualist doctrine (Berry, 2013; Helfer, 2002) which, strictly speaking, holds that international law and municipal law operate on different planes. It follows naturally, therefore, that for Caribbean countries, unless these international obligations are incorporated or transformed into municipal law they are not legally binding. Therefore, if one travels further along this continuum, the position of unincorporated treaties, which the Privy Council, CCJ, and ECCA have relied on in various judgments, should not be legally binding on Caribbean countries.

The point is clearly articulated by Berry (2013) while outlining the limited exceptions where courts may have recourse to them and reiterated by Ventose (2013) in his review of the route taken by CCJ judges took to establish rights based on the common-law doctrine of "legitimate expectation" on the part of the litigants in these capital punishment cases. Berry (2013, p. 103) argues that the common law rules for applying international law before the domestic courts invoked by the Privy Council and CCJ are not vague or contradictory. Rather these rules are precise, comprehensive, and comprehensible.

At this point, it may be important to state here the recent history of international law in some of the key death penalty cases from Pratt and Mor-

gan onwards. Lord Griffiths in Pratt and Morgan, in relying heavily on the
ECHR case of Soering v the United Kingdom, stated:

> "The total period of delay is shocking and now amounts
> to almost fourteen years. It is double the time that the
> European Court of Human Rights considered would be
> an infringement of Article 3 of the European Conven-
> tion and their Lordships can have no doubt that an ex-
> ecution would now be an infringement of section 17(1)
> of the Jamaican Constitution" (Pratt and Morgan, p. 23).
> "In arriving at this conclusion their Lordships do not
> overlook the reliance placed by the Solicitor-General
> on the dissenting judgment of Sir Gerald Fitzmaurice in
> The Republic of Ireland v. The United Kingdom (1978)
> 2 E.H.R.R. 25, 120 but prefer an interpretation of the
> Constitution of Jamaica that accepts civilised standards
> of behaviour which will outlaw acts of inhumanity, albeit
> they fall short of the barbarity of genocide" (Pratt and
> Morgan, p. 23–24).

A few years later, Sir Dennis Byron's leading judgment in the landmark decision in Spence and Hughes v The Queen contain profound statements
on the applicability and weight of the international law on the regional
court. He opined:

> "However, it is also well settled law that domestic provi-
> sions whether of the Constitution or statute law should
> as far as possible be interpreted so as to conform to the
> state's obligations under international law (Neville Lew-
> is and The Attorney General of Jamaica and Matadeen v
> Pointu (1999) 1 AC 98, 114G-H)" [para. 37]. Both St.
> Vincent and St. Lucia are signatories to the above-men-
> tioned ACHR, UDHR, and ICCPR and are bound by
> their provisions in International Law. The ACHR pro-
> vides in Article 5[2] states as follows:

> "No one shall be subjected to torture or to cruel, inhu-
> man, or degrading punishment or treatment ...." [para.
> 38]. "Not long after, in the 2006 CCJ case Joseph and
> Boyce, De La Bastide P and Saunders J in delivering the

joint judgement made the two telling statements on the courts view of international law in municipal law."

"Over the last sixty or so years, however, it has become quite common for treaties to grant to individual human beings "rights" directly enforceable by them with the result that, far from being passive subjects, individuals can now become active players on the international plane pursuant to treaties entered into by their Governments. These treaties contain provisions that are legally complete under international law. They provide the process by which individuals may enforce the rights conferred by them and no refinement is required by a State Party in order for nationals to take advantage of such provisions. Pursuant to the ACHR for example, without formal incorporation by Parliament, individual citizens may initiate proceedings and obtain relief from an international body" [para. 105].

"This development has been accompanied by the promotion of universal standards of human rights, accepted both at the domestic and on the international level. Citizens are now at liberty to press for the observance of these rights at both levels. At the domestic level, the jurisprudence of international bodies is fully considered and applied. In determining the content of a municipal right, domestic courts may consider the judgments of international bodies. Likewise, on the international plane, the judgments of domestic courts assist in informing the manner in which international law is interpreted and applied. There is therefore a distinct, irreversible tendency towards confluence of domestic and international jurisprudence" [para. 106].

These decisions as well as Privy Council decisions such as Thomas v Baptiste, Lewis v AG [2001] 2 AC (PC), Reyes v R UKPC 11 [2002], Fox v R [2002] UKPC 13 [2002] and Hughes v R UKPC 12 [2002] have been roundly criticized by Berry (2013) as misapplications of the rules of international in the municipal courts. In fact, Ventose (2013, p. 146) agrees "that the decision runs counter to the constitutional principle that international treaties do not form part of the domestic legal process until they have been incorporated by the legislature"; however, he contends that "the CCJ's approach is forward thinking."

Discussion and Analysis: Rationalizing the Jurisprudence

The Privy Council's track record on the death penalty in the English-speaking Caribbean countries has resulted in patchwork in the jurisprudence. The fact that the death penalty has been abolished in every country in Europe, except Belarus, the European Union's abolition prerequisite for membership and the momentum of the global abolition movement should not be discounted as factors in the London-based court's decisions.

On the other hand, many Caribbean people were left wondering as the CCJ's ruling in Joseph and Boyce, appears to have continued along the Privy Council's continuum on the death penalty jurisprudence, despite its exhortations on the limitations imposed on Pratt and Morgan regarding both the 5 year time limit for execution and 18 months to exhaust all international human rights appeals. The judgment in Joseph and Boyce and presence of Byron, Saunders, and Barrow suggest that we can expect more of the same from the CCJ. However, in rationalizing the death penalty jurisprudence in the ESC it is important to understand the jurisdiction of the courts because of the various intersecting jurisdictions of the Privy Council, CCJ, and the ECCA which is lower ranking court but is placed in a peculiar position in the region.

Jurisdiction

Privy Council decisions are binding only on those countries that currently retain it as their final appellate court (Antigua and Barbuda, The Commonwealth of the Bahamas, Grenada, Jamaica St. Kitts and Nevis, St. Vincent and the Grenadines, Trinidad and Tobago, and all British Overseas Territories). The CCJ is the final appellate court for Barbados, Belize, Guyana, and the Commonwealth of Dominica. While the Eastern Caribbean Court of Appeal is an Appellate court with jurisdiction for the OECS countries and overseas territories, it is not a final appeals court. As such, its decisions are reviewable by the CCJ in the case of the Commonwealth of Dominica and by the Privy Council in all other cases from the remaining Member States. It is important to note the weight the CCJ will attach to Privy Council decisions highlighted in the judgment of De La Bastide P and Saunders J in Joseph and Boyce. Therefore, Privy Council decisions in Barbados, Belize, and Dominica prior to their membership in the CCJ will continue to be binding on those jurisdictions until they are overruled by the CCJ, and later Privy Council decisions on the relevant issues carry persuasive weight in the CCJ.

LEGALITY OF THE DEATH PENALTY

Despite the various Privy Council decisions the death penalty continues to be lawful. This is contained in the various pieces of legislation throughout the English-speaking Caribbean (ESC) (De La Bastide P and Saunders J in Joseph and Boyce and prescribed by the American Convention on Human Rights and the Optional Protocol on Civil and Political Rights of the United Nations (Tittemore, 2004). This view is also reflected in the decision of Boyce v The Queen (Barbados) Watson v The Queen (Jamaica) and Matthew v The State (Trinidad and Tobago). However, it must be applied in a manner that is consistent with the guidelines laid down in the various judgments of the Privy Council and the various international treaties of the human rights bodies coupled with their Protocols and Advisory Opinions, whether incorporated or not, following Spence and Hughes and Joseph and Boyce.

DISCRETIONARY APPLICATION OF DEATH PENALTY

There is no longer any mandatory death penalty in the English-speaking Caribbean following the decisions of Spence and Hughes of the ECCA and The Queen v Spence and Hughes in the Privy Council. These decisions were followed in Reyes v R (Belize), R v Bowe, R v Forrester (Bahamas) Joseph and Boyce (Barbados), Lambert Watson v R (Jamaica), and Nimrod Miguel (Trinidad and Tobago), see Table 3.4.

RIGHTS OF PERSONS ON DEATH ROW

Almost 20 years before Pratt and Morgan, the Privy Council established that convicted persons have rights even after conviction in Abbott v A-G of Trinidad and Tobago. Lord Diplock opened the door in Abbott in his leading judgment when he stated:

Table 3.4 *The mandatory death penalty in the Commonwealth Caribbean*

Country	Is the death penalty mandatory?	Legal authority	Legislation or decision of highest appeal court
Antigua and Barbuda	No	*Spence and Hughes*	Privy Council decision
Barbados	No	*Joseph and Boyce*	CCJ decision
Bahamas	No	*R v Bowe, R v Forrester*	Privy Council decision
Belize	No	*R v Reyes* *Joseph and Boyce*	While this is a Privy Council decision. The CCJ is now the highest appeal court
Dominica	No	*Spence and Hughes* *Joseph and Boyce*	Privy Council decision CCJ is now the final appeals court
Grenada	No	*Spence and Hughes*	Privy Council decision
Guyana	No	Criminal Offences (Amendment Act) 2010, Joseph and Boyce	While the CCJ decision is Joseph and Boyce, Guyana also has legislation
Jamaica	No	*Lambert Watson v R* *Offences Against Person Act 1992*	The Privy Council rule the death penalty is discretionary
St. Kitts and Nevis	No	*Spence and Hughes, R v Fox*	Privy Council decision
St. Lucia	No	*Spence and Hughes*	Privy Council decision
SVG	No	*Spence and Hughes*	Privy Council decision
Trinidad and Tobago	No	*Nimrod Miguel v The State*	The PC ruled that the death penalty is discretionary some murders

Source: Fieldwork, 2017 as created by author using data from Seetahal
(2014, p. 366–368) and the CCJ decision in *Joseph and Boyce*

"That so long a period should have been allowed to
elapse between the passing of a death sentence and its
being carried out is, in their Lordships' view, greatly to
be deplored. It brings the administration of criminal

justice into disrepute among law-abiding citizens. Nevertheless, their Lordships doubt whether it is realistic to suggest that from the point of view of the condemned man himself he would wish to expedite the final decision as to whether he would die or not if he thought there was a serious risk that the decision would be unfavorable. While there's life, there's hope. At any rate, as in *de Freitas v. Benny* [1976] A.C. 239, it has to be conceded that the applicant cannot complain about the delay totalling three years preceding his petition for pardon caused by his own action in appealing against his conviction or about the delay totalling two years subsequent to the rejection of his petition caused by his own action in appealing against the sentence on constitutional grounds. His case as advanced before their Lordships has depended solely on the period of somewhat less than eight months sandwiched between the two longer periods, which was allowed by the state to elapse between the lodging of his petition for pardon and its rejection by the President. This it is claimed amounted to delay so inordinate as to involve a contravention of his constitutional rights" (p. 20).

Sentencing Guidelines after Murder Conviction

Once convicted of murder, sentencing guidelines and factors of the particular convicted person must be considered in determining whether to impose the death penalty of another appropriate sentence *Spence and Hughes* and Article 4 of the American Convention (Tittemore, 2004). Additionally, the death penalty must only be imposed in the most serious cases where there is no prospect for rehabilitation *Spence and Hughes* and Article 4 of the American Convention (Tittemore, 2004).

In Riley v Attorney General, the Privy Council ruled that whatever the reasons for or the length of the delay in execution a sentence of death lawfully imposed, the delay can afford no ground for holding the execution to be in contravention of section 17(1). However, following the decision in Pratt and Morgan it may be inferred that if the death penalty is applied more than 5 years after conviction, it would normally be deemed to be an inordinate delay. However, Lord Griffith, who delivered the judgment in Pratt and Morgan did not rule out the possibility of shorter periods being considered inordinately long or longer periods in circumstances where the condemned persons contributed to the delay being considered to be lawful [p. 13]. This view was echoed by Privy Council in Guerra v Baptiste (Rediker, 2013) and De La Bastide P and Saunders J joint judgment with Bernard J concurring in Joseph and Boyce.

Must be fair and just exercise of Prerogative of Mercy

The Prerogative of Mercy must be exercised in fair and just manner and can be reviewed if challenged Neville Lewis v A.G. and Joseph and Boyce departing from the earlier position in De Frietas and Benny and Reckley v Minister of Public Safety and Immigration (No. 2). However, the decision in Reckley (No. 2) partially relied on "a full and careful review of authorities throughout the world and Jamaica's obligations under the American Convention on Human Rights" (Morrison, 2006, p. 16) and has attracted negative reviews from Caribbean scholars (Berry, 2013; Ventose, 2013) as running afoul of constitutional principles.

International Law Principles will Inform Death Penalty

The decisions in Spence and Hughes in the OECS and Joseph and Boyce regarding the role of unincorporated treaties in the Caribbean region dictate that all appeals to the human rights bodies must be exhausted before the death penalty can be implemented. This underscores the critical role of international law in the evolving death penalty jurisprudence in the Caribbean. The key decisions are contained in Table 3.5 which provides a timeline of some of the key death penalty decisions.

THE ABOLITION ISSUE

Abolition of the death penalty in the Caribbean is a very controversial issue. At the heart of the problem is the hurdle that many Caribbean governments and the public at large support the death penalty (Amnesty International, 2012; Burnham, 2005a, 2005b; Helfer, 2002; Hood & Seemungal, 2009, 2011; Norris & Chadee 2001). This is primarily because of the high levels of murder and other types of serious crimes and the inability of the state to provide effective sustainable solutions. As such, many politicians wave the death penalty to appease public anxiety.

Table 3.5 *Evolution of the jurisprudence on the death penalty in the Caribbean*

Year	Case	Court	Jurisdiction	Issue	Finding
1976	*De Freitas v Benny*	JCPC	Trinidad and Tobago	Prerogative of Mercy	No right of appeal
1977	*Abbott*	JCPC	Trinidad and Tobago	Rights of convicted persons	Convicted persons retain rights even after conviction
1993	*Pratt v Morgan*	JCPC	Jamaica	5 years delay on death row	Illegal
1996	*Guerra v Baptiste*	JCPC	Trinidad and Tobago	5 years delay in not a yardstick	Four years and 10 months could amount to delay
1999	*Thomas and Hilaire v Baptiste*	JCPC	Trinidad and Tobago	Local safeguards for international protection	1. The protection of the due process of law under national constitutions extend to the procedures before the Inter-American Human Rights System, 2. Eighteen months might not be sufficient to exhaust petitions to the international bodies
2000	*Desmond Baptiste Neville Lewis & AG of Jamaica*	JCPC JCPC	Jamaica	Mercy	The prerogative of mercy is reviewable
2001	*Lewis and the AG* *Spence v The Queen*	JCPC JCPC	Jamaica	Reviewability of exercise of mercy Mandatory death Penalty	Prerogative of mercy can be reviewed Is unconstitutional
2002	*Reyes Hughes Fox*	JCPC	Belize St. Lucia ECCA	Legality of the mandatory death penalty	Unlawful
2002	*Hilaire, Constantine & Benjamin et al. v Trinidad and Tobago*	IACHR	Trinidad & Tobago	Mandatory death penalty	Contrary to the ICCPR and ACHR

2003	Balkisoon Roodal	JCPC	T&T	Legality of the death penalty	Death penalty is unconstitutional
2004	Boyce v The Queen Matthew v The State Watson v The Queen	JCPC	Barbados T&T Jamaica	Legality of the death penalty	Lawful because of the savings clause in the constitutions
2006	AG and others v Joseph and Boyce	CCJ	Barbados	Mandatory death penalty	Unlawful because violates the right to life arbitrary and ignores application only to most serious cases
2011	Nimrod Miguel v The State of Trinidad and Tobago	JCPC	T&T	Legality of death penalty	Mandatory death penalty unlawful
2015	Hunte and Khan v The State	JCPC	Trinidad and Tobago	Can Courts of Appeal commute death sentence while the case is before the PC	No

Source: Fieldwork, 2017 (created using decided cases from
the ECCA, CCJ, UKPC, and IACHR).

To compound matters, regional governments have been criticized for
their public security policies that are heavily focused on suppression and
reactionary strategies but fail to address the root causes of the problem
(Amnesty International, 2012; UNDP, 2012; UNODC/WB, 2007). Additionally, many have argued that it is our law and should be respected
notwithstanding the many incursions by the Privy Council, Inter-American Court on Human Rights and more recently, the CCJ, the ECCA, and
local courts in the OECS region.

On the other hand, abolitionists agree that the death penalty is contrary
to international law; it is cruel and unusual punishment, unconstitutional
and contrary to the right to life. One of the more convincing arguments
against the death penalty is the lack of research which supports it as an
effective tool in the fight against crime; however, this argument does not

seem to be too persuasive in the region. In that regard, there seems to be little research and advocacy in the region from the leading academic intuitions on this subject which I feel would add currency to the abolition discourse. In fact, one study has shown that while one Caribbean country executed persons annually within a given a time frame the murder rate remained fairly constant.

The fact that all Latin America countries (except Cuba and Guatemala) have abolished the death penalty also does not seem to bolster the case for abolition. Many of these countries have very high murder rates, with Central America leading the globe (UNODC, 2014). However, the United States retention of the death penalty may be a critical factor and it is arguable that if the United States abolishes the death penalty the remaining Caribbean might follow their lead, though there have been several calls by Amnesty International to abolish the death penalty on various grounds.

CONCLUSION

Despite abolitionists' pleas and scathing judgments from the highest courts and international tribunals, it appears that Caribbean countries will not abolish the death penalty in the near future because of the high levels of violent crime in the region and lack of effective crime reduction strategies. Moreover, there is no political support at the regional level in CARICOM that is equivalent to the EU's mandatory abolition of the death penalty prerequisite for membership to act as a buffer to these retentionist states of the Commonwealth Caribbean. Additionally, despite decisions that further limit the application of the death penalty in every CARICOM Member State, it is noteworthy that the death penalty remains the law in all of these Caribbean countries (De La Bastide P and Saunders J in Joseph and Boyce). However, there are many limits to its application.

To begin with, following the decisions in *Spence and Hughes* (in the OECS countries), Joseph and Boyce (Barbados, Belize, Dominica, and Guyana) and (The Commonwealth of the Bahamas Jamaica, Trinidad and Tobago), the decisions of the Inter-American Commission and Court on Human rights have further restricted the instances when the death penalty can be lawfully implemented on issues such as pregnant women and persons over 70 years old. In this regard, the judgment in Hilaire represents a watershed moment and part of the Inter-American Human Rights System's monumental contribution to the region's death penalty jurisprudence.

Despite some of the drawbacks of the influence of international law highlighted by Berry (2013) and Ventose (2013), the noble attempts by jurists in the region (ECCA and CCJ) and further afield in IACHR, are commendable, as they continue to find innovative ways to protect individual human rights where the written law and the constitution seems lacking. In this regard, the judgments of the various courts, though conflicting at times, have consistently limited the applicability of the death penalty stopping short of outright abolition. The courts have pushed the envelope on the death penalty and it is now left to the politicians to make the next move.

REFERENCES

Amnesty International. (2012). *Death penalty in the English-speaking Caribbean: A human rights issue.* United Kingdom: Amnesty International, International Secretariat.

Anderson, W. (2011). The role of the Caribbean court of justice in human rights adjudication: International treaty law dimensions. *Journal of Transnational Law & Policy, 21,* 1–34.

Anthony, K. D. (2003). *The Caribbean court of justice: Will it be a hanging court?* Address at The Norman Manley Law School, June 28, 2003.

Antoine, R. M. B. (2005). Waiting to exhale: Commonwealth Caribbean law and legal systems. *Nova Law Review, 29*(2), 141–169.

Barrow, D. (2016). Developments in the CCJ and the Caribbean and the application of international law to domestic cases. *Caribbean Journal of International Relations and Diplomacy, 4*(1), 63–68.

Berry, D. (2013). Transitions in Caribbean law: An introduction. In D. Berry & T. Robinson (Eds.), *Transitions in Caribbean law: Lawmaking constitutionalism and the confluence of national and international law* (pp. vii-xxvii). Kingston, Jamaica: Ian Randle Publishers.

Berry, D., & Robinson, T. (Eds.). (2013). *Transitions in Caribbean law:*

Lawmaking constitutionalism and the confluence of national and international law. Kingston, Jamaica: Ian Randle Publishers.

Birdsong, L. E. (1999). Is there a rush to the death penalty in the Caribbean: The Bahamas says no. *Temple International and Comparative Law Journal, 13*, 285.

Birdsong, L. E. (2005). The formation of the Caribbean court of justice: The sunset of British colonial rule in the English speaking Caribbean. *The University of Miami Inter-American Law Review, 36*(2/3), 197–227.

Broadbent, G. (2004a). Trinidad and Tobago: Murder-constitutionality of constructive malice and mandatory death sentence Khan v The State. *Journal of Criminal Law, 68*(4), 301–305.

Broadbent, G. (2004b). Barbados: constitutionality of mandatory death penalty. *Journal of Criminal Law, 68*(6), 484–497.

Burnham, M. A. (2005a). Indigenous constitutionalism and the death penalty: The case of the Commonwealth Caribbean. *International Journal of Constitutional Law, 3*(4), 582–616.

Burnham, M. A. (2005b). Saving constitutional rights from judicial scrutiny: The savings clause in the law of the Commonwealth Caribbean. *The University of Miami Inter-American Law Review, 36*, 249–269.

Byron, D., & Dakolias, M. (2008). The regional court systems in the organization of Eastern Caribbean states and the Caribbean. In E. M. Favaro (Ed.), *Small States, Smart Solutions: Improving Connectivity and Increasing the Effectiveness of Public Services. Direction in Development; Public Sector Governance (pp. 91–126)*. Washington, DC: World Bank.

Campbell, J. (2015). Murder appeals, delayed executions, and the origins of Jamaican death penalty jurisprudence. *Law and History Review, 33*(2), 435–466.

Carozza, P. G. (2003). My friend is a stranger: The death penalty and the global ius commune of human rights. *Texas Law Review, 81*, 1031–1089.

Concepcion, N. P. (2000). Legal implications of Trinidad & Tobago's withdrawal from the American convention on human rights. *American University International Law Review, 16*(3), 847–890.

Cross, J. E. (2014). Matter of discretion: The de facto abolition of the mandatory death penalty in Barbados-a study of the Boyce and Joseph cases. *University of Miami Inter-American Law Review, 46*(1), 39–59.

Eidson, W. (2008). The Caribbean court of justice: An Institution Whose Time Has Come. *Chicago-Kent Journal of International and Comparative Law, 8,* 166–199.

Fraser, A. (2006). From forgotten through friction to the future: The evolving relationship of the Anglophone Caribbean and the Inter-American system of human rights. *Revista Instituto Interamericano de Derechos Humanos, 43,* 207–237.

Frost, S. (2014). DaCosta Cadogan v. Barbados. *Loyola of Los Angeles International and Comparative Law Review, 36*(1/6), 155–172.

García Ramírez, S. (2010). The Inter-American court of human rights and the death penalty. *Mexican Law Review, 3*(1), 99–127.

Gifford, A. (2009). Death penalty: developments in Caribbean jurisprudence. *International Journal of Legal Information, 37*(2/7), 196–203.

Greenberg, D. F., & Agozino, B. (2012). Executions, imprisonment and crime in Trinidad and Tobago. *British Journal of Criminology, 52*(1), 113–140.

Griffith, I. L. (1997). *Drugs and security in the Caribbean: Sovereignty under siege.* University Park: Pennsylvania State University Press.

Griffith, I. L. & Munroe, T. (1997). Drugs and democratic governance in the Caribbean. In I. L. Griffith & B. N. Sedoc-Dahlberg (Eds.), *Democracy and human rights in the Caribbean* (pp. 74–93). New York: Westview Press.

Helfer, L. R. (2002). Overlegalizing human rights: International relations theory and the Commonwealth Caribbean backlash against human rights regimes. *Columbia Law Review, 102,* 1832–1911.

Helfer, L. R. (2003). Constitutional Analogies in the International Legal System. *Loyola of Los Angeles Law Review* 37(2), 193–237.

Hill, S. (2013). The rise of gang violence in the Caribbean. In R. Seepersad & A. M. Bissessar (Eds.), *Gangs in the Caribbean* (pp. 36-79). London: Cambridge Scholars Publishing.

Hill, S. M., & Morris, P. K. (2017). *Drug trafficking and gang violence in the Caribbean*. In M. Raymond Izarali (Ed.), *Crime, violence and security in the Caribbean* (pp. 52–57). New York and London: Routledge.

Hodgkinson, P., Gyllensten, L., & Peel, D. (2010). *Capital punishment briefing paper. The centre for capital punishment studies*. London, UK: Westminster University Law School.

Hood, R. G., & Seemungal, F. (2006). *A rare and arbitrary fate: Conviction for the murder, the mandatory death penalty and the reality of homicide in Trinidad and Tobago*. Centre for Criminology, University of Oxford, UK.

Hood, R., & Seemungal, F. (2009). Experiences and perceptions of the mandatory death sentence for murder in Trinidad and Tobago: Judges, prosecutors and counsel. In R. Hood, F. Seemungal, D. Mendes & J. Fagan (Eds.), *A Penalty Without Legitimacy: The Mandatory Death Penalty in Trinidad and Tobago. Papers Prepared for a Conference held in Port of Spain on 7 March 2009* (pp. 1-30). London: The Death Penalty Project.

Hood, R. G., & Seemungal, F. (2011). Public opinion on the mandatory death penalty in Trinidad. A summary of the main findings of a survey. A report for the Death Penalty Project and the Rights Advocacy Project of the University of the West Indies Faculty of Law, 1–9.

Katz, C. M., Maguire, E. R., & Choate, D. (2011). A cross-national comparison of gangs in the United States and Trinidad and Tobago. *International Criminal Justice Review, 21*(3), 243–262.

Klein, A. (2001). Between the death penalty and decriminalization: New directions for drug control in the Commonwealth Caribbean. *New West Indian Guide, 75*(3–4), 193–227.

Lehrfreund, S. (2011). International legal trends and the 'Mandatory' death penalty in the Commonwealth Caribbean. *Oxford University Commonwealth Law Journal, 1*(2), 171–194.

Lofquist, W. S. (2010). Executions in the Bahamas. *The International Journal of Bahamian Studies, 16,* 19–34.

Maertens, F. & Anstey, C. (2007). Crime, violence, and development: Trends, costs, and policy options in the Caribbean. *United Nations Office on Drugs and Crime Latin America and the Caribbean region of the World Bank. United Nations: UN Latin America and the Caribbean Regional Office.*

Maguire, E. R., Willis, J. A., Snipes, J., & Gantley, M. (2008). Spatial concentrations of violence in Trinidad and Tobago. *Caribbean Journal of Criminology and Public Safety, 13*(1–2), 44–83.

McKoy, D. V. (2007a.) Reshaping Commonwealth Caribbean jurisprudence: From Pratt and Morgan to Joseph and Boyce. *West Indian Law Journal,* 32(2), 155–187.

McKoy, D. V. (2007b). Identifying the Chi in Commonwealth Caribbean Law: The contribution of the common law and human rights law to constitutional interpretation, 1-20. Retrieved from https://ssrn.com/abstract=1021627. Based on 'Reshaping Commonwealth Caribbean Jurisprudence: From Pratt and Morgan to Joseph and Boyce' (2007) 32 (2) West Indian Law Journal, 32(2), 155–187.

Montoute, A., & Anyanwu, D. (2009). *A situational analysis of gun related crime in the Caribbean: The case of Trinidad & Tobago; Antigua & Barbuda; St Vincent & the Grenadines and St. Lucia.* Coalition for Development and the Reduction of Armed Violence.

Morrison, D. (2006). The Judicial Committee of the Privy Council and the Death Penalty in the Commonwealth Caribbean: Studies in Judicial Activism. Nova Law Review, 30(3), 403–424.

Norris, M., & Chadee, D. (2001). Capital ideas: A cross cultural study on death penalty attitudes in and around the Caribbean. *Caribbean Journal of Criminology and Social Psychology, 6,* (1&2), 62–81.

Novak, A. (2014). The global decline of the mandatory death penalty: Constitutional jurisprudence and legislative reform in Africa, Asia, and the Caribbean. Surrey, England: Ashgate.

Phillips, F. (2009). The death penalty and human rights. Kingston, Jamaica: Ian Randle Publishers.

Rediker, E. (2013). Courts of appeal and colonialism in the British Caribbean: A case for the Caribbean court of justice. *Michigan Journal of International Law, 35*(1/6), 213–251.

Rupnow, J. (2013). The death penalty in the Greater Caribbean. Detailed Fact Sheet. 11th World Day Against the Death Penalty.

Schabas, W. A. (2003). *The abolition of capital punishment from an international law perspective.* Paper presented at the International Society for the Reform of Criminal Law 17th International Conference 'Convergence of Criminal Justice Systems—Bridging the Gaps', The Hague, August 24–28, 2003.

Seetahal, D. S. (2014). *Commonwealth Caribbean criminal practice and procedure* (4th edn.). London and New York: Taylor and Francis.

Simmons, D. A. C. (1999). Conflicts of law and policy in the Caribbean-Human Rights and the Enforcement of the death penalty-between a rock and a hard place. *Journal of Transnational Law and Policy, 9*(2), 263–287.

Tittemore, B. D. (2004). Mandatory death penalty in the Commonwealth Caribbean and the Inter-American human rights system: An evolution in the development and implementation of international human rights protections. *William & Mary Bill of Rights Journal, 13*(2/7), 445–520.

UNDP Caribbean Human Development Report. (2012). Human development and the shift to better citizen security. United Nations.

UNODC/WB. (2007). Crime, Violence, and Development: Trends, Costs, and Policy Options in the Caribbean. Report No. 37820 - A Joint Report by the United Nations Office on Drugs and Crime and the Latin America and the Caribbean Region of the World Bank.

UNODC. (2014). UNODC Global Study on Homicide 2013. UNODC Publications: Vienna, Austria.

Vasciannie, S. (2008). Decision of the judicial committee of the Privy Council in the Lambert Watson case from Jamaica on the mandatory death penalty and the question of fragmentation. *New York University*

International Law and Politics, 41, 837–869.

Ventose, E. D. (2013). Legitimate expectations, international treaties and the Caribbean court of justice in transitions. In D. S. Berry & T. Robinson (Eds.), *Caribbean law: Law-making, constitutionalism and the convergence of National and International Law.* (pp. 128–147). *Kingston, Jamaica:* The Caribbean Law Publishing Company.

CHAPTER IV

ANTIGUA AND BARBUDA

COUNTRY INFORMATION

A twin island state located in the northern part of the Eastern Caribbean, Antigua and Barbuda has a population of ~90,000 inhabitants. Tourism, the main industry, contributes about 80% of the gross domestic product (GDP). The Criminal Justice Systems in Antigua and Barbuda consist of the Police Force, the Magistrate Courts, The Supreme Court, the OECS Court of Appeal, and Her Majesty Prison. The highest judicial court in the island is the Judicial Committee of the Privy Council in the UK; therefore decisions taken are legally binding in Antigua and Barbuda. The principal legislation which addresses the crime of murder is the Offences Against the Person Act, Chapter 300 of the Laws of Antigua and Barbuda where, according to Section 2, "whosoever is convicted of murder shall suffer death as a felon." Section 3 of the said Act speaks to the sentence of a convicted murderer.

THE ROYAL POLICE FORCE OF ANTIGUA AND BARBUDA

The Royal Police Force of Antigua and Barbuda is the primary law enforcement agency in the country. The Police Act Chapter 330 of the Laws of Antigua and Barbuda Revised Edition 1992 provides the legal framework for the Force and outlines its constitution, powers, duties, and administration. In addition, Section 105 of the Constitution Order of Antigua and Barbuda makes provision for the establishment of a Police Service Commission, whose administrative responsibilities include appointments, promotion, transfers, and certain disciplinary controls. These responsibilities contribute to the general efficiency of the Police Force.

In order to provide effective services to the citizens, residents, and visitors, the primary Law and Order Agency has in total 577 members, of which 450 are male and 127 female. The work of the Police Force is also assisted by ~156 members of the Antigua and Barbuda Fire Service who are legally police officers. They serve to strengthen some departments by providing additional personnel to perform administrative duties or participate in major operations. According to Section 6(1) (a) of the Police

Act Chapter 330, the Police Force shall consist of a Commissioner of Police who, subject to the provisions of the Act and the general direction of the Minister shall have responsibility for the superintendence of the Force.

THE INTERVIEWEE

In January 2015, Mr. Wendel Robinson was appointed by the Police Service Commission as the Commissioner of Police (acting) of the Royal Police Force of Antigua and Barbuda. Mr. Robinson enlisted in the organization in 1989 and has worked in several departments namely the Criminal Record Department, The Traffic Department, The Special Services Unit, and the Prosecution Department. He also had the opportunity to work in the Office of the Director of Public Prosecution and the Office of National Drug and Money Laundering Control Policy (ONDCP).

Commissioner of Police (Ag.), Wendel Robinson holds a Bachelor's Degree in Law from the University of London and was called to the Bar in St. Vincent and the Grenadines in 1998 and Antigua and Barbuda in 2000. He also holds a Master's Degree in International Police Science from the University of Portsmouth. Additionally, he attended the Bramshill Police Staff College in England and the Jamaican Constabulary Staff College where he pursued Police Management and Leadership courses.

Mr. Robinson has stated in his discourse that in June 2015 it was his professional objective "to provide the best possible leadership in any circumstance, and develop the Royal Police Force of Antigua and Barbuda into an institution that ensures integrity, growth in human relations and offer best services securing the tranquillity of the fair state of Antigua and Barbuda."

In recent times, there have been few occasions where convicted murderers have been executed; in fact, the last convicted murderer was hung in 1991.

The following paragraphs in this chapter are the content of an interview with Commissioner of Police (COP) Robinson who was interviewed by Superintendent Atlee P. Rodney and who gave his opinion on the death penalty, crime prevention, and the role and responsibility of the Royal Police Force of Antigua and Barbuda to the community.

THE INTERVIEW

APR: In terms of violent crimes, in your view, have you seen an increase within the past 5 years in Antigua and Barbuda?

WR: In terms of violent crimes, yes, we have seen an increase except I would say for the past 4/5 months. We have seen an increase in terms of violent crimes. Some of these violent crimes emanated from domestic violence though they may start out small—issues of threats as the case may be. And also a situation where there is a turf war between different drug dealers and those have escalated. Of course, with respect to drugs, you would always see firearm annex to it. And so, some of these drug dealers find serious weapons, serious handguns and other weapons, which they can use as an instrument to perpetrate their criminal activities.

APR: Would you describe criminals today as a little more brazen that those in the past?

WR: I don't think there is any doubt about that. They are more brazen and the way in which they are committing the crimes are even more blatant and obvious. I'll give you one typical example. Ten years ago when we would have had housebreakings, you would not normally know of persons breaking into a house using a mask. It has become a norm now that when persons such as criminals are breaking into houses they don't do so unless they are masked or unless they have a gun with them or at least an imitation of a firearm. It shows that they are trying to catch up with technology and the whole issue of identification. So they are gloved and they are masked and that is only to show you how much violent crimes have been graduating and is graduating.

APR: And in terms of the violent crime, what are you seeing more prevalent in Antigua in terms of the choice of weapon?

WR: The choice of weapon is a firearm. And it appears as if 9-millimeter weapons are being used. Rarely will you find firearm of a higher calibre. But that seems to be the position, 9-millimeter weapon and in one or two cases you will see even a .45.

APR: From where you sit, do you sense that the criminals today are thinking about penalty or just the desire to commit the crime? Do you see anything that indicates that?

WR: I really don't think that penalty—the penalty of the crime really means much. Of course the good thing that penalty—if you raise the penalty of the crime does, is that when a person is convicted they will be away for a very long time, but I really don't think that they considered that. Because even though they are arrested and they are on bail, even if they are remanded for a while and they go on bail, they commit the same crime and that gives me the clear impression that the penalty doesn't mean one thing to them.

APR: Now, let's come to this ticklish situation of the death penalty. Because of the increase of homicide in the region, your personal policing philosophy on the death penalty—what are your views on the death penalty?

WR: It is difficult for me to speak from a policing point of view since I am also an attorney and since I would have had some experience in human rights. But my view from a policing perspective is that the death penalty should remain. And I would tell you the reason why. In a twenty-first century, we have the safeguard of DNA which is available. We also have a number of defences which are available for a person who has been charged with murder. We have a court system whereas between the High Court and the Court of Appeal we still have the Privy Council. All these are thresholds where persons who would have defences to a charge of murder can raise these defences and discuss these defences and argue these defences strenuously. And if having had the opportunity to argue these defences before a jury, before their peers, before a High Court judge, before a Court of Appeal and before a very eminent panel as the Privy Council and they fail those tests, then I don't see why in truth and in fact that they should not be hanged. The space or the avenue for a mistake is extremely rare especially in the twenty-first century.

So where these defence of provocation, diminished responsibility, self-defence, mistake, intoxication, automatism, all these defences are available in the legal system as well as the twenty-first century mechanism of DNA. When they would have failed all those particular arguments, I can't see why they should not be hanged. That is from a policing perspective, I must warn you.

APR: The next question I would ask is, how effective do you see the death penalty? Do you see it as an effective way of reducing crime in a society?

WR: No. I think most of the time when persons are considering committing the offence, the issue of the death penalty or any penalty don't come in front of them. What comes in front of them might be anger. What comes in front of them might be frustration, stress, depression, as the case may be, and they kill out of that anger, frustration or that violence. There lurks within all of us that temptation to commit violence, and during that time when we have that temptation, we do not consider the penalty. And we do not consider the repercussion unless, if God helps it, that somebody sees what is about to happen and decide to speak to you and guide you and tell you well, listen this is what the consequences are. Do you really want to? Other than that, I don't think criminals think about the penalty at all.

APR: But in the so-called modern society we live, do you think we have reached the stage where you would say that it's something that should be totally abolished, the death penalty?

WR: No, no, no. I am not in agreement that the death penalty should be totally abolished. The present situation in the Caribbean courts is such that the courts seem to divide it in two. (1) That there are certain cases which if it is the most brutal and the most severe of all the cases, should be reserved for the death penalty. But where the case is not that severe then the person can get life imprisonment or at least would have done or should do maybe 25/30 years imprisonment. So the courts within the Eastern Caribbean jurisdiction at least and within the Caribbean, virtually within the whole Caribbean, reserve the death penalty for the most brutal of cases.

I think what the courts are trying to do is to come to a common ground, a compromise, strike a compromise. Because we have the Privy Council, which is the highest court of the land, and in England itself where the Privy Council sits, the death penalty has been abolished for several decades. And how does/how should our legal jurisprudence develop in such a way as to strike a compromise between a court that sits in the very country where they don't have the death penalty and in the Eastern Caribbean where many of us within the Eastern Caribbean still believe that the death penalty should hold. So I think the courts within the Caribbean strike a compromise. And certainly, except for Justice Redhead, I think it was Justice Saunders and Chief Justice Byron who tip on the scale that the mandatory death penalty is abolished, but they still reserved the death penalty for the most brutal cases. And I—as far as this jurisdiction is concerned, I am yet to see since then that the death penalty has been imposed. So in a way, it seems virtual so that the death penalty has been abolished. But the legal position is, at least in theory, and at least according to precedence, that the mandatory death penalty is abolished and that the death penalty is reserved for the most serious and the most brutal of the murder cases.

APR: But on that note, when you talk about the murder cases, do you see there is any room to include other serious crime/offenses for the death penalty?

WR: Well, I would say cases of treason, cases of terrorism. Those are cases that the death penalty should be reserved to because of the threat of terrorism and at least the fear of terrorism is such that it can have a devastating effect upon society. And, yes, in those cases the death penalty should be reserved for those kinds of cases. Perhaps—, I wouldn't want to go as far as to say that robbery or kidnapping should go for the death penalty because there is still that provision where persons can be sentenced for a very, very long time for offenses of aggravated robbery and kidnapping as the case may be.

APR: So you do not think that the death penalty is cruel and inhumane and so forth?

WR: Well, no. I do not think so. Because you live by the sword you die by the sword. That is a concept that I think is reserved. If you finished the life of another person abruptly, then you should only—it is only reasonable that you should anticipate that your life should be ending somewhat the same way.

So an eye for an eye and a tooth for a tooth, though it may seem not to be a concept in modern biblical terms, and the more—how should I put it? The more realistic view these days based on the New Testament is that if somebody slaps you on your right cheek you turn your left cheek. I don't think the bible meant it to be that simple and I think sometimes we tend to use these biblical terms to suit ourselves. I think the concept of an eye for an eye and a tooth for a tooth should remain where the death penalty is concerned.

APR: From your experience now, what are some of the policies now you think that can be used from where you sit as Commissioner of Police to reduce not only homicide but maybe crime generally? What are some of the things you think from your experience and what programmes that can be used?

WR: Well, you would appreciate that I am Commissioner of Police only for 5 months. What I have introduced is the concept of visibility policing. It will call for more resources, more vehicles, and more petrol use. But I think the idea where the police are seen in the community both in the night and in the day gives that sense of reassurance. And do remember that the fear of crime can be as devastating as the crime itself. Of course, since I became Commissioner of Police we have seen one or two violent crime still but it has been reduced so drastically and I think it is because of policing, visibility policing, reaching out to the community, response time, which is very critical, and also following up on reports.

One of the things that I have introduced as well is that I developed the idea that many of the murders do not occur in a vacuum and, therefore, it is some of the simplest reports that are made to the police that sometimes are not followed up that result in serious injuries and murders. A threat, a person makes a report of a threat to another, a domestic violence situation between a boyfriend and girlfriend, husband and wife at the home, little skirmishes. One drug dealer threatening the other drug dealer, the police hears about it, the police don't get involved and at the end of the day, a murder occurs and the police have to investigate it. So if we nip these in the bud early o'clock, deal with these minor reports, one it would be seen that the police have no tolerance with some of these incidents however simple they may be; and two also, it might nip things in the bud early o'clock that the police get involved, the police deal with the matter either to quell the social disturbance between individuals in the society or to arrest and charge persons. So I have rung that through the ears of the district stations, deal with the minor reports or they become major ones for us to handle.

APR: And based on what you have been doing so far, what would you consider are some of your main challenges in getting to implement it and to sustain it?

WR: Well, one of our main challenges, of course, is resource, and also to have money to pay for intelligence and information. Because some of the persons who bring in information are criminals themselves and are persons who may have little brushes of the law and they might not be persons who are working. They are persons who are from a society who are struggling and if they give a piece of intelligence or a piece of information—they might not be asking for $500 or $600. They might be asking for $100 or $200 and we better have something in the kitty to assist or else they wouldn't come back. And what I have done is that whereas in the past we would have deposited money into the consolidatory fund for firearms training for those persons who have been qualified or deemed qualified and who have been approved to obtain firearms licence that is $500 from each applicant goes to a police account that would pay for these things. I call it a training development account. It goes back to buying ammunition and equipment and to assist in the investigation of cases as well as training.

APR: In terms of your effort as Commissioner of Police, how would you describe the relationship or the assistance you are getting from the general public in terms of crime reduction?

WR: I will tell you this, if the general public gets the impression that the police are working closer with them that the police has a no nonsense approach that the administration is trying to clean up the police in terms of corruption, and in terms of police brutality and these types of things, rest assured that members of the public are going to come forward. Members of the public are going to see the police visibility; you are going to see the police effort in the community. They are going to see that, okay, there have been some changes in the organization however simple the changes are, once there are changes that the public can see, it will have a positive turn around. And I think, these are some of the things that I always try to instil in the senior officers. I have regular meetings and also I developed the approach where members of the public come to me for satisfaction. I try to help them as far as I can legally possibly do so.

APR: When we were talking earlier on about homicides, when we have cases of that nature, do you still feel the presence or the assistance of the general public in terms of giving information.

WR: Well, the three homicides that we have had so far in 2015, we got a lot of assistance from the public in terms of information, members come forward. There was one matter which I do not know if it's because of the fact that it took us a while before we could verify whether or not this was a murder when the person went missing, the young 18-year-old boy. That apart, we did get some information on that but it is still sketchy and we are still working towards that. But that apart, I find that the general public is assisting a lot.

APR: And now not only the general public, let's go back to the whole criminal justice system in terms of when they are sentenced to death. Are you satisfied or dissatisfied with how things are working when we have cases where persons are sentenced to death, the whole process. What's your take on that?

WR: There is a substantive delay in Antigua and Barbuda of these serious criminal cases. When I was Crown Counsel or acting in that capacity when I was seconded to the office of the Director of Public Prosecution, on an average a case would take between 1½ to 2½ years before it was tried. Now cases are taking 5 and 6 years before they are being tried or before they are put on the list of cases to be tried. There is a substantive delay and I do not think in as much as there has been a greater volume of cases that are going before the Crown Court, I do not think it is so high that it could not be manageable. There could be a number of factors which may have accounted for it, but certainly, the delay is unsatisfactory and the sooner the authorities nip this, the better.

APR: What are some of the things you think within the court system that can be done to improve?

WR: One, you have to speed up the committal proceedings and the time the delay from the committal proceedings to the cases reaching the Crown Court. As it stands now you might need to have criminal cases going all year "round as oppose to assizes." You may need another additional judge as well, as well as additional Crown Prosecutors. It may also call for a reclassification of some of the offenses. So, therefore, the Magistrate's Court could be given a wider jurisdiction to deal with several other kinds of cases which normally would have been dealt with at the High Court. So in terms of property offenses, perhaps a magistrate should be able to deal with matters up to $25,000–$40,000. With respect to an offense against a person, perhaps a Magistrate should be able to deal with wounded with the intent that would carry a penalty of up to 7/8 years. So it cuts down on the number of cases that are going before the High Court. Do remember, though, that the Magistrates Court in all these jurisdictions still would resolve at least 94% to 95% of all criminal cases. So there is no need for the backlog of the High Court if it is managed appropriately.

APR: As we conclude this interview, generally, from the police, the justice system and the public points of view, what are some of the things that you feel can be done right now to reduce, not only violent crimes but crimes generally in your society.

WR: I think there needs to be more public police involvement in terms of community sharing of problems and how you deal with problem solving. But community policing is not a mere ticking box exercise. I think you cannot be a good community police if you are just merely playing football in a community or you are merely having meetings with the churches or a committee within the community. It has to go much further than that, real problem solving.

Perhaps the churches are not doing enough. Perhaps there is a certain degree of mistrust between the police and the public. Perhaps the police is not helping the situation when they would have committed acts of violence upon persons who are taken into custody, keep people in custody unnecessarily long, do not respond to incidences however simple, and perhaps do not reach out to the community as much as they should, and the way in which they talk to members of the public. So I think what needs to be done is for us to go back to the drawing board, between the police and the public, speak frankly as to what are some of the problems and the ways in which they can address them. Perhaps policing should not be just seen for strictly speaking police officers or law enforcement officers, but policing should be seen as a community social problem or social issues that must be resolved albeit by police, the government agency, or the community on a whole.

I think also that there is a certain level of mistrust between law enforcement agencies. And similarly this has happened all over the world which have resulted in deaths, terrorism as the case may be where customs may have information and do not share with immigration, immigration have information and does not share with police, police have information do not share with ONDCP, ONDCP have information but because of certain level of mistrust about police officers do not share the information and as a result nothing get solved. And these are some of the ills that need to be corrected.

APR: Mr. Robinson, finally, I would just ask you to just give me your perspective on the importance of crime prevention as it relates to homicide or other serious crime, what's the value of crime prevention itself?

WR: Crime prevention is critical. Most of the time policing is seen as trying to solve the crime. Now, if we can prevent the crime it is better because the prevention helps with respect to the fear of crime. And that is why I have introduced within the police force the whole idea of all the police vehicles, once they have on the lights, to put on the lights in the night. And, of course, the jury is still out where some persons are concerned and think that oh, the criminals when they see the police they would hide. Statistically it has been shown that once they (the criminals) see the police vehicle every few minutes passing through the community in the night with the vehicle police swivel lights on there might be some level of discomfort, but at the end of the day, that police visibility—that is a way of preventing crime. And you would rather know that you prevent the crime than the crime occurring and you solve it. The fact that the crime occurs in and by itself might be some cause for trauma and sudden level of distress and invasion of privacy upon people. So prevention of crime is much more critical that solving the crime itself.

APR: My final question for you, if we don't prevent the crimes, what would you consider as your three most important proposals to fight them?

WR: Well, apart from the fact that you have to have the resources and the DNA capabilities because this is twenty-first century policing, I think one of the critical importance is that 24, 48, 72 hr after the crime occurred it would be good to collect all your statements, and you interview all the persons that you need to interview. If you have a suspect in mind, you deal with the suspect early o'clock and at least come up with a theory as to how the crime would have occurred and start to reconstruct within your mind-set as to how the crime occurred. I think if you do that it is important.

It's also very critical to have what is we would call a follow-up. Sometimes a victim of a crime may not recall certain things, but then 2/3 days after or even a week after they recall certain other things.

Also, you follow the crime trend may show a particular modus operandi. A criminal leaves behind a particular way in which he commits the crime and even though he might try to change that particular modus, two/three other acts down the road there might be a common trend and you have to look sometimes for that common trend to see which group of criminals operate this particular way, also a careful study of the major criminals, those criminals that keep re-offending. It is always good to keep on top of them and do a careful study.

So every now and then you have to put a trail on them, trace their whereabouts and conduct surveillance and sometimes do the sporadic search warrants as the case may be. You will never know because at least—at the very least —they know that the police are still on their tail part so to speak. These are some of the simple methodologies, following through with crimes that are critical 48–72 hr, and also bring your best investigators to bear on serious criminal investigations.

CONCLUSION

The interview with the Commissioner of Police (Ag.), Mr. Wendel Robinson was very cordial as he was very open and forthright with his answers and was never evasive. It is evident that Mr. Robinson is an intelligent individual who has a clear vision for his organization. He is unambiguous on his stance on the death penalty and pointed out that there are sufficient safeguards to obtain fairness and justice with convicted murderers.

He strongly supports the approach of proactive policing and recognizes the value of community policing and having a good relationship between the police and the public. Adhering to his recommendations can greatly reduce serious crimes, especially homicides in Antigua and Barbuda and allow the state to be a place of tranquillity for every citizen, resident, and visitor.

REFERENCES

The Antigua and Barbuda Constitution Order. (1981). Chapter 23 of the laws of Antigua and Barbuda (Revised Edition 1992).

The Police Act Chapter 330. (1992). Laws of Antigua and Barbuda Revised Edition.

CHAPTER V

BARBADOS

COUNTRY INFORMATION

B arbados, a former British colony, gained its independence from Britain in 1966. It is the most easterly island in the Caribbean chain and has a population of 277,821 (Barbados Statistical Service Census, 2010). Barbados is made up of 11 parishes. Bridgetown is the capital of Barbados and is located in the parish of St. Michael. Barbados operates as a constitutional monarchy and is governed on a parliamentary democracy, modelled on the British Westminster system, with Elizabeth II, Queen of Barbados, as Head of State.

The Head of State is represented locally by the Governor-General, Elliott Belgrave and the Prime Minister, Mr. Freundel Stuart as the head of the government. There is a three-tiered court system, starting with the Magistrates Court, the Supreme Court, and the Caribbean Court of Justice. An accused can appeal his sentence at the Caribbean Court of Justice, which is the final appellate court in the Caribbean and which is based in Trinidad and Tobago. This court replaced the Privy Council of England which was the final appellant court in the region and its operations began in 2005 (http://www.caribbeancourtofjustice.org/).

Barbados' system of criminal justice is based on common law and national statutory laws, using an adversarial method of trial. The criminal justice system is similar to the system that exists throughout the English-speaking Caribbean. An accused goes from arrest to trial, where he has the right to an attorney-at-law. In the event that he cannot afford one, he is entitled to an attorney who is provided through the Community Legal Services. The accused can be granted bail, which can be permitted for all types of crime, including murder. However, this is left to the discretion of the Magistrate or Judge, depending on the antecedents and criminal history of the offender and his propensity to re-offend.

Prior to sentencing, an accused is given a pre-sentence report prepared by the Probation Department. This report outlines mitigating and aggravating factors that can affect his sentence. Magistrates and Judges require these reports to assist in the sentence of the convicted person.

INTRODUCTION

Capital punishment has been in Barbados since colonial days. Barbados like almost all Commonwealth Caribbean nations has a mandatory death penalty. In other words, a conviction for murder is currently an automatic death sentence. However, a death sentence can be commuted to life sentence by the Governor-General. Barbados "saved" death penalty after independence in 1966 even though the UK had abolished the death penalty in 1965 because Barbados had not incorporated that abolition into its laws. This is referred to as the "saving clause." In the Laws of Barbados under the Offences Against the Persons Act 1994, capital punishment is prescribed as the mandatory punishment for the crime of murder.

In the past, a juvenile (someone under the age of 18) could not be sentenced to death and if found guilty of murder, was sentenced to Her Majesty's Pleasure. This is a sentence where someone is kept in prison until it is officially decided that it is safe to release them. However, over the years there has been a shift in policy as it relates to the death penalty and sentences of murder. While it is still on the statute books as the ultimate punishment for persons convicted of murder, there has not been a hanging in Barbados since 1983. The death penalty is a notoriously debatable topic for politicians. Successive governments both locally and regionally have faced pressure from both international communities as well as their electorate on the issue of the death penalty. Research has shown that 8 in 10 Barbadians are in support of the death penalty. However, Barbados has signed international treaties such as the Inter-American Commission on Human Rights (IACHR).

There have also been precedent cases which have worked in favour of persons who have been sentenced to death. For example, in Barbados, there was the landmark ruling *Boyce and Joseph v the Queen* where in April 1999 Marquelle Hippolyte was murdered by Jeffrey Joseph and Lennox Ricardo Boyce and two others. Boyce and Joseph pleaded not guilty for the murder of Hippolyte, while the other two accused pleaded guilty to manslaughter (Cross, 2015). The latter were sentenced to 10 years' imprisonment, while in 2001; Boyce and Joseph were found guilty of murder and sentenced to death.

In 2002, they appealed to the Court of Appeal in Barbados and their appeal was dismissed. Through a series of appeals, all of which were dismissed, Boyce and Joseph filed an application in 2002 to the Judicial Committee of the Privy Council (JCPC) which is an arm of the Privy Council in England to spare their lives, as death warrants were earlier read to them. The JCPC upheld the mandatory death penalty (see OAS Case 12.480). They then took their application before the Inter-American commission on Human Rights for a declaration that their rights were being violated under the American Convention on Human Rights. The Inter-American Court provided measures which required Barbados to save the lives of the two condemned men pending the outcome of their appeal to the Commission. The case then went to the Barbados Court of Appeals which commuted the sentences to life imprisonment.

It is worthy to note that Joseph was released from prison in May 2015. However, it was unlikely that Boyce and Joseph would have been executed. Another landmark case, the 1993 precedent of *Pratt and Morgan* would have prohibited the execution of Joseph and Boyce. In this case, it prohibits execution of persons after 5 years had passed, and in this case, Boyce and Joseph had been on death row longer than 5 years.

The issue of the mandatory death penalty has recently been revived. The Government of Barbados currently has a bill before Parliament in which it is being argued that there should be varying degrees of murder, such as first, second, and third degree murder and that the mandatory death penalty is removed from the constitution as the sole punishment for murder. This, however, does not mean that the death penalty will be removed from the books; it just opens options to judicial officers when it comes to sentencing a person found guilty of murder.

Barbados also had on its law books the sentence of Her Majesty's Pleasure. This was a sentence given to persons under the age of 18 years who were found guilty of murder but were too young to be executed. This sentence came from English law. However, England had repealed this law. This sentence was deemed unconstitutional in Criminal Appeal No. 34/2002 in the case of Mormon Scantlebury v R and was implemented into law on April 13, 2005 as it stated that a juvenile cannot be sentenced to an indeterminate sentence by an executive of Government (the Governor General) who also sits on the same executive that reviews such sentences. Section 18(1) of the Constitution, however, guarantees the right of an individual to a fair hearing by an independent and impartial court established by law. This was seen as an anomaly and therefore unconstitutional.

THE ROYAL BARBADOS POLICE FORCE

The Royal Barbados Police Force (hereinafter referred to as the RBPF) is a 1,400 strong Force headed by the Acting Commissioner of Police, Tyrone Griffith. Mr. Griffith has been acting Commissioner of Police since June 17, 2013. He received extensive training in police-related subjects including Criminal Investigation Course at West Yorkshire Police Academy, Law Enforcement Management at the Federal Bureau of Investigation (FBI) National Academy, Quantico, Virginia, Executive Development Course at the Canadian Police College, Ottawa, Canada, Hostage Negotiations Training in Trinidad and Tobago, Assessment Centres Training, Florida, United States and Project Management Training at the Training Administration Division, Barbados. Mr. Griffith has worked in most areas of the force, including the Criminal Investigation Division, Drug Squad and Operations Support. After being promoted to the rank of Assistant Commissioner, he held the portfolio of Assistant Commissioner in charge of Operations Support and Assistant Commissioner in charge of Territorial Policing.

Structure of the RBPF

The RBPF is headed by the Commissioner of Police who has a Deputy Commissioner of Police. There are also four Assistant Commissioners of Police: Assistant Commissioner (Human Resources), Assistant Commissioner (Crime), Assistant Commissioner (Operations Services), and Assistant Commissioner (Administrative Services). The Commissioner of Police is responsible for the entire RBPF and reports to the Attorney General. Outside of the Deputy and the Four Assistant Commissioners of Police that report to him, there are four departments/individuals that report directly to him: Special Branch Truth Verification, Interpol, Public Information Officer, The Regional Police Training Centre, and the Police Sports Club. The Assistant Commissioner (Human Resources) is responsible for recruitment, training, performance appraisals, career development, social services, health and wellness, personnel records, chaplaincy, the police association, and the police credit union.

The Assistant Commissioner (Crime) is responsible for all three branches of the Criminal Investigations Department (CID), the Drug Squad, Major Incident Room, Major Crimes Unit, Forensics, Criminal Records, Certificate of Character, Financial Crimes, Family Conflict Unit, Digital

Evidence and Cyber Crime Unit, Human Trafficking and Sex Crimes Unit, Anti-Gang and Firearms Unit, Cold Case Squad, Document Examiner, and Copyright Infringement Unit. The Assistant Commissioner (Operational Services) is responsible for all territorial police stations, Community Policing, Special Operations Support Unit, and the Traffic Department.

The Assistant Commissioner (Administrative Services) is responsible for information, communication and technology department, operations control, the command centre, telecommunications, department of research and development, statistical department, accreditation department, the inspectorate, accounts department, the Registry, security of exhibits, asset procurement and stores, management of firearms, ammunition and explosives, provost general workers, plant management, and carpenter's workshop.

As indicated earlier, the Commissioner of Police (Acting) has been in the position of Commissioner since 2013. He has been a police for 39 years. His early years of policing were in the CID. His first 2 years of policing were at the main headquarters of the RBPF, which is Central Police Station beat control prior to his promotion to the CID where he spent 20 years of his career. He worked as a detective in CID and then in the Fraud Squad. Through the Acceleration Promotion Scheme, he was promoted to Inspector in 10 years.

It is against this backdrop that a study has been commissioned to examine Police Leaders' perspectives on the death penalty in the Caribbean. The Commissioner of Police (Ag), Mr. Tyrone Griffith was interviewed by Miss Kim L. Ramsay in his office in the Royal Police Force's Administration Division in Roebuck Street, Bridgetown in June 2015.

THE INTERVIEW

KLR: In your view, has violent crime and homicides increased within the past 5 years?

TG: No, violent crime and homicides have not increased within the past 5 years. This is because we have had programmes that address violent crime especially murders. We have always spent resources in murder investigations. People believe that generally if they are involved in a violent crime, they will be apprehended. We have averaged 23–27 murders over the past 5 years, so generally no we have not had an increase in homicides or any other violent crimes.

KLR: Are criminals now more brazen than before? Is it that criminal does not care about the nature of penalties for criminal violations?

TG: Yes, criminals are more brazen, but it's not that they do not care. The drug culture plays a significant part in the violence we are currently witnessing. You see more violent at all levels, whether major or minor (assaults, woundings). Assaults are the biggest increase in violence.

KLR: What are your views on the death penalty? How effective is the death penalty?

TG: In Barbados' context, it is difficult to say how effective the death penalty has been because it has not been employed for many years. There must, however, be some penalty reserved for those serious cases that are very heinous in nature. If you look around the world, we cannot say terrorists will not meet our shores. If persons are willing to use explosives which can take dozens of lives, then there must be some penalty reserved in the form of death. We do not have different degrees of murder. Having the death penalty on our statute will not deter if it is not enforced. If we look at Trinidad and Tobago, when they last executed Dode Chadee, I am sure it had an impact (deterring effect) at least in the short term. Trinidad and Tobago was a different place for a while.

KLR: Should the death penalty be abolished, restructured, and/or implemented more consistently?

TG: There should be different degrees/categories of murder, like first degree to third degree and the death penalty should be reserved for the most heinous crimes. We have sufficient heinous crimes in Barbados that it should be implemented.

KLR: If execution is unacceptable, what are the alternatives?

TG: The next best thing is an extensive period of incarceration, for example, life imprisonment. Given the nature of some murders, if you will not employ the death penalty, there should be life. We have people in the system on their third murder charge. The only thing that will deter them is the death penalty or life imprisonment.

KLR: Do you believe that the death penalty is cruel and unusual punishment, or is it just desserts?

TG: Cruel and unusual? No, I do not see it as cruel. The offender gets his just dessert.

KLR: In your experience, what policies or programmes have worked well and which have not in terms of crime reduction?

TG: Intelligence led policing as well as community policing have both worked well in reducing crime in Barbados. Intelligence led policing is very thorough at detection and over time it acts as a crime prevention strategy. On the other hand, strong arm tactics and other brutal methods have not worked. It is important to note that these methods are very individualistic, and not known of any administration that has used it as a policy in the Royal Barbados Police Force. It is important to reiterate that these tactics are individualistic. The reason that I believe that intelligence led policing and community policing have worked is that the statistics show that much of the success has been as a result of that.

KLR: What are three of your most important proposals for fighting crime?

TG: Intelligence led policing combined with strong community efforts in challenged communities. In the long term, it serves to build better relations, identify problems the community is having, and improve the plight as well as working with other agencies. It also provides good intelligence. Another proposal is great emphasis on forensics.

KLR: What would you consider to be the greatest problem facing the police at this time in terms of crime reduction?

TG: The greatest problem facing the RBPF at this time is the widespread incidences of burglaries and they are all around no particular pattern. This makes it difficult to put programmes in place. There is also not enough patrol. The RBPF cannot have enough patrol. There is also the need of the support of the public along with getting householders to increase security at their homes, such as putting in security devices as well as target hardening.

KLR: Are you basically satisfied or dissatisfied with developments in the Criminal Justice System after a sentence of death has been passed on murder?

TG: There is only so much one can do. We need to look at the root causes of crime. A number of institutions have failed. The level of crime will always have a bearing on what is happening in society such as economic and social issues. You will always have crime as long as you have these issues. Drug selling is one of the things that offer people an alternative to poverty and seen as an opportunity. We need also to tighten up firearms getting into the country. The public needs to be more supportive of law enforcement. People in "high" places are very influential and would say and do things that will destroy an organization trying to do right.

KLR: Have strict legal procedures eliminated arbitrariness and discrimination associated with the death penalty?

TG: Yes, it has eliminated a lot of concerns and arguments that people will use that the right man is before the hangman. There are enough checks and balances, for example, various stages that the case goes through, pre-trial disclosures where everything is declared to the accused. Expertise is also required that he is entitled to have at the expense of the Government.

KLR: Should the death penalty be reserved for murder only, or for other crimes like treason and kidnapping?

TG: Kidnapping in our statue books is not the same as in other countries like Trinidad and Tobago. Kidnapping is not conducted in the same violent way or for ransom, yet we have cases of kidnapping which can be quite minor in terms of the adverse effects on the victim. However, conspiracy to commit murder and terrorist acts are just as good for the death penalty. We do not have to wait until a life is taken.

THE INTERVIEW

The interview was extremely cordial and thought provoking. While initially, it was difficult to secure the interview, the Commissioner put aside an hour out of his busy schedule and we met in his conference room. He was very cooperative, engaging, and willing to share information. He was relaxed during the interview.

CONCLUSION

Numerous themes emerged from the frank and open discussion with Mr. Tyronne Griffith. The themes that emerged from the interview are as follows:

1. Social and economic causes of crime

The Commissioner agreed that one must not utilize only law enforcement tactics to solve the crime, but one must examine the social and economic causes of crime. Criminological research has always indicated that the solution to crime must be tackled using various approaches, from the sociological, psychological, and even biological approaches.

2. Public support needed for crime reduction

The Commissioner noted that they need the help of the police to solve crime in Barbados. There is always a correlation between crime and public support. The police rely heavily on the public to assist in crime reduction. Without the support of the public, healthy relationship, chaos and high crime is an inevitable result (National Task Force on Crime Prevention, 2015).

3. The abolition of the mandatory death sentence

There is increasing pressure across the world for countries to abolish the death penalty. It appears that countries in the Caribbean are acceding to this pressure as the replacement of mandatory capital sentencing schemes with discretionary ones is the clear trend among countries who continue to keep the death penalty on its statute books (Novak, 2012, 2014).

4. Intelligence led policing and community policing

The Commissioner noted that intelligence led policing and community policing were the best evidence-based approach to solving crime in Barbados from the law enforcement's perspective. However, while the Commissioner stated that there has not been an increase in violent crime, it was believed that he formed this opinion based on the relatively stable rate of homicides. However, he later went on to note that there was an increase in violent at all levels, mostly in assaults and woundings.

The Commissioner of Police is in support of the death penalty. This is not surprising as research has shown that police chiefs are generally in support of the death penalty (Dieter, 1995). However, The Commissioner of Police in Barbados believes that the death penalty is not deterring criminals because it is not enforced. While it appears that police chiefs generally support crime, research has shown that some police chiefs do not believe that the death penalty deters crime (Bailey & Peterson, 1994; Radelet & Akers, 2005).

REFERENCES

Bailey, W., & Peterson, R. (1994). Murder, capital punishment, and deterrence: A review of the evidence and an examination of police killings. *Journal of Social Issues, 50*(2), 53–74.

Barbados Statistical Services Census. (2010). Retrieved from http://www.barstats.gov.bb/files/documents/PHC_2010_Census_Volume_1.pdf.

Caribbean Court of Justice. Retrieved from http://www.caribbeancourtofjustice.org/.

Cross, J. (2015). A life and death compromise: The mandatory death penalty in the Caribbean court of justice—Unpublished article. Retrieved from https://www.bu.edu/law/nepoc/.../JaneCrossMandatory.ppt.

Dieter, R. C. (1995). *On the front line: Law enforcement views on the death penalty*. United States of America: Death Penalty Information Center.

National Task Force on Crime Prevention. (2015). Royal Barbados Police Force 2014 Customer Satisfaction Survey. Government of Barbados.

Novak, A. (2012). The abolition of the mandatory death penalty in Africa: A comparative constitutional analysis. *Indiana International & Comparative Law Review, 22*(2), 267–295.

Novak, A. (2014). The abolition of the mandatory death penalty in the Commonwealth: Recent developments from India and Bangladesh. *ExpressO*. Retrieved from http://works.bepress.com/andrew_novak/3/.

Pratt and Morgan v Attorney General. (1993). 43 WIR 430.

Radelet, M. L., & Akers, R. L. (1995). Deterrence and the death penalty: The views of the experts. *The Journal of Criminal Law and Criminology, 87*(1), 1–16.

CHAPTER VI

GRENADA

COUNTRY INFORMATION

Grenada is a tri-island state, consisting of Grenada, Carriacou, and Petite Martinique, with Grenada being the largest of the three islands. Grenada is the most southerly of the Windward Islands, located 12 degrees north and 61.4 degrees west. Affectionately referred to as the "Isle of Spice," Grenada's economy is greatly influenced by its location and vulnerability to annual hurricanes. Grenada is one of the world's largest exporters of nutmegs and mace. The population of Grenada is ~104,000 (UN, 2009). There are six parishes in Grenada namely St. George, St. Andrew, St. Patrick, St. Mark, St. David, and St. John. The capital of Grenada is St. George's and is located on the south west coast of the island. The population is predominantly a Christian society. In February 2013, the New National Party won all 15 seats in the general elections. At the time the interview was conducted, the Head of State was Dame Dr. Cecile La Grenade and the Prime Minister was Dr. The Right Honourable Keith Mitchell.

Grenada does not have a major issue with drugs and offences committed as a result of drugs (Alexander, 2008). For example, between the years 2008 and 2012 most murders were committed using knives, cutlasses, and bottles. One was due to strangulation, three involved the use of firearms (one by police, one by prison officer, and one by civilian). According to Alexander (2008), none of the homicides were as a result of, or connected to drug trafficking. Instructively, Grenada is used primarily as a transit point for drugs but there is a serious problem with the use of alcohol. Alcohol consumption and abuse have caused major disruptions in society and at times has been the end result of murders being committed.

INTRODUCTION

The interview with Superintendent Trevor Modeste, presently the acting (Ag.) Assistant Commissioner of Police was conducted on Tuesday, September 22, 2015 at the Police Headquarters, Fort George, St. George's, Grenada. Before the start of the interview, Acting ACP Modeste and the author discussed elements of the study and what were the expected outcome. He was informed that the interview will be recorded and that the information obtained would be transcribed to highlight his perspectives on the death penalty and crime reduction in Grenada.

THE INTERVIEWEE

Ag. ACP Trevor Modeste is a 35-year veteran of the Royal Grenada Police Force (RGPF) having joined the RGPF in 1980. He has had extensive training in 13 forensic fields such as finger printing photography, crime scene investigations, and shoe print identification. To date, he has given evidence in court in 10 of these forensic areas. From 2012 to present he was the officer in charge of the Criminal Investigations Department (CID) in St. George's and before that the Criminal Records and Forensic Section of the RGPF. Ag. ACP Modeste possesses a wealth of knowledge and experience on the job and has been trained in policing practices in Cuba and Canada.

THE INTERVIEW

PF: How do you view Grenada in the context of crime in the Caribbean and what accounts for your views?

TM: Due to Grenada being a religious society, the crime/homicides rates in Grenada is relatively low when compared to other Caribbean countries. It is my opinion and belief that a religious foundation is most important for daily life and living for without the basic religious foundation there wouldn't be any respect for human life. The protection of human life is the most important function of police officers. The presence of family is important. Indeed, the importance of family life in society and/or the absence or presence of a mother and father in the home is key. Involved and decent parents in a home do make a difference in the lives of their children. Children who are properly corrected and trained from infancy grow up to be proper citizens with respect for themselves, each other and basic human life.

PF: What law would like to see implemented or strengthened to combat crime in Grenada?

TM: I would like to see laws in relation to domestic violence, use of offensive weapons, disorderly conduct, and other serious offences which may at times lead to murders be strengthened. People have to know that their actions have serious consequences. Stiffer penalties on the law books can be used as a deterrent to crime.

PF: What are your views on capital murder and non-capital murder in relation to the death penalty?

TM: Capital murder is planned murder and the treatment of a person for a capital or non-capital murder needs to be taken into account when looking at the death penalty. Murders cannot be seen as just a killing because there are planned murders as well and there are instances where there are accidental murders where one's emotions come into being. In these instances, the murder is not planned. In fact, according to a study conducted by Cornell University in April 2, 2011, there are 10 prisoners on death row at Her Majesty's Prisons in Richmond Hill, St. George's (Grenada's only prison).

The last hanging in Grenada took place in the year 1978 but hanging is still on the law books in Grenada. In fact, as of November 25, 2015 there have not been any executions in Grenada since 1978. Between the years 2005 and 2010, no death sentences were pronounced. The study all went on to say that in the year 1993, the Judicial Committee of the Privy Council (JCPC) ruled that any prisoner under sentence of death for longer than 5 years had presumptively been subjected to cruel and unusual punishment necessitating commutation of his/her death sentence and the courts in Grenada have applied this principle.

PF: What is the murder rate like in Grenada and what accounts for the high or low rate?

TM: For the last 5 years or more, the average number of murder per year in Grenada is less than eight and this is mainly due to the religious foundation or activities that can be seen throughout Grenada. Presently the court system is overcrowded. It is important that there are judges that can be effective in handing down harsher punishments to suit the crime at hand. In my opinion, when the perpetrators are caught and they serve their prison sentences, crime is usually reduced after that period. I believe that these harsh sentences can be used as a deterrent to criminal activities.

PF: What do you believe are some of the best methods that can be used to deter crime and murder in the Caribbean?

TM: I believe that closed-circuit television or CCTV is one of the best deterrents of crime. Although very costly, it is the most effective way to solve major crimes including murders. In my experience, in Grenada today, a lot of persons are buying and installing infra-red cameras on their properties and there have been successes in solving crimes. These cameras will definitely come at a cost but they have helped citizens feel more safe and secure both in their homes and places of business.

PF: What are some alternative sentences that can be used for murder besides the death penalty?

TM: I cannot comment on alternative sentences for murders as was mentioned in the questionnaire or as asked by you as I do not know of Grenada having any alternative sentences for committing a capital or non-capital murder. Further, Grenada does not have any facility at the moment to consider alternative sentencing. Before this is taken into consideration, appropriate measures including budgets, infrastructure, etc. must be looked and put in place. This would cost the government a lot of money.

PF: What are some crime reduction strategies that you would recommend to regulate and reduce crime in Grenada?

TM: Education, family life and well-being, strengthening laws for offences that may lead to serious crimes are some tactics that can be used to regulate and can cause a reduction in homicides in Grenada. I also believe there should also be an acceptance of the death penalty so citizens of Grenada will ultimately accept it as punishment for their crimes. The victims and their families are also important aspects to be taken into consideration at all times.

PF: What do you think is the best punishment for someone who is convicted of murder?

TM: I believe that for capital murders, the appropriate punishment is the death penalty. There aren't statistics to prove that the death penalty significantly reduced homicides in Grenada but it should be noted that after the last hanging in 1978, it took a number of years before another murder was committed. In the last 5 years, homicides have decreased in Grenada. There has been a reduction in assaults on Police officers and as such a reduction in crime in general.

PF: Do you think that the criminal element in Grenada has become more brazen with time?

TM: I have seen respect for persons from the Executive to the Judicial level in society and this has significantly contributed to the respect that currently exists for law and order in Grenada. With a community that respects and works together with the police in solving and reducing crime, successes will definitely continue. Criminals to a point have been less brazen in Grenada as it relates to harmful offences.

PF: What do you think contributes to most crimes in Grenada?

TM: The level of alcohol in one's system, peer pressure, and social occasion at the time of the incident all contribute to the circumstances and the type of offence committed. This is mainly due to the circumstances and the type of violent crime.

PF: What have the Grenada police implemented by way of policies to attempt to reduce crime?

TM: In the last 5–10 years, one of the programmes implemented by the Royal Grenada Police Force is the zero tolerance for threatening language, domestic violence, and offensive weapons public order policing programme. This programme has greatly contributed to a reduction in crime. For example, this programme was beneficial in the parish of St. Mark's where police officers of the Victoria Police Station engaged offenders about the use of threatening language. The offenders realized that time spent on processing and dealing with issues at the police station was too much and caused them, for example, time away from the job. The result of this programme was a reduction in crimes such as threatening language and causing violence, offences which can lead to serious offences and even murders. This does not mean that if a person makes up his/her mind to commit a crime he/she will not, but there was a reduction in crime from that programme.

CONCLUSION

Ag. ACP Modeste believes that the death penalty should remain on the law books of Grenada especially for instances of capital murders. He is of the view that the retention of the death penalty may or may not mean a reduction in the murder rate but it can be used as a deterrent to would-be offenders. Ag. ACP Modeste proffered the view that offenders need to know that there are harsh punishments for murders and their actions do have serious consequences. He further stated that there are a number of things that can be done to reduce crime in Grenada, among them are solving the crime, strengthening the laws, support for the magistrates and judges, better equipment for policing, automated finger print system, use of crime mapping apps, and crime linkage apps.

CONDUCT OF THE INTERVIEW

Though Ag. ACP Modeste was evidently busy due to his position within the Royal Grenada Police Force (RGPF), he was quite interested in sharing his wealth of knowledge and experience. The interview was very cordial, informative and enlightening as well as a learning experience based on the wealth of information that was received.

REFERENCES

Alexander, D. (2008). An Analysis of Homicides in Grenada 2008 to 2012. Retrieved from www.gov.gd/egov/pdf/ncodc/docs/AN_ANALYSIS_HOMICIDES_GRENADA_2008_2012.pdf

United Nations. (2009). Population Ageing and Development 2009. Department of Economic and Social Affairs. Population Division. www.unpopulation.org.

CHAPTER VII

GUYANA

COUNTRY INFORMATION

The Co-operative Republic of Guyana or Guyana, a country on South America's North Atlantic coast, is defined by its dense tropical rainforests filled with many species of distinctive plants and trees, teeming with exotic birds, insects, and mammals—are a big draw for eco-tourists. Guyana is situated in Central North of the South American continent with a coastline at the North Atlantic Ocean. Guyana shares international borders with Brazil, Suriname, and Venezuela, and shares maritime borders with Trinidad and Tobago and Barbados. The country is part of the Guianas, a region in the north-eastern part of the continent on the Guiana Shield, an old stable geological formation that forms a portion of the northern coast. The Guianas are bounded by the Orinoco, Negro, and Amazon rivers and the Atlantic Ocean. It includes Guyana, Suriname, and French Guiana.

Though located on the South American continent, Guyana is culturally connected to the Caribbean region. Its capital, Georgetown, is known for British colonial architecture, including tall, painted-timber St. George's Anglican Cathedral. Guyana became independent in 1966 and its population is largely descended from African slaves, imported by the Dutch to work on sugar plantations as well as indentured East Indian agricultural workers brought in by the British after slavery was abolished. English is the official language of Guyana.

INTRODUCTION

Guyana has experienced an increasing prevalence of crime, social violence, and insecurity among citizens over the past two decades. These have had enormous costs that jeopardize Guyana's economic development, human development, and governance, which was most painfully evident between 2002 and 2006 when the security situation deteriorated to crisis proportions. With limited financial resources, Guyana has been largely incapable of responding effectively to the onslaught of criminal violence.

Guyana is particularly vulnerable to crime as it is geographically located between the world's main source of illegal drugs, particularly cocaine (the Andean region of South America) and its main consumer markets (the United States and Europe) (UNODC/World Bank, 2007). Further, the country is enormous in land mass with large uninhabited and unprotected borders that are impossible for the small sized security forces to patrol and cover. Additionally, with a small population whose tertiary educated citizens migrate at a rate of over 85%, there are limited human resources. Crime in Guyana is multifaceted in nature and some of the most serious crimes are disorderly and domestic murders, narco and gun trafficking and robbery under arms (Griffith, 2002).

DEATH PENALTY APPLICATION IN GUYANA

Guyana's current status regarding the death penalty is ambiguous. Although death penalty laws are legally permissible and even mandatory for certain crimes, with no executions by the state since 1997, using the legally prescribed method, hanging, the status in Guyana is in effect de facto abolitionist.

Guyana's laws for some capital crimes do not provide an alternative sentence to death upon conviction. It states that an individual convicted of a capital offence "shall be liable to suffer death as a felon." Additionally, the law provides that murder and felony murder in the course of terrorism are "punishable by death." Article 19 of the Criminal (Offences) Law does not allow courts to substitute punishments not specifically stated for death-eligible offences (Criminal Law (Offences) Act of Guyana, 1998). In essence, courts do not have discretion in sentencing. Further, Article 164 of the Criminal (Procedure) Law provides that in circumstances where an individual is convicted of an offence punishable by death, "the Court shall thereupon pronounce [the] sentence of death" (Criminal Law (Procedure) Act of Guyana, 1998).

The death penalty is not applicable to three categories of citizens in Guyana, namely children under the age of 18 at the time of the offence, pregnant women, and the mentally ill. For all others, the following crimes are punishable by death in Guyana:

- Murder.
- Other offences that result in death including: (a) supplying, ad-

ministering, or causing a child to take drugs, (b) piracy, (c) hijacking, or (d) armed robbery.

- Terrorism-related offences that lead to death.
- Drug trafficking that leads to death.
- Treason.
- Specific military offences of a treasonable nature (Criminal Law (Offences) Act of Guyana, 1998).

Notwithstanding the preceding, the successive Guyana governments have taken steps towards abolishing the death penalty by effectively placing a moratorium on hanging since 1997 and by making commitments to the UN in 2013 and reiterating this commitment in 2015 to abolish the death penalty and erase capital punishments from its laws. Successive governments' ambiguity to the death penalty is in part dictated by high serious crime rates and citizens' strong support for a hard line approach to crime fighting including support for the death penalty. In a 2011, UNDP study, 61.1% of Guyana citizens surveyed "strongly agree[d]" and "agree[d]" with the statement "I support the death penalty" and 80.2% agreed and strongly agreed that criminals should be more harshly punished. An unsubstantial percentage (32.2) also supports the police given a free hand to kill criminals and 32.1% believe that human rights are obstacles to more effective crime control (UNDP, 2012).

Public support for hard line approach for crime fighting has coincided with persistent allegations of grave human rights violations by the Guyana Police Force (GPF). The force has been accused of torture, brutality, and extra judicial killings. These accusations have been bolstered by the perception that the force's culture is characterized by corruption, indiscipline, prejudice, and political partiality. These excesses all occur in the context of a technologically and administratively antiquated, underfunded, and understaffed organization that merely renders the force more incapable of stemming the upsurge in organized, narco- trafficking, gun, and domestic violence crimes.

STRUCTURE OF THE GUYANA POLICE FORCE

A paramilitary Police Force was established under Public Ordinance 10 of 1891 in British Guiana and in June 1939 this force was renamed the

British Guiana Police Force. In 1977, the former was repealed and replaced and the Guyana Police Force was established under section 3(1) of the Police Act, Chapter 16:01 as a public body. Subsection 3(2) of the Police Act, Chapter 16:01 outlines out the mandate of the Guyana Police Force as:

> The force shall be employed for the prevention and detection of crime, the preservation of law and order, the preservation of the peace, the repression of internal disturbance, the protection of property, the apprehension of offenders, and the due enforcement of all laws and regulations for which it is directly charged and shall perform such military duties within Guyana as may be required of it by or under the authority of the Minister.

The GPF, which is managed by a Commissioner of Police under the control of the Ministry of Home Affairs is responsible for maintaining internal security and is comprised of a regular force along with supernumerary, rural and special constables and has responsibility for national security, traffic control, passport, and immigration, registration of aliens and firearms control. The force is geographically divided into six police divisions, each commanded by an assistant commissioner:

"A" Division: The city of Georgetown and the East Bank of the Demerara River including the Cheddi Jagan International Airport, Timehri, 25 miles from Georgetown. The A Division comprises nine police stations and seven outposts.

"B" Division: Mainly the County of Berbice but excluding Kwakwani. This Division comprises 12 police stations and 5 outposts.

"C" Division: The County of Demerara, East of the Demerara River but excluding "A" Division. The "C" Division consists of eight police stations and four outposts.

"D" Division: The County of Demerara, West of the Demerara River, and a portion of the East Bank of the Essequibo. "D" Division comprises six police stations and one outpost.

"E&F" Division: Upper Demerara including the area surrounding the bauxite holdings of the Linden, Ituni, and Kwakwani areas and the Interior. This Division comprises 30 police stations and 6 outposts.

"G" Division: The Essequibo Coast including the Islands of the Essequibo and Pomeroon Rivers. The "G" Division comprises six police
stations.

The Commissioner and Deputy Commissioners of Police are appointed
by the President upon the recommendation of the Police Services Commission (PSC). The PSC has jurisdiction over the appointments and dis-
cipline of police that are higher than the rank of inspector while the Commissioner of Police has control over other ranks (Griffith, 2002). The
GPF, however, has a longer historical heritage as it the first policing structure established in 1839. From its inception in 1839, the Police Force was
linked to and supported the governing colonial elite at the expense of the
majority newly freed Africans. It was imposed by the ruling minority to
restrict and restrain the advancement of the majority since this conflicted
with the desires of the former.

In essence, it was birth in bias and oppression and it is argued that 171
years later, notwithstanding changes in structure, role, and function, its
colonial precepts persist in that the dominant power controls and directs
state and police power and the elements of violence that accompanied
policing in the colonial era have been perpetuated until contemporary
times. In other words, the dominant perception even today of the GPF
is that it favours and protects the interests of the elites within the society and the average citizen is left unprotected or even violated. Despite
changes in regimes in the post-independence era, the GPF is seen as a
symbol of the state's authority, oftentimes in its most inhumane, abusive
form. This perception more-so has been reinforced by corruption, indiscipline, prejudice, brutality, illegality and human rights violations and political partiality among the members of the force. These excesses all occur
in the context of a technologically and administratively antiquated, underfunded, and understaffed organization that merely renders the Force
more incapable of stemming the upsurge in organized, narco trafficking,
gun, and domestic violence crimes (Griffith, 1997).

It is within the preceding context that this chapter canvasses the views of
the Crime Chief of the Guyana Police Force, Mr. Wendell Blanhum on
the crime situation in Guyana and more specifically, the applicability and
utility of the death penalty as a tool for crime prevention and crime fighting in Guyana. Mr. Blanhum has emerged as one of the few young pro-

fessionals within the Guyana Police Force who has maintained a spotless reputation and not been tainted by the prevailing corrupt culture within the force. His views were progressive and he displayed an appreciation for human rights based policing methods which are not perceived as characteristic of many senior officers of the force.

THE INTERVIEWEE

Mr. Wendell Blanhum has been serving the Guyana Police Force for the past 16 years. He rapidly moved through the ranks, with his latest promotion being that of Senior Superintendent in 2014. Before serving as the second in Charge of the Criminal Investigation Department, Blanhum had attended several training programmes both locally and overseas, including Crime Prevention Policing, Organized Crimes for the Americas, Policing and Management, Intelligence-led Policing, Organized Crimes, Law Enforcement Leadership; and with the Federal Bureau of Investigation. Blanhum holds a degree in Public Management and a post-graduate diploma in Development Studies. Mr. Blanhum had served as the Divisional Detective in the Police "A" and "C" Divisions and was responsible for spearheading several high-profile investigations.

THE INTERVIEW

MI: Good morning Mr. Blanhum, I know that you are busy so I appreciate the opportunity to conduct this interview as I know how busy you are. Can we start by you telling me a bit about your career? From public records, I know that you have ascended the ranks of the force fairly quickly. Tell me a little bit about your career journey: the length, the divisions you've worked in, specializations, etc.

WB: Thank you. As you know I am a Senior Superintendent of Police and was appointed recently as the Crime Chief. I joined the force 16 years ago and my progression has been fairly rapid. I think my journey has been facilitated by my training and educational achievements. I have a degree in Public Management and I am completing a Master's Degree in Public Administration. I have also benefitted from training at several overseas law enforcement academies and institutes including the FBI. I have served within several Divisions and before this appointment was second in charge of the Criminal Investigation Division. So I think that I have had a well-rounded experience in several divisions and in various capacities within the force and so I am prepared for this appointment.

MI: In your view, has violent crimes and homicides increased within the past 5 years?

WB: No. Crime statistics have actually decreased from a very violent period Guyana experienced between 2002 and 2006.

MI: Are criminals now more brazen than before?

WB: During the period 2002–2006, criminals were very brazen and attacked and killed many police officers and citizens. Once that crime wave was arrested, criminals, on the whole, aren't as brazen anymore—though a few are.

MI: Do you think the reason for the decrease is that criminals are concerned about the nature of penalties for criminal violations?

WB: Yes, I do think that they care. I also think the decrease is because of the increased capacity of the force.

MI: What are your views on the death penalty?

WB: We have it. We haven't applied it in a while but it is on the books. Based on my experience on the force over the past 10 years, I think if the death penalty is enforced it will have an effect. I think harsh penalties tend to deter crimes. Criminal elements, in my opinion, pay attention to the sentences given for criminal activities and decide whether a particular crime is worth committing.

MI: How effective is the death penalty?

WB: It is not being enforced but I think it might be effective if it is.

MI: Does the death penalty deter crime, especially murder?

WB: I think criminals look at the consequences of crimes committed by other criminals and decide whether a particular crime is worth the punishment so I think if it were enforced it might be effective.

MI: Should it be abolished, restructured, and/or implemented more consistently?

WB: My personal view is that it should be eradicated. In a sense, I am on both sides of the fence. On the one hand, I believe in human rights. I believe a criminal can be rehabilitated. However, although I have my personal view, I think about the victims of crime. As a police officer, you have to explain to victims' families that their family members were murdered and the perpetrators of that crimes only get 10, 20 years rather than life sentence or even death. That is hard, as the families don't understand.

MI: If execution is unacceptable, what are the alternatives?

WB: I think the death penalty should be abolished and convicted criminals given the alternative sentence of life imprisonment without parole. I have also heard suggestions that corporal punishment could be used as well.

MI: Since you are somewhat conflicted, do you think the death penalty should be reserved for murder only, or for other crimes like treason and kidnapping?

WB: As I said, I think it should be eliminated for all categories of crime. Many people think that there are some crimes that are so heinous that the criminals don't deserve to live but I think most people can be rehabilitated.

MI: Should there be categories of murder with the death penalty being reserved for only the highest category of murder?

WB: No, I think the death penalty should be eliminated for all categories of murder.

MI: Do you think that the death penalty is cruel and unusual punishment, or is it just desserts?

WB: In my experience, if the crime is really horrendous, there is the tendency for the public to support the death penalty. The last instance when the death penalty was applied was 1997 when a young man stabbed and killed a 10-year-old boy and stole his bicycle who was riding to school. Most people were outraged and felt the death penalty was justified. But not all cases are clear cut so the application of the death penalty is a risk because there is a chance that the police and prosecutors could get wrong and the wrong individual could be convicted and put to death for a crime he didn't commit.

MI: In your experience what policies or programmes have worked well and which have not in terms of crime reduction?

WB: The Joint Services and security agencies collaboration, the social crime prevention programme, the training and capacity building of the police force have worked well.

MI: What are three of your most important proposals for fighting crime?

WB: 1. Intelligence—the intelligence gathering capability needs to be superior. It helps the force to be proactive rather than reactive.

2. Joint Services Collaboration—we have had several task forces formed with different agencies on different agendas—these involve the police, army, MORAD, GEA, and Ministry of Home Affairs [now Ministry of Public Security]. Task forces have been formed to address escalating criminal activities involving narcotics, contraband, illegal weapons, and fuel smuggling. The task forces are usually chaired by the Minister. I think these collaborations have been particularly useful.

3. Social crime prevention—we must get to the root causes of crime. As the saying goes, prevention is better than cure. It is better to reach at risk youths early with social programmes than to have to rehabilitate them after they have already turned to a life of crime.

MI: Could you expand a bit more on your perspectives on crime prevention? You report that there has been a reduction in serious crime. Do you believe that there have been any programmes implemented either by the force or by the state that has led to the reduction in serious crime?

WB: Three very effective crime prevention strategies have been intelligence gathering, capacity building and training within the force, and the introduction of new legislations. One of the things that have proven to be a deterrent is a number of new legislations that target gangs, terrorism, etc. The legislative tools were amended. The Gang Act referred to as Domestic Terrorism Act and the Piracy Act were amended. The penalties for a crime under these new acts and revisions are very severe including no bail and confiscation of assets. Legislation has helped in terms of gangs and those involved in narcotics.

We also now have witness protection legislation. While there is no structured witness protection programme in place, we do try to offer some forms of protection to witnesses and it has been working so far. Some gang members have been arrested and have offered some leaders up in exchange for less harsh penalties and we have provided protection for them. Additionally, working with members of the community in social crime prevention programmes I believe has had an impact. It is too premature to say definitively that the programmes are working. We started in Tiger Bay, Albouystown, Buxton—all divisions. The hot spots are targeted for social intervention and we focus on reaching the children.

Also, our intelligence division has improved greatly as well as our investigation and training divisions. The Force sent many officers for training—investigation training, prosecution training. Training was conducted by Scottish Police, FBI, the Canadians, French, and Brazilians. We are also now training in Russia, also in the Jamaican, and Trinidad and Tobago police training academies.

So our capacity has improved greatly in terms of investigation, prosecution, and computer training. We now have well trained crime analysts who can perform analysis of crime figures and analyse crime trends and offer advice and guidance to the leadership of the force. We have established computer centres in all three counties that make data storage, retrieval, and analysis easier. Management training is encouraged as well. Officers are encouraged to attend UG and other technical institutes.

Our immigration division has benefited from immigration and terrorism training as well. Marine training has also been launched to deal with piracy. The intensification of training occurred as a response to 9/11 and the rise in deportees and then the jail break in 2002. Intelligence determined that there was a collaboration between deportees and criminal elements and so we had to train our ranks to deal with these new security threats. We also do continuous training in Domestic Violence and Human Rights. We introduced modules in the course curriculum in domestic violence and human rights training or new recruits. We are improving police prosecutor training by encouraging prosecutors to attend the University. In other words, continuous training has led to notable improvement in the capacity of the force.

MI: What would you consider to be the greatest problem facing the police at this time in terms of crime reduction?

WB: I might be biased but I think societal values and morals are not as before. The family needs to play a greater role in ensuring children and youth go down the right path.

MI: Are you basically satisfied or dissatisfied with developments in the Criminal Justice System?

WB: From a law enforcement perspective, we are improving our investigations and charging persons for serious crimes, some career criminals however due to a backlog of cases, magistrates are forced to grant bail so criminals are back out on the street and reengage in crimes. The criminal justice system is not as efficient as it could be. Other sections of CJS—including the courts and the prisons—must also improve their functioning as well.

Prisons should be rehabilitative and correction centres but they aren't so that leads to high rates of recidivism. Better rehabilitation strategies are needed in the prison system. Some people say the solution is to build a bigger prison but that is not usually the best thing. Social prevention and rehabilitation are keys and we need to find best practices in other countries. For instance, some countries use the three strike law—the burden of proof is on the prosecution. Other societies place the burden on the accused. These are strategies that we can look at.

CONDUCT OF THE INTERVIEW

In order to fulfil the mandate as the researcher with responsibility for the Co-operative Republic of Guyana (for this chapter), an interview with Mr. Wendell Blanhum, Crime Chief of the Guyana Police Force (GPF) was sought and eventually granted. However, due to the extremely busy schedule of the Crime Chief, the interview was conducted over 2 days namely September 23 and 26, 2015 by the interviewer, Mellissa Ifill.

The interview with Mr. Wendell Blanhum, Crime Chief of the Guyana Police Force was conducted on two separate occasions, namely on September 23 and 26, 2015 by Mellissa Ifill. The interviews were conducted at his office and were conducted with professionalism by both interviewee and interviewer. Though very busy, Mr. Wendell Blanhum was very willing to share his wealth of experience on policing with the interviewer after being informed of the nature and scope of the research.

REFERENCES

Criminal Law (Offences) Act of Guyana. (1998). Section 19, Laws of Guyana Chapter 8:01.

Criminal Law (Procedure) Act of Guyana. (1998). Section 164, Laws of Guyana Chapter 10:01.

Griffith, I. L. (1997). Political change, democracy and human rights in Guyana. *Third World Quarterly, 18*(2), 267–285.

Griffith, I. L. (2002). Security, sovereignty and public order in the Caribbean. Security and Defense Studies Review.

UNDP. (2012). Caribbean human development report on citizen security.

United Nations Office on Drugs and Crime and the Latin America and the Caribbean Region of the World Bank. (2007). Crime, violence, and development: Trends, costs, and policy options in the Caribbean. Report No. 37820.

CHAPTER VIII

JAMAICA

COUNTRY INFORMATION

J amaica is an island in the Caribbean with a population of just over 2,800,000 and lies 145 kilometres south of Cuba and 161 kilometres west of Haiti. Its economic architecture is a mixture of free enterprise and regulation by a government modelled on the Westminster-Whitehall government structure. Jamaicans have long enjoyed the ethos of democracy that facilitates various human rights, which when violated see offenders receiving punishment by way of a criminal justice system that is retributive in nature. This system—comprising of the police, correctional services, and the court system—has at its epicentre, capital punishment as a form of retributory justice which has been a vexed issue in this Caribbean nation for decades.

Hanging as Jamaica's form of capital punishment predates its 1962 independence from Britain, and served as the appropriate form of punishment for murder. However, after the last person—Nathan Foster—was hung in Jamaica in 1988; the nation became an abolitionist *de facto* state (no executions in the last 10 years). This emanated from a ruling by the Judicial Committee of the Privy Council and has prevented a continuation of what was seen in some quarters as justice served, while human rights lobbyists breathed a sigh of relief to what they perceived as an "inhumane" method of punishment.

However, notwithstanding the Privy Council's ruling, in 2008 the Jamaican Parliament voted to retain the death penalty as a form of punishment for aggravated murder; since then there has been much discourse around the resumption of hanging in the face of the multiple cases of murder which have had a debilitating effect on the Jamaican society. This is a position promoted by the current Minister of National Security, Robert Montague who faces stout opposition from human rights groups and other government ministers. The ensuing debate surrounds—not just the "barbarianism" of capital punishment but—the need for adequate punitive measures for the heinous acts which seem to punctuate every report from the media.

THE JAMAICA CONSTABULARY FORCE (JCF)

As a vital part of Jamaica's criminal justice process, the local police—the Jamaica Constabulary Force (JCF) was established in 1867 out of the Morant Bay Rebellion and stands as the vanguard against crime and violence. The JCF is a paramilitary organisation with some semblance of British influence; it is the primary law-enforcement agency and is headed by a Commissioner of Police who commands just over 12,000 members. Within its purview, the JCF employs policing methods such as situational policing and target hardening to prevent acts of criminality. Such methods are implemented through the JCF's various divisions and non-geographical formations such as the Counter Terrorism and Organised Crime (C-TOC) Investigation Branch, headed by Assistant Commissioner of Police (ACP) Clifford Chambers. For the purpose of this research, it was deemed prudent to have an appreciation of ACP Chambers' perspective on the death penalty in Jamaica.

THE INTERVIEWEE

Assistant Commissioner of Police Clifford Chambers is a 28-year veteran of the JCF. He has served in various capacities throughout his policing career and has represented the JCF on various fronts to include his tenure as security attaché for Jamaica in Washington DC and also as the Jamaican representative at the Inter-American Defense Board. His current role at C-TOC sees him having command of over 280 police officers and straddling responsibilities associated with eight different sub-units. His views on the death penalty were captured during an interview and are presented hereunder.

THE INTERVIEW

AS: Tell me about your overall career; the divisions you have worked and your specializations.

CC: I started working in 1989 when I joined as a regular member; after completing 9 months of training I was posted at the Kingston Central Division where I was exposed to all aspects of policing; station guard, patrol, court process, and other aspects of basic policing. After about 4 years I became interested in investigation and I was accepted as a member of the

Fraud Squad where I worked for about 6 to 7 years. While at that division I rose directly from the rank of constable to sergeant and also spent time educating myself; I achieved a first degree in Public Sector Management and Accounting after which I was transferred to the Bureau of Special Investigation (BSI).

At the BSI, I investigated all aspects of police shootings and public sector corruption while taking the opportunity to pursue a Master's in Business Administration (MBA). At that time I also got the opportunity to participate in the Jamaica Constabulary Force's Graduate Entry Program and consequently did two examinations simultaneously as part of that process. Out of that program, I was promoted to the rank of inspector. I think I stand on record to be the shortest serving inspector because, after 2 weeks in the rank, I was elevated to assistant superintendent on the Graduate Entry Program. Now that program took us through a series of training because it is like entry management level to the organization and exposed us to strategic management, administrative policing, operational policing, and a plethora of other basic first year managerial skills that one should have when they are entering the managerial entry level of the JCF.

During the program I also did an on the job training in Clarendon and St. Mary as an administrative assistant, operation assistant, and the practicality of road policing. While I was in St. Mary, I instituted a traffic management system over there that saw some very good results. I was subsequently transferred to the Commissioner's Office as a staff officer to the Commissioner of Police and so I worked with—at the time—Commissioner of Police Francis Forbes. I was there for 2½ years with him and then Lucius Thomas became the Commissioner of Police. Staff Officer is kind of a very interesting position because though I was a Deputy Superintendent at the time I saw that I had some kind of influence over persons in higher office because of the position I was in. So as the staff officer, other senior officers have to come through me to see the Commissioner, so I had a lot of influence and authority at that time. I had the Commissioner's ear and I did his speeches; I would also accompany him to official functions at Jamaica House and Kings House.

I thereafter went to Washington DC on an external assignment, where I was the security attaché for Jamaican for 5½ years. During that stage, I was the Organization of American State Representative and also represented Jamaica at the Inter-America Defense Board. Whilst overseas I was promoted to the rank of Superintendent owing to a selection process I participated in. I subsequently returned to Jamaica and was in charge of the Fraud Squad for some time after which I was promoted to Senior Superintendent. Late last year (2016) just fast tracking to where I'm at—I was promoted to Assistant Commissioner; now I'm head of the Counter Terrorism and Organized Crime Investigation Branch (C-TOC).

C-TOC is a branch that has eight different units; Fraud Squad, Trafficking Persons, Intellectual Property, Cyber Crime, we also have the Financial Investigation Division Unit, we have a Court Evidence Gathering Unit, we have Special Operations and we have Transnational Crime Investigation Unit which works with the U.S. Embassy. So as it is right now I exercise control over 281 persons who operate island-wide. So between doing the Masters and going to Washington DC, I've also exposed myself to a higher level of legal training; I did a Bachelor of Law at the University of London. So in a succinct way, here I am today.

AS: Do you believe violent crimes have increased in Jamaica in the last 5 years, especially homicide?

CC: There is some amount of violent crime and when you take the aggregate figure there has been an upward trajectory.

AS: Do you believe criminals are more brazen now than they were before?

CC: Yes. Criminals are now more embolden and there are variables that might result in that. When you look at the ability of law enforcement—no fault of theirs, they don't provide the necessary resources—there were more resources then, than now comparatively. The population has increased, there are a lot of squatter settlements that have increased, yet the road infrastructure, the resources, and the police stations are all the same. The establishment of the police force remains unchanged as also our legislative arrangements. Most of our legislations are old and archaic; we accepted a Larceny Act from England that has remained unchanged since the 1930s. The police force is 150 years old; what modernization has come to it? Not much, to keep place with the current dispensation in society. So there are these gaps and until these gaps are brought up to speed with the reality of law enforcement we are going to be lagging behind, because you cannot be doing the same thing, using the same resource over and over and expect to get a different result, it just does not happen like that.

AS: It is clear then that there are certain deficiencies on the part of our criminal justice process and the organizations which make up our criminal justice system. Notwithstanding, do you believe that criminals are not mindful enough of the possible implications of their actions?

CC: There's a criminological theory that will tell you, justice should be swift, precise, and certain for crime to be impacted. A lot of criminals do what we could attribute to social choice theory; they look at the probability of being arrested, charged, and convicted before committing a crime. So when you look at the percentage of crimes that have gone unpunished, probably because of ineffective investigations; probably because of low-quality criminal justice system; probably because of how the High Court looks at things wherein every "I" has to be dotted and every "T" crossed; probably because of the threshold for criminal conviction, given that we have to prove all cases with circumstances beyond a reasonable doubt. Therefore, in a nutshell, criminals examine the probability of being convicted at times before they commit an offence. So the social theory I think is real. You're looking at criminals who are smart, they are intelligent and they weigh all the variables. So yes, the criminal justice system is an issue; some criminals look at their choices and certain probabilities of the outcome to advise and inform their decisions.

AS: The JCF has implemented measures to facilitate crime reduction. In your opinion, which programmes or initiatives have worked?

CC: Crime reduction strategies are varied and they are many. The crime reduction strategy that places huge numbers of law enforcement personnel in particular areas and situations don't work. Such a strategy may suppress a situation but will eventually have a balloon effect because criminals are moving around. It relates to the hotspot aspect of crime reduction; it works to an extent but it is temporary given that the criminals see hotspot policing in a specific place and so they migrate to another place. The strategy that will work—that we have seen elements of—is a legislative arrangement, giving law enforcement far more powers and authority which are used to contain criminal activities. So if you have, for example, an anti-gang legislation and you give law enforcement persons an avenue to charge persons for participating and recruiting and then you have very heavy sanctions, then we would see a greater impact in crime reduction.

We have to be mindful of the threshold to prove crimes beyond all reasonable doubts. There has to be an easier threshold—even though we understand the whole criminal prosecutorial system—there has to be a facilitation of the process that will assist investigators in presenting cogent arguments. But the way things are now we may not be able to prove in all cases beyond a reasonable doubt; there has to be some flexibility there. There also has to be straight and precise timelines for the trial of these matters; justice delayed is justice denied. So for example, we have developed the Lottery Scamming Legislation and it was done quite quickly. As a result, we had a lot of persons who are convicted on lottery scamming charges who were subsequently extradited, so you can feel the effect of such an Act. I think right now we have about 25% reduction in lottery scamming. So what I think would work is legislation wherein law enforcement is given the requisite space to enforce the law. Additionally, we need to have quick and precise sanctions that do not amount to just a slap on the wrist.

The problem with our anti-gang legislation is that it did not come with additional powers; you can't give law enforcement legislation and there is no enhancement of the authority that comes with such legislation. So again, legislation works, targeting persons committing crimes and not just the location works; these along with more authority to law enforcement to use technology to somehow enhance their investigating capability would have a tremendous impact. Additionally, with established sanctions in place so that at the end of the day a person will know that once they're convicted, they will receive such sanctions, there would be a huge dent in our crime situation.

For example, if you have a mandatory 20 years for simply been in possession of a firearm, an individual will probably see one but choose not to pick it up because he knows that once he takes it up the likely sanction is 20 years. So you need these major elements of deterrence that will prevent a person from behaving in a particular manner. Look at Singapore; you spit on the road and you go straight to prison; you are convicted of drug trafficking you get shot and killed. If people are aware that these are the sanctions they will face, they're going to think twice before getting involved.

AS: What are your views on human rights?

CC: I have no issue with that, the rights of an individual should be considered as sacrosanct. One of the things that we have to remember is that when you commit a crime against another person, the rights of that person have been taken away or are been trampled on. Once you do that then you are not being entitled to your rights anymore. It is said that an individual is innocent until proven guilty but at the same time the person who has been wronged goes through the issues and consequences of the offence committed against them. So law enforcement is the intermediary that can arrest, charge, and hold a person in custody until a person has been found guilty. Now even though we are mindful of that person's human rights, such rights should be suspended until the case has ended. So as not to trample on it the legal jurisprudence now has a responsibility to shorten the time period that the person may take to go through the process. If the person is not guilty then it is short, while if they are found guilty then you can start the sentence from the time when the person was taken into custody.

AS: Do you believe that we are impacted by an over observance of human rights to the extent that we are not able to operate as efficiently as we ought to, in order to stem our high crime rate?

CC: To some extent but it is not natural. The over extension of human rights is as a result of external forces which have been brought upon us. This is against the background that we have agencies locally which are funded internationally and so we have conditions which we must abide by. It is a known fact that in order to act on the dictates of these external agencies, local institutions give an outward expression of observing the rights of persons. However, if you speak to some of these persons outside of the entity of which they are a part of, they will open up and attest to the fact that they are being sponsored millions of dollars by these entities so they have no choice but to comply with their stipulations.

They will also tell you that the reality—given the criminogenic nature of Jamaica—is that our country requires a certain approach by law enforcement at times. They will not state this publicly but these are the monsters we are up against, these subtle monsters that impact the ease and freedom at which law enforcement can rise to the challenge of the criminal element that is out there. We have people moving around with shot guns, AK 47 and M16 rifles but then if law enforcement should match those weapons while maintaining their role then you may have the issue of personnel been too tactically charged to enter in certain environments.

You have the legislation that does not distinguish between the M16, the AK or the (Self Loading Rifle) SLR; so the illegal possession of a 9mm falls within the same sentencing range of the illegal possession of an AK47, SLR, or M16. These things need to be looked at because these firearms are not equal in velocity. One bullet from an AK47 rifle can kill several persons, while that is not the case with a .38 firearm. So it is clear that legislation must be looked at as the way forward so that police officers have the support they need. Law enforcement have to be mindful of the human rights of persons we have to be mindful of the Use of Force Policy of the JCF, we have to conform to the PLAN JM which looks at proportionality, legality, accountability, and all of those which are according to International Standards and I have no issue in conforming to all of that, but we have to realize that we are operating within an environment where the criminals do not abide by the same code of conduct.

When a policeman is out there, when a military person is out there when a law abiding citizen is out there and they're being attacked, the mental cranium at that time is sharply pushed into a survival mode and you have to respond. Sometimes only a few seconds make the difference between life and death; only seconds may sometime make a different between a good judgment call and a bad one; only a few seconds sometime decide if someone will be charged for murder as opposed to be seen as a legitimate fatal shooting. This is the predicament we are in. So when law enforcement personnel go through all of those variables and execute their duty, there needs to be legislation to give support, to give coherence to all of that and ensure that there is just sentence for a crime.

AS: We spoke just now about the rights of human rights, what are your views then on the death penalty?

CC: In my opinion, the death penalty has its place in law. The death penalty has its place in the judicial process; it has a place in the repercussion or consequences for crimes committed. The death penalty has its place in containing criminal activity; the death penalty, in short, is relevant but should only be operationalized in extreme circumstances. I believe that if the person is charged and convicted for capital murder then they should no longer be entitled to the rights or privileges of an ordinary person.

There are two sides to this; one is if you take a life then you practically gave up yours, and the other issue is you take a life and you are in a penal institution being fed by the families, spouse, relatives of the same person whom you have killed; how is that justified? That person is been taken care of by taxpayers' money; three meals a day in a secure facility at the expense of someone's life that you have taken. Now, where are the human rights aspects or elements in that? What justification can any human rights operative make that would justify a person killing another person, and causing that individuals children to grow without a father and those children becoming law abiding citizens and paying taxes to feed the man who killed their father? That is just not right.

AS: I know that the death penalty was a feature of our criminal justice process some time ago and the Privy Council to some extent had some input in amending that approach. As a result, it is not a prominent feature within our country anymore. However, based on what you have seen on the crime front, do you believe that the death penalty has a place in Jamaica?

CC: In my opinion, it should be brought back but with strict conditionality; the execution should be mandated to take place within a day and a month of conviction because once that time has exceeded it lessens the effect or impact.

AS: Ok. But there are some schools of thought around the notion that even if someone has committed murder the death penalty is cruel; this is normally the position of human rights advocates. What are your views on this?

CC: Again the penalty must equate to the crime. We have had circumstances where children have been killed, women have been raped and killed, we are seeing where bodies were decapitated, and we are seeing children being shot at point blank. Now those are heinous crimes and that's just to say a few, we have had persons who were responsible for over 25 murders and confessed, we have had persons who said that they have been a part of a criminal enterprise where they have been directed to kill, we have persons who had engaged in contract killings, the murder rate alone often by itself tells you how heinous our environment is. Now how can one not agree that those actions require an equal reaction? You cannot do those things without expecting that they are going to be done back to you. We are talking about human rights but we have to look at fairness.

AS: It has been said that there has been some bias and inconsistency and even discrimination associated with how the death penalty has been passed in various jurisdictions. Is there enough soundness and structure in our own jurisdictional processes at this time, to prevent this kind of discrimination or arbitrariness if we were to bring it back?

CC: Yes. I think there is, one of the things I like about our jurisprudence is that there is the independence of the judiciary and the prosecution has responsibilities to prove its case beyond reasonable doubt. The burden of proof lies on the prosecution and this standard of proof must come out of the evidence. There are legislations, there is precedence, they are case studies, and there are various avenues of appeal. I think that it is a balanced justice system that gives the accused person the equal right, equal footing to establish his innocence if he can and to establish a good defence if he can, and where that fails then the law must take its course. So if you do have legislation in place that states that if found guilty you should be hanged, having exhausted all the avenues, it is just a matter of going through the system that has been setup. The system is not classist, the laws are not classist, there's nothing in the law that distinguishes between the rich and the poor; it is not racist, the system is black and white, it is the legal structure it is the legal construct that is setup and has been tested and proven over the years. It is not biased and once you are found guilty and the penalty is death then it should follow through.

AS: Now in our own law enforcement architecture, there has been this view that we are very reactive, and there needs to be a more proactive front which should include social intervention. How do you see crime prevention? What do you think we should employ to promote more sound crime prevention strategies?

CC: Crime prevention is multifaceted and is one element in law enforcement. It starts at various levels. The first element of crime prevention is in the home where positive values are inculcated and you are exposed to right and wrong. Now when you move on to basic school, then you are exposed to other elements, in a wider external environment, because you have different people from different facets and also the school as an institution that should add to those values you already learnt at home. Given that the school environment is bigger than the home and the same values are shared—the value for life, you engender honesty and integrity and respect for other people—a foundation is laid.

Now growing up individuals may be exposed to peer pressure or other variables; they see things that they want and cannot achieve so they start to think of gaining them illegally. That is when other agencies become active in social intervention to create alternate avenues for such individuals. Therefore, crime prevention is everybody's business; it is everyone playing an active role in deterring, in educating, in advising, in suppressing the need for certain persons to become involved in criminal activity. There are many criminological thoughts that speak to it, there are those who believe that persons are predestined to be criminals, and there are sociological perspectives which suggest that persons are a product of their environment.

There is no society without crime but the police are there to suppress the elements considered wayward while looking at the bigger picture. Crime prevention is everybody's business; there are various social agencies that should see their role in—not directly tackling it but in—the building of a kind of sub-consciousness in persons they come in contact with on the virtues and values of good honest living.

AS: So there needs to be a more multifaceted approach to crime prevention including private agencies?

CC: Exactly! In some institution you have private agencies adopting locations, adopting roads, adopting schools and what they do is pump back some of their revenue into these locations to prevent them from becoming havens for criminal activity. So once you engage the public in alternative lifestyles outside of criminality there will be a positive impact on crime prevention. Every agency, every entity, every institution, should have an active role in crime prevention, every entity has a role to play it's just for them to identify what role they can play and how to play it because crime impacts everyone.

CONCLUSION

"The death penalty has its place in containing criminal activity ..." ACP Chambers clearly articulates a position of advocacy for capital punishment in particular situations. In asserting this position, he also attached the condition of expeditiousness to such a process when culpability for capital murder is clear and all avenues in the appellate process are exhausted. According to him, this swiftness in justice would have a profound impact in serving as a deterrent to others, thereby militating against the commission of some types of criminal activities. This expeditious serving of punishment has longed been echoed in the arena of criminology; according to Beccaria (2013), "The more promptly and the more closely punishment follows upon the commission of a crime, the more just and useful it will be." The stance adopted by ACP Chambers emanates from the view that a thorough retributive approach should be adopted for a horrific crime such as murder without any observance of human rights for the perpetrator. He qualifies this by offering the view that the offender relinquishes their rights when the rights of the victim are abused through the offence committed. Therefore, while he advocates for the sacrosanctity of human rights, a person who takes the life of another automatically surrenders such privileges. However, while he stoutly asserts his position on the rights of such an offender, human rights groups such as Amnesty International see the death penalty as, "... cruel, inhuman and degrading." These are sentiments which are also shared by local human rights group Independent Jamaican Council for Human Rights.

Notwithstanding the position of human rights groups on the death penalty, a country such as Jamaica with the crime rate spiralling out of control needs a crime antidote. The brazen nature of criminals has seen individuals been slaughtered in full view of onlookers and if a conviction is subsequently gained, the offender languishes in prison at the expense of taxpayers. As ACP Chambers indicated; an individual's decision to commit a crime is largely contingent on the likelihood of being caught and the possible punishment. His perspective here is akin to the theory of rational choice (Crawford & Evans, 2012; Hirschfield, 2005) wherein individuals assess the risk of being caught against the benefits of committing the offence. Therefore, given the certainty and finality of capital punishment—justly apportioned as the penalty for the heinousness of murder—even the most motivated offender may be deterred.

GLOSSARY OF TERMS

JCF—Jamaica Constabulary Force

C-TOC—Counter Terrorism and Organised Crime Investigation Branch.

ACP—Assistant Commissioner of Police.

Abolitionist De Facto State—No executions in the last 10 years notwithstanding retention of the death penalty.

Capital Punishment—Government sanctioned practice wherein a person is put to death as a penalty for a crime.

Morant Bay Rebellion—An event marked by the uprising of slaves against white authority in Morant Bay, St. Thomas, Jamaica on October 11, 1865.

Jamaica House—Official residence of the Prime Minister of Jamaica.

King's House—Official residence of the Governor General of Jamaica.

High Court—The highest court of Jamaica—the Supreme Court.

Rational Choice Theory—A Criminological school of thought suggesting that an individual's decision to commit a crime is contingent on the assessment of benefits and risks associated with the act.

REFERENCES

Beccaria, C. (2013). [1764]. On crimes and punishments. In E. Mclaughlin & J. Muncie (Eds.). *Criminological perspectives (3rd edn).* (pp. 5-15). London: Sage.

Crawford, A., & Evans, K. (2012). Crime prevention and community safety. In M. Maguire, R. Morgan, & R. Reiner, (Eds.), *The Oxford handbook of criminology* (5th edn). (pp. 769-805). London: Oxford University Press.

Hirschfield, A. (2005). Analysis for intervention. In N. Tilley (Ed.). *Handbook of crime prevention and community safety* (pp. 629–673), Willan, Uffculme, Devon.

CHAPTER IX

ST. LUCIA

COUNTRY INFORMATION

R esearch on police views on the death penalty was conducted on
the island of St. Lucia. The island is located to the north of Trinidad and Tobago, between the Caribbean Sea and North Atlantic Ocean. It measures 238 square miles with a population of ~182,973
people (as of January 2015). Although English is the official language of
St. Lucia, French patois is also spoken by most of the individuals on the
island. Manufacturing and agriculture have contributed significantly towards St. Lucia's economy over the years. However, the Tourism industry
accounts for 65% of St. Lucia's GDP and is the primary source of employ-
ment in the country and the main source of foreign exchange earnings
(CIA, World Fact Book, 2014).

As it relates to justice, criminal and civil cases are heard in St. Lucia's lower district court or in more serious cases the high court. In certain circumstances, further appeals are made to the Eastern Caribbean Supreme
Court (ESCS). The ESCS has its headquarters in St. Lucia and directs the
judicial system of the country (St. Lucia Country Profile, 2015).

Although St. Lucia is a signatory for the instituting of the Caribbean Court
of Justice, final appeals and rulings especially pertaining to the death penalty are heard by the Judicial Committee of the Privy Council located in
the UK. St. Lucia though a retentionist country of the death penalty, has
been referred by many journal authors as abolitionist in practice. This is
due to the fact that as of 2015, there has not been any execution. The last
execution in St. Lucia took place on October 17, 1995, when Joseph Solomon Vitalis who was sentenced to death was hung. Prior to the execution
of Vitalis, there had only been one other execution which took place in
1986.

As it relates to St. Lucia, the Judicial Committee of the Privy Council
(JCPC) and the Eastern Caribbean Court have alluded to cases such as
Reyes v, the Queen (2002) and Queen v Hughes to rule that the death
penalty amounts to cruel and unusual punishment. However, St. Lucia
has maintained its support for the death penalty as it did not vote in fa-

vour relating to a moratorium on the use of the death penalty at the UN General Assembly in December 2012. In addition, in a recent case concerning the death of a British National Oliver Gobat in St. Lucia in 2014, a request from the UK asking the relevant authorities to relinquish its death penalty in order to receive assistance to solve the murder case was rejected by the Government. Both the Prime Minister and Minister for Foreign Affairs felt this request from the UN foreign Affairs Office was unsuitable and indicated the request would not be granted.

THE ROYAL ST. LUCIA POLICE FORCE (RSLPF)

Organizational Structure (RSLPF)

The Royal Police Force of St. Lucia is led by a Commissioner of Police. Under the Commissioner are the Deputy Commissioner, Assistant Commissioner, Superintendents of Police, and Assistant Superintendents. There are two Deputies; one in charge of administration and the other in charge of crime and policing. There are three Assistant Commissioners; one assigned to crime management, the other two assigned to operations and territorial policing, respectively. The operational unit consists of the marine unit, special services unit, drug unit, etc. and the corporate unit covers territorial policing, training, etc. Under the assistant commissioners are superintendents and assistant superintendents. It must be noted that for territorial purposes, the island of St. Lucia is divided into northern and southern divisions.

The northern division is comprised of eight police stations whilst southern division is comprised of five police stations. Each division is headed by a Superintendent of Police. It is important to note that in St. Lucia, the Police Force also includes the Coast Guard, Immigration, and the Police Band. St. Lucia does not have a military. Superintendents are also responsible for the police band, training, as well as a special services unit. A superintendent undertakes the role of an administrative officer and is responsible for support services as it relates to the police force. Assistant Superintendents are assigned to similar divisions as well as some are in charge of smaller units such as beat and patrol, traffic and the marine patrol. The Police Force comprises of ~1,100 police officers (an exact figure was not given).

For the purpose of this research, the Acting Deputy Commissioner (DCP) of Police Mr. Severin Moncherry was interviewed. Mr. Moncherry has served as a police for 30 years and has worked in almost every department. His longest stint in the Police Service was in the Prosecution Unit where he spent 13 years. Mr. Moncherry also spearheaded the Anse la Raye Crime Fighting Committee geared at fighting crime committed by juveniles under the age of 16. He is also the current director of Community Policing in S Lucia. Mr. Moncherry had only been in the position of Acting Deputy Commissioner for about 3 weeks at the time of the interview. He has been a part of various crime fighting committees. Prior to his acting appointment as ACP, he had been acting in the position of Acting Assistant Commissioner of Police (ACP) for 6 months. Due to the absence of a second DCP, Mr. Moncherry has the responsibility of overseeing the administrative as well as corporate and operational affairs of the Police Force.

The interview with DCP Mr. Severin Moncherry was conducted on April 21, 2015, at the Police Headquarters in Castries, St. Lucia by Miss Milissa Dupres and was very cordial. DCP Moncherry was very enthusiastic and eager to share his wealth of experience and knowledge for the improvement of the Caribbean.

THE INTERVIEW

MD: Do you think violent crimes and homicides have increased within the past 5 years?

SM: Not exactly. There has been more or less some sort of fluctuation over the past 5 years based on the figures. In 2009 there were 39 homicides. Of these 39 homicides we had (two security-related shootings).

In 2010, there were 48 homicides (four security-related shootings).

In 2011, there were 52 homicides (13 security-related shootings).

In 2012, there were 44 homicides (eight security-related shootings).

In 2013, there were 34 homicides (two security-related shootings).

In 2014, there were 33 homicides (two security-related shootings).

There was an increase in the number of homicides for the period 2010–2011 followed by a decrease in the number of homicides in 2012–2014.

It is important to note that security-related shootings may or may not be police shootings. Security-related shootings include both police shootings and shootings by general security personnel.

MD: Do you think criminals are more daring in this present day as opposed to years before?

SM: Yes I think criminals are bolder in terms of the things they do and how they do it.

MD: Can you provide an example?

SM: For example, in the past, you hardly heard of criminals discharging rounds at police. But on the other hand, I believe it may be that way because of modernization and technology, persons have more access to weapons. In addition, in times before persons would have assaulted a police by using their hands, for example, punching, slapping. This may have been this way due to the lack of firearms which were available. Whereas I believe criminals have become bolder, I believe this may be due to the increase in technology.

MD: Do you think they care less about the nature of the penalties for criminal violations?

SM: I do not think it's a matter of them caring less about the nature of the penalties for committing a crime. I believe persons are just hell bent on committing crime and no matter what the consequences are they will commit crimes. In addition, some research has shown that an increase in penalty actually increases crime. The stiffer the penalty may result in increased crime. In my experience I have realised persons may not want to get caught so they may do anything even if it means killing someone.

MD: What are your views on the death penalty?

SM: I believe it's something we need to move away from. Whereas I'm not a full proponent of it I think it can have its place. But I don't think it should be carte blanche. If you want to use it as a deterrent I think you should qualify the circumstances in which it can be used. We have had it on our law books forever, and I have not seen any changes. It really makes no sense for countries like St. Lucia to be talking about the death penalty when they have no control over it.

MD: Do you think the death penalty is effective?

SM: No it's not, because it's in our law books but the last time it was used is 1998 when Solomon was hanged. As a matter of fact, I was the one who lead the inquest after the hanging. We have little control because of the interference by the Privy Council. Maybe we may have more control if we moved to the CCJ.

MD: Do you think it can deter crimes especially murder?

SM: Not just on its own. It depends on a number of other factors. It depends on the individual, why the person wants to kill, etc. Generally to the reasonable man yes.

MD: Do you think it should be used for crimes such as treason and kidnapping?

SM: To my knowledge, we have not had a case of treason in St. Lucia. Generally, I don't think so but for special circumstances, especially in cases of kidnapping, it can be used.

MD: Should there be categories of murder with the death penalty being reserved for only the highest category?

SM: Not being a proponent of it does not mean I am against it completely. Yes, I think there may be circumstances in which it can be used. In some cases of capital murders, I think it can be used.

MD: Should the death penalty be abolished, restructured, or implemented more consistently?

SM: I think the death penalty should firstly be restructured and then implemented more consistently.

MD: Do you think the death penalty is cruel and unusual punishment or is it just desserts?

SM: I think depending on the means used it can be considered cruel for example hanging. I think the lethal injection or execution should be used instead. In St. Lucia hanging has been the only method used. If the death penalty is used I think it should be used swiftly. But the first one needs to ensure that the individual has exhausted all legal avenues and have been found guilty. An individual may have committed murder but the circumstances surrounding the act should assist in determining whether the death penalty using hanging is used; for example, a woman who has been abused and kills the partner as opposed to a man who goes into a house and rapes and kill a woman. Therefore, I am not against the death penalty in all circumstances but more so the means by which it is used.

MD: Have strict legal procedures eliminated arbitrariness and discrimination associated with the death penalty?

SM: We have not experienced this in our jurisdiction since the last hanging was in 1998, so this a question that does not apply.

MD: Are you basically satisfied or dissatisfied with developments in the criminal justice system after an individual has been placed on death row?

SM: I am dissatisfied with it. This is one of the reasons we have not been able to use the death penalty. Some of the cases take so long before they even get to the high court, some do not even get to the Privy Council. It takes 5-7 years sometimes, and so I am not satisfied at all.

MD: In your experience what programmes have worked and have not worked in terms of fighting crime in St. Lucia?

SM: What has really worked for us is Community Policing. Also, police presence in terms of patrol has worked. But lately one of the main crime fighting tools that have really assisted is technology in terms of intelligence driven policing.

MD: What is intelligence driven policing?

SM: It's basically collecting information from various sources, analysing it, and using it as a crime fighting tool. Community policing, however, is one of the most effective crime fighting tools that we have used. The problem in St. Lucia is the misconception of community policing. The police and the community working together do not necessarily amount to community policing.

Community policing involves working with specific groups, stake holders, etc. in an effort to fight crime, for example, working with the Ministry of Youth and Sports, mother and fathers groups, etc. One of the first things that are done is community profiling, where you go into the community and find out what the issues and problems are in the community. After you have identified the problems then you identify the stakeholders that you need to work with and then you will form partnerships in developing programmes to adjust to the needs of the community. You do not throw out traditional policing because you have introduced community policing. What may work in one community may not necessarily work in another community.

MD: In which communities have you seen the most positive results?

SM: We have seen good results in Choiseul, Babonneau, Micoud, and Vieux-Fort.

MD: Which programmes have not been successful?

SM: I do not think one can say any have not been successful, because some of them you cannot measure the success like others. I am not aware of any that haven't worked because we have very few. Due to fiscal challenges and the rate of attrition that we have, there is a reduction in police presence.

MD: Any challenges with the Community Policing?

SM: One of the challenges is that we sometimes bring the same programmes into each community and that may not work. Also, community policing may be more effective in some departments if there is confidence in the police and in some instances, the level of confidence may be low and some individuals in the various communities may not be receptive.

MD: Was operation restore confidence a special programme? What are your views on operation restore confidence?

SM: Without going into too much detail, the programme in itself may not have been a problem. If there was a problem, it may have been in the execution of the programme.

MD: What was the aim of the programme?

SM: From my limited knowledge the program was an initiative geared at reducing crime and restoring public confidence. If there was a problem it may have been how it was executed, but I repeat the initiative in itself was not a problem. About 95% of St. Lucia say that operation restores confidence was a good initiative it is only now as this new revelation has come about persons are saying if this is how it was done then it was not good.

Operation restore confidence was intelligence led operation. When you conduct intelligence operations it is very likely that you will have deaths whether it is on the police side or on the side of the criminal. And the reason for that is when you do intelligence lead operation, you are actually going in based on intelligence. Intelligence is when you have information that has been analysed and accessed information and you have the final product. For example, through intelligence the police may know that a certain individual is planning to rob a bank, now if the police decide to try to catch the individual in the act, it is likely that if the criminal is armed if he gets the chance he may shoot the police. During intelligence driven operations you fight criminals not a crime so it is likely there will be more injuries and deaths. A lot of crimes committed are committed with fire-arms and weapons so both persons are at risk, i.e. police and criminals.

MD: What are your perspectives on crime prevention in terms of what you think should be done in St. Lucia to prevent crime?

SM: In societies like ours we may be faced with little resources. Therefore, most times I don't think resources are the problem. Sometimes it is how we manage the resources we have to prevent crime. There is abuse or mis-management of resources in many instances such as misuse of police ve-hicles. In terms of crime fighting strategies, I think one of the major chal-lenges we face is that the criminals may have resources and many times more sophisticated equipment which are superior to that of the police. Another major challenge we have is the type of criminal we deal with. One of the problems is the increase in deportees.

MD: Why do you think increase in deportees is a challenge in crime pre-vention?

SM: You would have trained your law enforcement officers at a particular level, and then you have all these sophisticated types of criminal activities coming from the states. There has been an increase in crimes never seen before and by the time you are able to figure it out and put in place a crime fighting strategy, it may be very difficult. Casing point, one of the latest things is persons who order credit card readers and drain out credit cards. An individual can walk next to another person with one of these readers and get their information by reading their credit card number, then go online and order, etc. There are these chips they place in the ATM, and one can go in there and put in their card and the criminal can get their pin number.

Another problem is that the same technology that works in our favour works against us. One can go right now and Google how to make a bomb.

Individuals can now monitor the police conversations, know exactly where the police are, what they are doing, etc. It also goes back to unscrupulous cops or crooked crops.

MD: Based on what you mentioned as it relates to the problems facing the police in terms of crime reduction what are your most important proposals for fighting crime?

SM: I think we need to look at our penal system/correctional system. But it needs to be reviewed at the first level. We need to look at our Boys Training Centre first thing. I think my main strategy would be to introduce at the lowest level or earliest stage, a diversion from the criminal justice system.

MD: Could you explain a bit further?

SM: We have clearly seen that whatever mechanism that is in place for our young people have failed them greatly. About 98% of the young people who go to BTC end up at Bordelais. They do not just end up at Bordelais but come out as real trained criminals. These people have not failed themselves, it is the system. Now the diversion from the criminal justice system means in the case of first offenders, rather than sending them to prison or detention centres, mechanisms should be put in place in order to avoid them from facing the CJS.

Programmes should be put in place so that they do not have to go through the courts and even if they go through the courts they should not have to face the penal system. Rather than sending young boys to the Boys Training Centre, what should be done is to enrol them in some programme where there is training to guide them away from committing a crime. The rate of recidivism at Bordelais is very high; it tells one that it is not serving its purpose. Another proposal is to review the programmes and the structure at Bordelais. We need to definitely use community policing. It should not be a short-term or medium-term programme but long term. It should begin at even kindergarten. In addition, I believe there should be a zero tolerance for crime on the whole. Allowing someone to go through the red light may be seen as nothing but it may amount to bigger problems in the future if it continues.

MD: What is most needed now to reduce the rates of violent crime and murders in your jurisdiction?

SM: Community policing can help at all levels. If you were to examine the stats about 80–90% of persons who commit or are victims or murders are young people. Community policing can be used in tackling these young persons. We have been having town hall meetings, meet the commissioner, among others. Due to the manner in which our homicides occur, I think community policing along with intelligence driven policing is essential. Doing community profiling, assessments, doing problem solving models, collaborating with stakeholders, and tackling the problems from the onset is important.

THE INTERVIEW

The interview with DCP Mr. Severin Moncherry revealed insights not only on the position of the DCP as it relates to the death penalty but his views were equally focused on strategies that would ensure that one avoids the justice system in the first place. Although the Deputy Commissioner indicated he is not a proponent of the death penalty, his reasoning suggests that the death penalty in itself is not something he is totally against but rather the methods in which persons may be put to the death and the amount of time on death row. This is similar to many of the arguments brought up by human rights activists.

Unlike proponents of deterrence theory who believe people who commit less crime if the punishment is swift, certain and severe the DCP Moncherry believed individuals would commit crime regardless. In addition, his arguments suggest that the death penalty does not have a deterrent effect and is consistent with research by Radelet and Lacock (2009) who concluded that "the death penalty does not add any significant deterrent effect above that of long-term imprisonment" (p. 504).

His arguments for crime fighting and his approach to the death penalty lean towards the classical theory of Hobbes who argued that excessive severity would not reduce crime, but would only increase crime. Additionally, he is a proponent of the rehabilitative approach and does not appear to follow the retributive approach as a core crime fighting strategy. Although the DCP has complete faith in community policing similar to Deosaran (2002), he understands that effective police–community partnerships require at least an 80% public satisfaction level.

DCP Moncherry's strategy to crime fighting is consistent with Wilson and Kelling's (1982) broken windows theory. Highlighting the importance of non-tolerance for all types of crime as well as focusing on community policing, he alluded that small signs of the disorder may communicate a lack of social control and result in increased criminal activity and should be addressed from the primitive stages.

GLOSSARY OF TERMS

Carte Blanche: complete freedom to do something (Cambridge Dictionary Online).

Community policing: Community policing entails a collaborative effort between the community and the police in order to identify and solve community problems. In community policing, the police are no longer solely in charge of enforcing the law, but the community becomes active participants in the thrust towards ensuring the safety of themselves and the neighbourhood as a whole (Bureau of Justice Assistance, 2004.

Intelligence-led policing: "Intelligence-led policing is crime fighting that is guided by effective intelligence gathering and analysis—and it has the potential to be the most important law enforcement innovation of the twenty-first century" (Kelling & Branton, 2006).

REFERENCES

Bureau of Justice Assistance. (2004). Understanding community policing. U.S. Department of Justice, Office of Justice Programs. Retrieved from https://www.ncjrs.gov/pdffiles/commp.pdf.

Cambridge Dictionary Online. Retrieved from https://dictionary.cambridge.org/.

Central Intelligence Agency. (2014). *World fact book.* Retrieved from https://www.cia.gov/library/publications/the-world-factbook/geos/st.html.

Deosaran, R. (2002). Community policing in the Caribbean: Context, community and police capability. *Policing: An International Journal of Police Strategies & Management, 25*(1), 125–146.

Kelling, G. L., & Bratton, W .J. (2006). Policing terrorism. *Civic Bulletin, 43,* 1–10.

Radelet, M. L., & Lacock, T. L. (2009). Do executions lower homicide rates: The views of leading criminologists? *Journal of Criminal Law and Criminology, 99*(2), 489–508.

St. Lucia Country Profile. (2015). ISSAT. http://issat.dcaf.ch/phantomjs/create_pdf/20024/A4.

Wilson, J. Q., & Kelling, G. (1982). Broken windows: The police and neighborhood safety. *Atlantic Monthly,* March 1982, 29–38.

CHAPTER X

St. Vincent and the Grenadines

COUNTRY INFORMATION

St. Vincent and the Grenadines (SVG) is an archipelagic state situated in the Eastern Caribbean. The Island of St. Vincent is the largest island with the Grenadine Islands comprising of Bequia, Mustique, Canouan, Mayreau, Union Island, Palm Island, and Petit St. Vincent among 32 islands and cays. The country covers some 150 square miles, and has a total population of ~111,380 (1998, updated figure) with the overwhelming majority being of African descent. SVG gained political independence from Britain on October 27, 1979, instituted a Parliamentary Democracy on the Westminster model and has since remained a part of the Commonwealth. Queen Elizabeth II, head of state of the UK of Great Britain and Northern Ireland is also the head of state of St. Vincent and the Grenadines but is represented by a resident Governor General.

The legal system of St. Vincent and the Grenadines was inherited from England and is based on English common law. This common law system was developed through the practice of the early customs and norms of the English society that were recognized and enforced by the judgments and decrees of the courts. Over time, the term "Common Law" came to include not only those early customs and norms but also all legislative enactments and the judicial decisions interpreting their application. It must be noted that the death penalty is included in the national laws of SVG.

Based on the doctrine of Stare Decisis ("let the decision stand"), it means that the courts in the Common Law system are obliged to follow the decisions and rulings in previously decided cases, or precedents, where the facts and issues are substantially the same. This doctrine provides certainty, uniformity, and predictability which essentially promote a stable legal environment. In St. Vincent and the Grenadines, therefore, a court's decision is binding authority for similar cases decided by the same court or by lower courts within the Court Structure. The decision is not binding on courts of higher rank but it may be considered as persuasive authority. Decisions from courts outside of SVG and the Eastern Caribbean are not binding, but may also be referred to as persuasive authority if there is no local case which has settled the point in issue.

STRUCTURE OF THE JUDICIAL SYSTEM IN SVG

The administration of justice in SVG is carried out through a network of courts that is structured on a four-tier judicial system. The first tier consists of the Magistrates Court which also includes the Family Court. This court is an inferior court of record and, is governed entirely by statute. Magistrates have the jurisdiction to try cases summarily as well as on indictment. The level of sanction, in terms of fines and imprisonment, is lower than that which may be imposed in the High Court. Appeals from the Magistrates Court are to the High Court Division or by way of case stated to the Court of Appeal Division both of the East Caribbean Supreme Court.

The second tier is the High Court which is the highest first instance court. It is a superior court of record and has unlimited jurisdiction. It has both inherent and statutory jurisdiction. Appeals from the High Court are also made to the Court of Appeal. The third tier of the court structure is the Court of Appeal, which is the court to which all appeals are first referred. The Court of Appeal may confirm, overturn or vary judgments in any cases in which there are appeals from any of the first-instance courts.

The Judicial Committee of the Privy Council is the fourth and highest tier of the SVG court system. This court, which is the final court of appeal, is based in London, England. The Privy Council hears appeal relating to criminal and civil matters from the Court of Appeal and makes a recommendation to the Sovereign as to the manner in which the appeal is to be resolved. It may recommend confirmation, overturn or variation of the judgment of the Court of Appeal. Appeals to the Privy Council are restricted to cases of a certain monetary value or where they are of exceptional public importance.

STRUCTURE OF THE ROYAL ST. VINCENT AND THE GRENADINES POLICE FORCE (RSVGPF)

The RSVGPF has a total of 1,074 members spread across three areas—Police, Fire, and Coast Guard services. It is headed by a Commissioner of Police who is assisted by a Deputy Commissioner and three Assistant Commissioners. Each Assistant Commissioner is in charge of one of three principal functions of policing namely: Administration, Operations, and Training and Crime. The operations function of the Police Force comprises of seven geographical divisions namely: Southern Grenadines, Northern Grenadines, Central, South Central, Western, Eastern, and South Eastern. Each division is headed by a Superintendent of Police who reports to the Assistant Commissioner of Police in charge of operations.

THE INTERVIEW

The interview with Michael Charles, Police Commissioner of the RSVG-PF was conducted on Thursday June 11, 2015, at the office of the Commissioner by Mr. Steve Eugene Stewart.

SES: Tell me a little bit about your career in terms of the length of time working, and movements within the force.

MC: My name is Michael Charles and I was enlisted in the Royal St. Vincent and the Grenadines Police Force on the February 28, 1981, 34 years ago. After graduating from the Police Training Academy in Barbados, I was placed on the Beat and Patrol Unit for 6 months. I was later transferred to the Special Service Unit (SSU) where I spent 9½ years. During that time I was also an instructor at the Regional Security System (RSS) Training Institute in Barbados where I was a specialist in Map Reading and Field Craft. Though I was a Constable in the RSVGPF I attained the rank of Sergeant Major with the RSS. I also travelled extensively throughout the RSS region.

SES: How did you progress through the ranks of the Police Force?

MC: After leaving the RSS and upon my return to St. Vincent, I was placed with the Narcotics Unit where I spent 10 years. During that time, I attained the rank of Sergeant. In 2001, I was transferred from the Narcotics Unit to head the Prime Minister's Security Details. In 2004, I was reassigned back to the Narcotics Unit and was promoted to Station Sergeant.

SES: Was it because you were so good why you were transferred back to Narcotics?

MC: Because of my experience working all those years in that field before and since the person who headed the Unit at the time was about to retire, I was then asked to return. In 2004, I was promoted once again to the rank of Inspector and again in 2006, to Assistant Superintendent of Police while still at the Narcotics Unit. In 2007, I was promoted to the rank of Superintendent (Ag.) and in that same year, I was reassigned back to head the Prime Minister's Security Details. In 2008, I was confirmed in the rank of Superintendent. In 2010, I was placed in charge of Special Branch, which is responsible for internal security and was made Commandant of the Police Training School. In 2011, I was promoted to Assistant Commissioner of Police (Ag.) in charge of operations.

In 2012, I was promoted to Deputy Commissioner of Police (Ag.) and also acted as Commissioner of Police from December 2012 to January 2013. Both holders of these substantive posts were out of state—the Deputy Commissioner of Police was on study leave and the Commissioner of Police was on vacation at the same time. On the return of both the Commissioner of Police and the Deputy Commissioner, I reverted back to my substantive post. Then upon the retirement of the Commissioner of Police some time later, I acted as Commissioner of Police from July 2013 and was confirmed in that position on January 16, 2014, with effect from November 1, 2013.

SES: Can you tell me about any training which you have received during your career?

MC: Over the years I received several types of training. In 2009, I did a Management Development Programme in Trinidad and Tobago. During the period 2011–2012, I completed the Staff and Command Programme at the Jamaica Staff College. I also completed a series of short-term training programmes in St. Vincent and the Grenadines.

SES: You have worked in a number of areas of the Police Force before your final promotion of Commissioner of Police, what area(s) did you enjoy most?

MC: I enjoyed working in the Narcotics Unit where I spent the greater part of my time as an enlisted officer. I often share the story of how I first met the present Prime Minister of St. Vincent and the Grenadines. During my time at the Narcotics Unit, Prime Minister Gonsalves was then a defence lawyer. We would often come up against each other on drug-related cases in the Court. That's where we actually met each other and formed a relationship.

SES: Let us turn to the subject of crime. In your view has there been an increase in violent crimes and homicides within the past 5 years?

MC: I would say that while there has been a reduction generally in the overall crime rates, somehow there has been an increase in homicide within the past 5 years.

SES: Are criminals more brazen now than before?

MC: Yes, I would say that.

SES: Is it that criminals do not care about the penalties for committed crimes?

MC: From some of the conversation we often hear, criminals don't seem to care about the penalties for crimes committed. What we see happening now is that a person who is convicted of a violent crime, let say murder, generally doesn't care what happens to him/her. Some would even go so far in making comments such as "I'll take you out and go around there (in reference to Her Majesty's Prisons which is located directly behind the Court House Building in Kingstown), sit down, eat and get fat."

SES: Do you think the death penalty deters or prevents serious crimes, especially murders?

MC: I'll say both; it deters and also prevents violent crimes, especially murder.

SES: If that is the case how is it that you have such an increase in the homicide rate?

MC: Stemming out of the Pratt and Morgan case, what we see happening now is that, a person who is convicted for a violent crime and sentenced to hang, he/she would have to go through the stages. The appeals may reach up to the Privy Council. By the time all the legal processes have been exhausted, 5 years would have gone by then Pratt and Morgan steps in. So everybody is well aware of that so they would use it to their advantage. Basically, as we see it, if we continue in this way then no convicted murderer would be hanged unless a country decides to go ahead and hang them and in the process breaks the law by the disregarded precedent established through the Pratt and Morgan Case. So with that, a person knows that he is not likely to be hanged because of the length of time allowed for the appeal process coupled with the implications of Pratt and Morgan.

SES: Do you think the death penalty is effective? If not, why?

MC: In my view yes.

SES: Should the death penalty be abolished or should it be more consistently enforced?

MC: I don't think it should be abolished. I am a firm believer in the bible which advocates that "if you live by the sword you should die by the sword."

SES: When was the last time we had an execution?

MC: It's been quite a while since; many years; I can't remember exactly the year. But it may be over 20 years ago if my memory serves me right.

SES: In that period of time you would have seen a spike in the number of murders being committed?

MC: The numbers have been ebbing and flowing, up and down. I think in 2004 and we had some 32 murders which were noticeably high.

SES: Of that number how many convictions were secured by the State?

MC: I think we would have gotten a fair amount of convictions; I won't say half. Some were sentenced to hang and some of them appealed.

SES: How many murderers are presently on death row?

MC: There is just one murderer on death row and he has exhausted all his appeals; you also have to take into consideration that many of them are going through the stages of appeal which often takes time.

SES: Is execution by the state acceptable in our society? If not, what is the alternative?

MC: This is a serious debatable issue. We are generally a religious society. Though someone is wrong it depends on which side of the fence you are. If a family member becomes a victim due to murder, that family would no doubt seek justice and would want the defendant to be convicted of murder. If on the other hand, the victim is unrelated or a stranger, one may be more inclined to suggest a life sentence rather than the death penalty. But listening to people, if you go around the community I think the majority of people in St. Vincent and the Grenadines are not for the death penalty but a fair amount of people are still supportive of it.

SES: We have not had the death penalty by hanging being carried out in the last 20 years or so, coupled with the fact that in that period there has been a spike in the murder rate with only one person on death row, it would appear that the State does not have the will nor the appetite for carrying out the death penalty for convicted murderers. How do you respond to that?

MC: It would appear so; the mere fact that if a person is sentenced to hang he/she is likely to go through all the stages of appeal, which takes time. So it would depend on the outcome of the case on final appeal to the Privy Council. I must also tell you the Human Rights lawyers here do a lot in respect of the death penalty. Whenever the subject of the death penalty comes up these lawyers are usually "up in arms"; they are against it.

SES: What policies or programmes in your view, have worked well and those that have not in relation to reducing crime?

MC: The programmes that we now put in place and we have started with the schools making presentations to students on drugs and violence. We also have a few "Police Youth Clubs" where the youths would meet the police in their respective communities, particularly when schools are on vacation; we usually have summer camps.

Some 10 years ago it was evident that the police was separated from the communities in which they work. The relationship then was not this good. With the coming on stream of the police youth clubs what we are seeing now is that there is a better relationship with the police; some parents would even come in to observe what is happening. At present we have about 24 clubs including one club on Bequia in the Grenadines.

We also have a Government sponsored programme called "Pan Against Crime," which is also geared towards the youths. There are greater activity and involvement in this programme during the summer. I must say that my daughter was a beneficiary of the pan music programme in her school since her love for pan music developed while at secondary school. She played many instruments which had a positive impact on her academic performance.

Another programme is the DARE—Drug Awareness Resistance Education. We have commenced this programme in the primary schools and it has since been extended to secondary schools because of its popularity. There are presently four police officers in the DARE Unit who would collaborate with the Ministry of Education which would provide the names of the schools that should be visited. This programme has been running now for over 20 years and the Unit has visited all primary schools on mainland St. Vincent and just one school in the Grenadines, and that is Bequia. We have even done visits to some private schools. If a secondary school requests a visit then we would oblige. We've just started the secondary school programme in the last 2 years.

SES: How have the programmes been implemented in the rest of the Grenadines?

MC: Well, although the police was not instrumental in setting up the Pan Against Crime in Union Island and Canouan, the schools on these islands have set up their own steel orchestras; nevertheless, officers from time to time would journey to these islands to give assistance in the practice and theory of pan music.

SES: Which programmes in your view have not worked in the fight against crime?

MC: I would say that all the programmes we have implemented have worked.

SES: Are there any proposals on the table which the police are considering to be used in fighting crimes?

MC: The leadership of the police would meet from time to time where we would discuss certain strategies. But I would not want to disclose them at this time.

SES: What do you see as the greatest problem/challenge facing the police with respect to crime reduction?

MC: With our limited resources, for us to have the requisite tools to effectively fight crime; our main challenge is getting witnesses who are reluctant, to come forward to give evidence in criminal matters especially murders. However, to get around that challenge it means that we now have to consider obtaining forensic evidence, which is not really pursued at this time because of our limited resources. However, we have received some assistance from the United States for fingerprinting evidence. We would also send some of our officers from the Criminal Records Office on attachment to St. Lucia since that country has a relatively good crime fighting unit.

SES: It would seem to me a little bit strange if not contradictory that you have all these programmes that are designed to improve the relationship between police and community and still there is a fair amount of distrust by eyewitnesses to come forward to give evidence in criminal matters.

MC: I must say that the relationship is getting better; there is still some reluctance but some people though they may not come forward, would nonetheless, drop hints for the police to pick up on.

SES: Are you satisfied generally with developments in the criminal justice system after a sentence of death has been imposed on a murderer?

MC: Well, I think our criminal justice system is working well, functioning properly; prosecutors can only proceed on the basis of what is evidence the investigators bring before them. I have no issue with our justice system; once the prosecutors do proper investigations then I would be satisfied with the outcome.

SES: Are you happy with the length of time it often takes for a criminal matter in particular homicides to conclude a case in its entirety?

MC: As police officers, we are trained to carry out a proper investigation, arrest the suspect then charge him/her with an offence. It is then left to the courts and the system to determine the outcome. But I think it is too lengthy at times. While that may be so, I also think people would be generally satisfied if the offender is convicted following the outcome of the trial notwithstanding the length of time of the appeal process.

SES: Are there cases where some offenders were convicted of murder and sentenced to hang but later had their sentence commuted to life imprisonment?

MC: There aren't that many cases like that; I can only think of three such cases.

SES: What is most needed now to reduce the rates of violent crimes and murders in our jurisdiction?

MC: We are supposed to be a Christian society; there needs to be a return to a spiritual pathway; the churches and civil society need to begin a serious conversation and to build a stronger relationship among themselves in terms of using more appropriate means of settling disputes. I would say that we need education and getting back to being "our brothers' keepers."

SES: Do you think there are too many illegal firearms in the country?

MC: I would say definitely yes—too many; of the 36 murders which were committed last year; 27 were done with the use of such firearms. One may ask the question, why are there so many illegal firearms in the country. By and large, it has to do with the fact that we have a large and extensive maritime boundary to patrol and the issue of limited resources does arise. Unlike for example a country like Barbados which consists of one island and has more resources at their disposal, St. Vincent and the Grenadines is made of a number of islands that extent over a much larger maritime boundary with very limited resources.

SES: Some years ago the Police Department had in place for a short period of time an amnesty programme for the recovery of illegal firearms? Would you consider implementing such a programme again?

MC: Some people called for that programme back then but from the response, it did not have the kind of results that we were hoping to get. But it is still something that we might want to look into over the course of time.

SES: Is there a backlog of criminal murder cases?

MC: I think the judiciary is trying; there are so many cases and right now the high court is going full speed. From time to time the Government brings in retired justices to assist with the back log. There are a lot of cases, though I won't want to use the word "backlog" but that's what it is. If we had adequate resources of the state then things would have been better. But we have to work with what we have.

SES: Commissioner I want to thank you very much again for granting me the opportunity to conduct this interview with you.

MC: You are welcome

PERSPECTIVE ON THE DEATH PENALTY

COP Charles' perspective is that the death penalty is an appropriate punishment for a convicted murderer and that it should not be abolished since as a firm believer in the bible, he subscribes to the principle that "if you live by the sword you must die by the sword." It is his belief that the death penalty both deters and also prevents violent crimes, especially murder notwithstanding the fact that only one murderer is presently on death row and that it was more than 20 years ago that the last execution occurred. During that same period the number of murders committed on a yearly basis has been ebbing and flowing with 2004 and 2014 being particularly significant as some 32 and 36 murders were committed, respectively, making 2004 and 2014 two of the deadliest years on record.

The police leader explains the apparent contradiction between the death penalty being an effective deterrent to violent crimes, particularly murders and the increase rates of homicide by pointing to the impact of the Pratt and Morgan case as precedent. He stated that everybody is well aware of the lengthy process of murder trials and appeals and the implications of Pratt and Morgan and, a convicted person may use them to his advantage. He admits that if things were to continue in this way then no one is likely to be hung unless the country goes ahead and hangs the murderers thus in effect disregarding judicial precedent. The effect of the Pratt and Morgan case is that an individual who has spent more than 5 years on death row cannot be executed.

When asked whether he thinks state execution is acceptable, Commissioner Charles acknowledged that it was a serious debatable issue and that it depended on which side of the fence one sits. He explained that if a family member becomes a victim of murder that family would no doubt seek justice and would want the defendant to be convicted of murder. If on the other hand, the victim is unrelated or a stranger, one may be more inclined to suggest a life sentence rather than the death penalty. He believes that the majority of people in St. Vincent and the Grenadines are not for the death penalty but a fair number of people are still supportive of it.

PROBLEMS AND SUCCESSES EXPERIENCED

Charles indicated that the genesis of the programmes which are now implemented in an attempt to reduce the crime situation came out of the need to bridge the gap between police and the communities in which police officers work. The relationship then was particularly not a good one. With the coming on stream of programmes such as the Police Youth Clubs, Pan Against Crime, and DARE, there is some evidence of improvements in the existing relationship. He is of the opinion that all the programmes implemented, have worked.

Charles has cited the Department's limited resources as the greatest challenge in the fight against crime. He has also identified the general reluctance of witnesses to come forward to give evidence in criminal matters especially murders. He explains that while there is still a fair amount of distrust between the police and the public and that the relationship is not where they would like it to be at the present time, he feels that it is definitely getting better. Notwithstanding the distrust, some eyewitnesses are still willing to drop hints for the police to pick up on.

The Commissioner's general assessments are that he is basically satisfied with the functioning of the Criminal Justice System in St. Vincent and the Grenadines after a sentence of death has been passed on a murderer. His view is that once the investigators and prosecutors execute their jobs properly to the extent where a conviction is secured then that brings satisfaction to him irrespective of the appeals process thereafter. He is of the view that there are too many illegal firearms in the country. However, appears not willing to implement an amnesty programme because his assessment of a previously implemented programme was that it was not satisfactory.

CONCLUSION

Mr. Michael Charles, Commissioner of Police (COP), was interviewed on the June 11, 2015, at the Police Commissioner's Office in Kingstown, St. Vincent. The interview covered a range of topic areas geared towards ascertaining the Commissioner's perspective not only on the death penalty as a deterrent to violent crimes and homicides but also on the challenges which his Department faces in dealing with the criminal justice system and criminality in general in St. Vincent and the Grenadines. The interview also sought answers to questions on effective police strategies to control crime in the island. The interview was very open and cordial and the COP expressed his views openly.

The major themes covered in the interview were: the Commissioner's assessment of the state of violent crimes, his personal views on the death penalty, problems and successes experienced in relation to the reduction of crimes, and his overall assessment.

COP Charles is of the view that although there has been a reduction generally in the overall crime rates, there has also been an increase in homicide within the past 5 years. He also believes that the criminals are more brazen now than before and concludes that criminals do not seem to care about the penalties for violent crimes committed as it appears to them that the operation of the judicial system is such that a convicted criminal is more likely to remain behind bars for quite a long time rather than be put to death.

GLOSSARY OF TERMS

CRU: Criminal Records Unit

COP: Commissioner of Police

DARE: Drug Awareness Resistance Education

PAC: Pan Against Crime

PYC: Police Youth Clubs

RSVGPF: Royal St. Vincent and the Grenadines Police Force

RSS: Regional Security System

SSU: Special Service Unit

SVG: St. Vincent and the Grenadines

CHAPTER XI

TRINIDAD AND TOBAGO

COUNTRY INFORMATION

The twin-island Republic of Trinidad and Tobago is considered to be one of the wealthiest and most developed Caribbean countries. It is the most southerly of the Caribbean Islands and after gaining its independence in 1962, became a Republic in 1976 but still kept the Privy Council as its final Appellate Court. Tobago is the smaller of the two islands and whilst Trinidad accounts for ~93% of the total land mass, together both islands comprise a total of 5128 square kilometres. With a population of ~1.3 million (Clement, 2012), Trinidad and Tobago is a cosmopolitan society, with many varied religions, cultures, and ethnicities. Whilst the major ethnic groups are persons of African (34.2%) and East Indian (35.4%) origin (Clement, 2012), Trinidad and Tobago has seen over the years an increase in its mixed population from 20.5% in 2000 to 22.8% in 2011 (Clement, 2012).

Trinidad and Tobago has been for many years and continues to be heavily dependent on the petroleum sector but over the years they have seen the significant growth in the manufacturing sector and attempts made at diversification of the economy have seen some investment in the tourism industry. Trinidad and Tobago has a bicameral Parliamentary System based on the Westminster model. An Electoral College elects the President who acts as the Head of State, whilst the Prime Minister represents the head of the government. The electoral system is one that is based on first past the post and the 41 members of the House of Representatives are elected for a term not exceeding 5 years.

The mandatory death penalty for murder in Trinidad and Tobago still forms part of the statutes in accordance with Section 4 of the Offences Against the Person Act, Chapter 11:08. Whilst Trinidad and Tobago is not a party to a moratorium on executions, and has consistently voted against the United Nations General Assembly Moratorium Resolution (United Nations, 2012), the last executions occurred in 1999 when 10 persons were hanged over a 6-week period. It is quite evident that Trinidad and Tobago intents to maintains its right to execute criminal offenders. This is demonstrated by their refusal to accept the recommendation for a moratorium on executions in the Universal Periodic Review (United Nations, 2011) as well as their withdrawal from the ICCPR's First Optional Protocol (American Convention on Human Rights, 1969) and their denouncement of the American Convention on Human Rights in 1998 (Amnesty International, 2012), 1 year before the hanging of 10 took place. However, prior to 1999, the last hanging occurred in 1994 (Allum & Delzin, 2003). Although murder is the most prevalent offence for which the death penalty is prescribed, other offences for which it is prescribed include treason, terrorist acts resulting in death and genocide where members of the group targeted have been killed.

THE INTERVIEWEE AND SETTINGS

Mr. Jason Forde, Acting Senior Superintendent of Police, Head of the Homicide Bureau of Investigations in the Trinidad and Tobago Police Service was interviewed by Mrs. Karen Lancaster-Ellis. The interview commenced at 1:00 p.m., concluded at 2:20 p.m. and was conducted at an office of the Police Administration Building, Port-of-Spain on Friday April 15, 2015. The air-conditioned office was clean, well-lit, and the ergonomic design was of the highest standard which created a sense of comfort. The interviewer made the arrangement for the use of the office space with an Assistant Superintendent of Police 2 days prior to the interview being held. At no time prior to, during or following the interview did the interviewee show any signs of unwillingness. He was enthusiastic, forthright, cooperative, and amiable, which created a comforting environment and facilitated an ease in questioning. The interviewer first informed the interviewee, the purpose of the interview, assured him of confidentiality, and assured him that she will not invade his privacy or cause any embarrassment to him. The interviewee was also advised that at any time before or during the interview he can choose to no longer participate. The interviewer sought and obtained permission from the interviewee to tape record the interview, so as not to negatively impact on the flow. Given the interviewee's position as a law enforcement officer in the Trinidad and Tobago Police Service and her level of responsibility, there was seemingly a very high level of trust developed.

The author conducted the interview with the interviewee, Mr. Jason Forde, an Acting Senior Superintendent of Police who is attached to and leads the Homicide Bureau of Investigations in the Trinidad and Tobago

Police Service. The interviewer first communicated to the Assistant Commissioner of Police in charge of the Homicide Bureau of Investigations to obtain authorization for the interview to be conducted. Having received the required authorization she made a request of the interviewee, for the interview 2 days prior to the interview being held. Due to his recent posting to the Bureau, the interviewee was initially apprehensive when asked to participate and felt that another senior officer (his subordinate) may have been the better option since that individual had in excess of 20 years' experience working at the Bureau. Despite such plausible reasoning and the interviewee's extremely hectic schedule, he subsequently elected to avail himself to be interviewed.

Mr. Forde is approaching his 35th year of policing in Trinidad and Tobago having joined the Trinidad and Tobago Police Service in 1980. Following his training at the Police Training College, the interviewee worked in several divisions throughout Trinidad but spent most of his early years of policing in the Northern Police Division. The interviewee also performed policing duties at the then Narcotics and Firearm Control Bureau, today called the Organized Crime Narcotics and Firearms Bureau, the Guard and Emergency Branch and in the year 2000 as a Police Constable, he was transferred to the Homicide Bureau of Investigations and has been there up to today. The interviewee now holds the rank of Superintendent of Police, acting in the capacity as the Senior Superintendent in charge of the Homicide Bureau of Investigations. The interviewee received his first promotion to the rank of Police Corporal, after 23 years of dedicated service to the people of Trinidad and Tobago. Following that first promotion, the interviewee was promoted four times within a 10-year period, with his last promotion being in 2013.

Although the interviewee suggested that by virtue of his recent posting he may not have been the most suitable officer at the Bureau to be interviewed, it was discovered during the interview that the interviewee had in fact been working at the Bureau for almost 15 years and to the mind of the interviewer was sufficient to constitute significant experience at the Homicide Bureau although it may not have necessarily meant investigative experience. The interviewee is the holder of a Bachelor of Science Degree in Political Science from the University of the West Indies and a Certificate in Human Resource Management from the same institution and he has also participated in several internal and external training courses and workshops.

STRUCTURE OF THE TRINIDAD AND TOBAGO POLICE SERVICE (TTPS)

The Trinidad and Tobago Police Service (TTPS) is required to police the island of Trinidad and Tobago and to ensure efficiency and effectiveness of the administrative arrangements, the country is demarcated into four police regions which are further sub-divided into nine geographic police divisions, with eight being in Trinidad and one in Tobago. The breakdown of this arrangement is illustrated in Table 11.1. Each of the nine police divisions are led by a Senior Superintendent of Police, whereas each region is led by an officer of the rank of Assistant Commissioner of Police. There are 77 police stations and posts and 23 branches, sections, and units.

Table 11.1 *Demarcation of police regions—Trinidad and Tobago police service*

Number of divisions	Divisions	Number of regions	Regions
1	Port-of-Spain	1	North West
2	Western		
3	North Eastern	2	North East
4	Northern		
5	Eastern		
6	Tobago	3	Tobago
7	Central	4	South
8	Southern		
9	South Western		

Source: Fieldwork, 2015

The TTPS consists of 10 ranks that fall within the First and Second Divisions. The most senior officers from the rank of Assistant Superintendent of Police to Commissioner of Police form the First Division, whilst the most junior officers from the rank of Police Constable at the lowest end to Inspector of Police fall under the Second Division. Currently, the TTPS has a complement of a little over 6,500 officers and is supported in great measure by Special Reserve Police (SRP) Officers. The rank structure of the TTPS is shown in Table 11.2.

Table 11.2 *Rank structure of the Trinidad and Tobago police service*

No.	Rank	Division
1	Commissioner of Police	First Division
2	Deputy Commissioner of Police	
3	Assistant Commissioner of Police	
4	Senior Superintendent of Police	
5	Superintendent of Police	
6	Assistant Superintendent of Police	
7	Inspector of Police	Second Division
8	Sergeant of Police	
9	Police Corporal	
10	Police Constable	

Source: Fieldwork, 2015

THE INTERVIEW

KLE: Good afternoon and thank you for facilitating this interview today. My name is Karen Lancaster-Ellis and I am the author of a chapter in a book which looks at the death penalty and its deterrent effect. I would like to assure you that the information you provide to me will be held in confidence. It will be, the information you provide will also be part of research being conducted as it relates to the death penalty, am, because the same information basically would be provided by other law enforcement officers throughout the Caribbean so the information you provide would be just your views based on that Trinidad and Tobago experience as a law enforcement officer. Before we start I just need to get a little information from you, I would like you to tell me a little bit about your career, how long you have been in the organization, where you have worked, where you have moved to, the specialist section you have worked in, how long, what year you started, that sort of standard information.

JF: Well, good afternoon, my name is Jayson Forde. I have been a police officer for the past 34 approaching 35 years. I had the pleasure of joining the Trinidad and Tobago Police Service in 1980. I worked in several Divisions most notably in Northern Trinidad. I worked in the then Narcotics and Firearm Control Bureau, today called the Organized Crime Narcotics and Firearms Control Bureau. I worked in various Divisions. I worked at the Guard and Emergency Branch and in the year 2000, I was transferred to the Homicide Bureau of Investigations and I have been there since that time to the present date. When I was transferred there, I was a Constable; today I hold the rank of Superintendent, acting in the capacity as a Senior Superintendent in charge of the Homicide Bureau of Investigations.

KLE: Mr. Forde how many persons were in your batch?

JF: In excess of 300.

KLE: Was it more than 400?

JF: Not to my recollection.

KLE: When did you receive your first promotion? Do you recall?

JF: Twenty-three years after joining the service, that would have been the year about 2003 or thereabout, 2003.

KLE: And your 2nd promotion?

JF: Two–three years after that. It has been like that yuh know, ever since.

KLE: And the last time you received a promotion, could you say how long ago that was?

JF: That was in 2013.

KLE: I know you said you have been working at the Homicide for the past 10 years, 10 years or 15 years.

JF: 14 going into 15 years.

KLE: 14 going into 15 years, okay. Prior to joining the Homicide Bureau which Department, Section, or Division you would have worked in for the longest period of time?

JF: To give you a period of time will be difficult because to my pleasure, I was a regular mover, because I worked at the Guard and Emergency Branch, I worked at the Honour Guard, I worked in Western Division, I worked in Narcotics, then I went in to North Eastern Division, I would not be able to give you an exact period of time.

KLE: When you worked in those specific Divisions, was it uniformed duties or was it in Sections?

JF: Well, Guard and Emergency and Honour Guard are uniformed areas. Western Division, I worked uniform, charge-room, then I did some administrative work in the office. In North Eastern Police Division I worked Task Force, uniform.

KLE: Alright, tell me something I am looking at some other things, other questions that I will like to ask you now? In your view has violent crimes and Homicides increased within the past 5 years, in your view? Do you think it has increased?

JF: Actually, in the past 5 years homicides have been decreasing. Violent crimes too have been decreasing in the past 5 years in Trinidad and Tobago.

KLE: Is your view based on statistical data or just based on a hunch or observation?

JF: Well the last time that I had the opportunity to glean some information there was statistical data showing that we have been having a reduction. As a matter of fact, I recall the Commissioner saying that he had been seeing a downward trend. It has been the greatest decrease for the past 15–20 years or something like that.

KLE: And you can attest to that?

JF: Yes.

KLE: But do you think criminals are now bolder than before?

JF: Think? Yes, I think that they are bolder than before.

KLE: What has led you to that thinking?

JF: Two things. One would be personal interaction and two, I find there is more reporting. Because of the explosion of technology and you have reported taking place via the media you get a sense that criminals and criminal activity yuh know are bolder than before.

KLE: I know you said interactions right when you say interactions, could you explain expand on that ah little bit? Interactions with whom and those interactions, what am, what happened during those interactions that led you to believe they are bolder than before?

JF: In the area that I work, in the Homicide Bureau of Investigations, you would appreciate that at times I will interact with suspects I will also engage in conversations with my Supervisees and based on those interactions the feedback is that criminals are bolder than before. Additionally, you have a lot more criminals committing a crime without masking themselves. In the past, criminals committed most of their crimes under the cover of darkness and many of them wore masks. Today it is as though they are using the local parochial term "look meh," when they are going through there unmasked and crimes are committed in the day. So certainly if you add all those variables together, one can reasonably come to a conclusion that they are bolder than before.

KLE: Could you give me an example of an instance where a criminal was bold that you would have interacted with, that you would have experienced?

JF: Approximately, about 5 years ago there was a Homicide that took place at Independence Square, Port-of-Spain, where a young man was shot and killed and a young lady received an injury to her calve from a bullet in the same incident. It is ironic that crime took place in broad daylight and there was the presence of police officers in and around Port-of-Spain, but because the criminal wanted to exact revenge, he had no compunctions about pulling out his firearm and shooting and the young man died, the target died, and a young lady was injured in that scenario.

KLE: Now there are penalties for violations of the law, right. Do you think that criminals don't care about those penalties for criminal violations?

JF: It seems as though they do not care about those penalties.

KLE: Why do you think they don't care?

JF: Yuh know, the question throws me back to my youthful days and just like you because I don't think we are too, we share too many, too big ah difference in age, although women they say, don't ask woman her age and although yuh look as though you are 16 (laughs) right, I recall that as a younger man I felt invincible and I felt as though nothing could have conquered me and I think every generation goes through that feeling of invincibility but back then when we had differences to settle we fought it with either kid's fight or we pelted each other with stones or bottles. Today the firearms are more easily accessible and you have a very easy access to firearms with young people having a sense of invincibility and as such, they are willing to commit criminal acts. I guess back then I did not consider the repercussions for my actions. Young people to me in every generation do not really consider repercussions. The sad thing is that back then when we fought with fists we could have gone home and you know taken something for the cuts we got and call that the game. But the criminal today uses weapons, guns, well mostly guns or knives, but mostly guns. So that feeling of invincibility and access to lethal barrelled weapons namely firearms, add that to the discussion we had earlier.

KLE: And Mr. Forde what are your views then on the death penalty looking at the personal policing philosophy on the death penalty. What are your views on the death penalty?

JF: Now, the law in Trinidad and Tobago says that if yuh convicted of murder yuh shall suffer death. Personally, I wonder how much of a deterrent the death penalty is. Because that law has not been struck off of our law books and still persons are willing to shoot at each other with intention to kill and I believe that they are aware that the penalty for murder is death but I don't think it is a strong enough deterrent today.

KLE: On a scale then of 1–10 how effective is the death penalty?

JF: It would be difficult for me to give yuh that rating and let me tell you why. I think one of the deterrents to crime is if justice is swift. Besides being caught, justice has to be swift. As far as my memory serves me the last time we executed anybody in Trinidad and Tobago was in 1999 that is how many years ago. In the absence of data, it will be difficult for me to give you a proper answer. And I qualify it further by saying that it would be interesting yuh know with 20/20 vision, to see that if you were executing people periodically if that might have been a deterrent to persons committing that most serious kind of murder. In the absence of executions between 1999 and today and persons believing that they would not hang anybody in Trinidad and Tobago and they doh hang people in Trinidad and Tobago, am, my rating might be low but am, I cannot give yuh a proper rating.

KLE: Do you think then even based on, in light of what you have just said, the death penalty deters persons from murdering someone else?

JF: I will have to say no and I will qualify that answer by saying that Trinidad is a country governed by rules and regulations and our laws clearly state that the death penalty is there for anyone who is found guilty of murder and persons are committing murders and I believe in the full knowledge that the death penalty exists and they still commit murder as though they have a certain level of impunity. I do not think that it is an effective deterrent at this time.

KLE: But why do you think they have the full knowledge that death penalty will be for murder. Why do you think that they are aware of that, that's the penalty, death is the penalty for murders?

JF: Why I think that they are aware? Well, our media, our responsible media ever so often bring it to our attention that the penalty for murder is death. There are discussions on street corners; there are discussions in bars that the penalty for murder is death. I am hard-pressed to believe that young people who are engaging in that violent type of crime will be unaware that the penalty for murder is not death. Keep in mind that my view is subjective because I haven't interviewed them, but Trinidad and Tobago being the small society that it is, I am of the view that most persons are aware that the penalty for murder is death.

KLE: I have asked that in light of the fact that am, as you said earlier that nobody has been hanged since 1999, so persons who would have committed crimes within recent times right, may not have been exposed, or may not have known about those persons who would have been hanged, hung in 1999.

JF: Probably.

KLE: Probably. So are you saying then that they would have been made aware that the penalty for murder is death just by virtue of the information on the media as well as those persons on the street corners?

JF: Well, I cannot say that they were made aware as I said my view is subjective but I repeat that Trinidad and Tobago being a small country, ever so often the media highlight the issue of the death penalty. Every so often debate takes place on the value of the death penalty, also whether it is an effective deterrent or not, to murder and we have a very educated population in this country called Trinidad and Tobago and I am saying again I am hard pressed to believe that many of those persons will be unaware that the penalty for murdering another person is death.

KLE: Then, in light of that fact do you think the death penalty should be abolished?

JF: That's an interesting question, I think murders should be categorized and the death penalty should be retained for the most heinous of murders.

KLE: Then do you think the death penalty should be restructured?

JF: Well, I think we are saying the same thing there, that it should be restructured in that murders should be categorized and we keep the death penalty for the most heinous of murders committed.

KLE: And do you think it should be implemented then more consistently?

JF: Yes I do.

KLE: For what purpose?

JF: Well, based on my suggestion, if yuh have ah categorization of murders and we retaining the death penalty for the most heinous as I tell you about swift justice and the assurance that you will be punished for crimes against the society, I think in that way you can look at it and see if it can be a deterrent because there are murders committed that certainly, you would not want to administer the death penalty for, for example, self-defence. Someone acting in self-defence you wouldn't want to hang that person for acting in self-defence, notwithstanding that it is a defence that can be used in presentation in Court. But I think it can have ah, it can have, I think it can have, I say that tongue in cheek I believe it can have some type of deterrent effect for some of the more heinous murders.

KLE: For example, could you give me an example of a heinous murder?

JF: I sit and plan your execution, leave and acquire the means to execute you, I acquire a firearm, I acquire bullets for the firearm and I have periods of time when I can change my mind. I hunt you down wherever you are and I kill you in cold blood. I think that is the most heinous of murders that we can commit. I believe that something like that, there should be some type of severe punishment for that.

KLE: If let's say executions were unacceptable what other alternatives do you think could be considered?

JF: The way they look at our education system because we can go into the area of what we call retributive justice or probably another dispute resolution method and if as you say executions were unacceptable then you are speaking about, to me, educating a population in the acceptance of a loss of a loved one with some type of compensation, not necessarily cash, but some type of compensation that would be acceptable to that person who experienced that loss to allow that person to continue on with their life or his or her life. So I think it makes a case for retributive justice for alternative dispute resolution for conflict resolution methods. Cause, loss of our loved ones not an easy thing to stomach, there would always be that urge to avenge that death and there has to be some type of system I do not have the answer, some type of system to bring about resolution for that, the party who suffered the loss can in some way accept and forgive even if he or she could not forget but forgive for taking the life of their loved one.

KLE: So in terms of, so if we are saying that no longer would we have that death penalty right, are you suggesting then that the offender pays a fine for the loss of somebody's loved one?

JF: Well, there can be a scale, nah a wouldn't put a fine, ah doh think yuh could put ah price, put a price on the life of a human being especially in that circumstance. You have terms of imprisonment. For example, you have life imprisonment that you can start with, depending on, as I said, the rating of the murder and yuh can look at terms of imprisonment for committing the act of murder.

KLE: Do you think strict legal procedures have eliminated punishment from being arbitrary or discriminatory as it relates to the death penalty?

JF: Strict legal procedures?

KLE: Strict legal procedures have eliminated that arbitrary discrimination associated with the death penalty?

JF: Explain that question, please.

KLE: Okay, if we have, do you think that having strict legal procedures in that legislative framework eliminate persons from being arbitrarily punished or discriminated against as it relates to the death penalty? Yuh understand? So if yuh have strict legal procedures, as in the death penalty ....

JF: As in the law?

KLE: Right. So it removes the possibility for the judicial officer from using their discretion yuh know, in terms of arbitrariness or discriminatory so you may say, 1 year am, because they committed this murder or 15 years for yuh know, for somebody else who committed a similar murder under similar circumstances. Do you think those strict legal procedures have eliminated that arbitrariness and discrimination?

JF: I want to feel that I jumped ahead of that question now that you have explained it. I would say probably yes and that's why I propose we should have a categorization of murder so that the judicial officer would have discretion as to how to impose sentencing upon a person found guilty of murder.

KLE: And that discretion will be based on? What will that discretion be based on?

JF: Well, certainly the categorization will be written into law, so that the law lords in our country will work out for a particular type of murder you have a window of X amount of years that you can convict a person to and you can use it going up according to the category that the murder has been given.

KLE: Alright, do you think the death penalty should be reserved for murder only or should it be used for other crimes such as treason and kidnapping and those crimes?

JF: Kidnapping—no (KLE's phone rings). Treason, sedition, and murder, wouldn't they qualify for the death penalty?

KLE: I am asking.

JF: (He laughs) Right.

KLE: Should kidnapping be reserved for murders only or should it be used for other crimes such as treason and kidnapping? What are your views?

JF: I think probably treason, kidnapping—no.

KLE: Treason, why treason and not kidnapping?

JF: Well, the nature of the offence yuh actually turn against the State and you can cause others to turn against the State and death sometimes can occur so I think probably for that, but kidnapping, I say no, for forcibly taking someone against his or her will and moving him away from one place to the next, once death doesn't occur, doesn't our law books have terms of imprisonment for kidnapping, I think that could continue.

KLE: I know we would have discussed this before, but I will still ask the question again just in case you would like to add something to it in retrospect. Should there be categories of murder with the death penalty being reserved for only the highest category of murder?

JF: A resounding yes.

KLE: You would like to add anything to that?

JF: I think, it might facilitate more persons probably experiencing the death penalty than what obtains right now. I do think so.

KLE: It will facilitate more ...

JF: More persons experiencing the death penalty than occurs right now.

KLE: Are you saying then that there are more persons who actually carry out heinous crimes?

JF: No, I am not saying that, but if our last execution was in 1999, the question needs to be asked as to why we probably might wonder is it because we have different categories of murderers in Death Row or not, I do not have the answer to that one.

KLE: Do you think that the death penalty is cruel and unusual punishment or is it deserved?

JF: The death penalty depending on how it is administered, I can consider it to be cruel and inhumane punishment, I say depending on how it is administered.

KLE: Meaning. Could you expand on that?

JF: I think death by hanging is cruel and inhumane. I think lethal injection is not cruel and inhumane.

KLE: Are you suggesting then that the death penalty should be used as a method of lethal injection?

JF: Yes something like that.

KLE: But not by hanging?

JF: As opposed to hanging. We have graduated from firing squad. We have graduated from public hangings. We have, in our jurisdiction, what we call semi-private hangings. I think lethal injection or you're put to sleep in a chamber, I think that would be less cruel and inhumane.

KLE: But, it is deserved, do you think it deserved the death penalty for persons who commit murder?

JF: Yuh know that is ah kind of yes and no answer. Yuh judge a society by its criminals, the way it takes care of its less fortunate and who has the most wealth. There are other markers. When a society is producing plenty of killers, it says something about the society. Those are things that need to be addressed in a society and that is why I say that murders should be categorized and the death penalty retained for the most heinous of the murders, of murders committed.

Because the way we devious in society, there are some persons who are bent on committing crime, bent on committing a murder, and a lesson should be sent somehow to others who may have that leaning, so that the death penalty should not be for everybody but I think that, work also should be done to find out why we, why any society, any society at all would be producing persons who are so willing to resolve their conflicts using that high level of violence, taking the life of another, something has to be going wrong with that society that is willing to solve its disputes in a violent way.

KLE: But based on the frequency of murders that we have and the levels of murder, what does it say about our society, in your view?

JF: That we are very disrespectful, we are confrontational, we are very violent, that is what I thought about our society.

KLE: I want to understand, some of our problems and successes that you have experienced, right. In your experience what policies or programmes have worked well and which have not in terms of crime reduction?

JF: An initiative that has taken a lot more traction lately, will be the police youth club. That is a wonderful initiative that could be translated into a policy to get at many of the youths before the criminals get at them. One of the things that we need to consider. For a policy that I think has not worked well is sometimes, there might be an interpretation that there is an inequality in the justice system where young offenders might be sent off to prison. When you have young persons who are exposed to criminal behaviour and they find themselves on the wrong side of the law and they pass through the judicial system and they are sent off to prison there is the possibility of easily being influenced by hardened criminals and many times persons like that become angry at society, even though they might have contributed to where they are, and we have to be careful that we do not end up creating more criminals as opposed to valuable citizens.

So sometimes the sentencing system that can be looked at, that might not always be the best method where sometimes young persons find themselves incarcerated with hardened criminals. As I say, the police youth club programmes, the community policing programmes, a programme that I believe is bearing fruit because they are trying to get to the young offenders they are trying to get to the citizenry to work with the police. That could augur well for the future of crime reduction in Trinidad and Tobago.

KLE: And the police youth clubs, they are one of the successes that you have experienced, are there any others? But before you go to the other successes, could you speculate what are the reasons for the success of the police youth club?

JF: I once saw a slogan that said, if you catch them when they are young they are yours forever and I spoke earlier about youth and feelings of invincibility. And if you have any young, any younger people venturing into what we call blue collar crime, violent crime, yuh have to try and catch them earlier, to share with them the virtues and values of being a civic-minded citizen of living a life of up-righteousness. As any programme that can get young people coming together for positive purposes I think is guaranteed to yield success. I think that it has been one of the major reasons that the police youth clubs have borne the fruit that it is bearing.

KLE: Are there any other successes that you have experienced?

JF: I spoke about the community policing effort that has been a success, probably as I go forward I will think about it, but right now I can't think of any.

KLE: What about problems in your experience. Let me read the question, in your experience, what policies or programmes that did not work well, in terms of crime reduction and why?

JF: Policy and programmes? Well, I spoke just now about the sentencing programme of having young offenders sentenced to terms of imprisonment, spending jail time with hardened criminals; that is not a programme that should be continued for sure.

KLE: And you say that was a programme in terms of crime reduction?

JF: That was a programme that will not reduce crime that can only cause crime to be inflated or increased.

KLE: But what other policies or programmes that may have been implemented that did not work well in terms of crime reduction?

JF: Right now, none comes to mind yuh know.

KLE: Yuh think everything that was implemented worked well?

JF: Not that but right now none comes to mind.

KLE: Okay, what for you what are three of your most important proposals for fighting crime?

JF: Way back in 1829, Sir Peel the founder of policing made a statement "the police are the people are the police" and we must never lose sight of that. The police must be legitimate in its actions, the public must trust the police, the police must be fair in the execution of its duty and they must be fair consistently. If the police perform as a professional body and perform fairly, the public will trust us. When the public trust us they will interact with us closer, much closer than they are right now and with that interaction, crime will be reduced because the public will have the confidence that they can call and report crimes and know that one, their confidentiality will not be breached and two, action will be taken in a timely manner to deal with the crimes that are occurring in their neighbourhoods.

KLE: Okay, could you now summarize those three points, identify the three most important proposals for fighting crime?

JF: Professionalism in the execution of our duties that will build trust and legitimacy. That will now come with what yuh call collaboration or a community effort with the police and the population will work as one. That then allows the police or the public to have the confidence to report crime so I will say professional in the execution of their duty, collaboration then we have trust and confidence.

KLE: Okay, if those are the three proposals for fighting crime what are your views in terms of its implementation, professionalism how are we to incorporate professionalism, collaboration, trust, and confidence, give me examples of what you will do?

JF: You need to have constant training and retraining or retooling of police officers in customer service and public relations. That will incorporate inter-personal skills and all of that. That will be more or less pushed by a vision of what the police service is supposed to deliver to a population. So we have training, retraining. The police service has a vision, it has a mission, it has a motto to protect and serve with PRIDE. I am of the view that before any team leaves the police station to go on any report or any exercise, the vision, mission, and the motto should be drummed into the heads of police officers and a constant reminder of a raison d'etre or reason for existence in the society, there must be reviews of all actions that were taken during the execution of our duties to see if we had achieved our goals and if we have fallen short, why we have fallen short and what we can do to improve with a view to achieving those goals the next time we are called for service. So I think that to summarize, if we are reminded of our vision, our mission and our motto, regularly, ad nauseum, if we are trained in customer service and public relations, if we do periodic reviews of our actions, I think we can have a better performing Police Service.

KLE: Mr. Forde, what are your perspectives on crime prevention?

JF: I think it is a valuable concept, if we can prevent crime from occurring I think you have won the battle.

KLE: And the Police Service current status in terms of crime prevention, what are your perspectives?

JF: We are doing a great job at present, the last figure we had about 30% decrease in crimes nationwide, that's an average, so we have been doing a great job on crime prevention.

KLE: What standard do you use to measure the greatness of the job that you do?

JF: Crime prevention?

KLE: Yes.

JF: Statistics provided by the Crime and Problem Analysis Branch. That is what I base my utterances on.

KLE: Is it then that, do you just compare previous years as opposed to current?

JF: No, I think they have been doing comparisons for about, from 5, 6, more, more than 2 years, they have been doing that comparison.

KLE: Over the years?

JF: And we have been seeing a trending downwards where crime is concerned.

KLE: Only as it relates to our local situation, meaning in Trinidad and Tobago?

JF: Yeah, I am speaking about Trinidad and Tobago.

KLE: Have you ever compared it with international standards, the crime rate, with other countries?

JF: Well, I can tell you I compared it with Honduras. Honduras has a murder rate of 177 per 100,000 (laughs) compared to us who ah think have about 30 something, great. So compared to a country like Honduras, whose population is more than us yuh know we ... (laughing).

KLE: Is it only Honduras you compared our crime rate with, Mr. Forde?

JF: No, I have not, but unfortunately, I do not have the data with me otherwise I would have furnished you with that information. I have done comparisons with other countries of the northern clines and the southern clines but I do not have that data with me at present.

KLE: When you say clines, what do you mean?

JF: Okay, like the northern hemispheric countries, like Norway, Sweden, Switzerland, compared to the Americas and then the southern, like the Latin Americas and ...

KLE: So you have compared it with Sweden?

JF: Yes I have.

KLE: What did you find?

JF: I do not have the data with me so I cannot give you that information.

KLE: Have you looked at countries around the world with the lowest crime rates?

JF: Yes I have.

KLE: Have you inquired in terms of their crime prevention strategies?

JF: Yes I have.

KLE: Have you been able to implement any of those crime prevention strategies and if not, why?

JF: Well I personally, have not implemented any and you will understand that where I sit I am driven by policy communication. I also function based on the laws of the land. So the laws of Trinidad and Tobago, I function within those laws. If a policy or law is formulated and comes and is given life and is communicated then I will go along that line but until such time again I have to function within the laws of Trinidad and Tobago.

KLE: Have you made any enquiries in terms of strategies that would have been implemented in any of those countries where they may have had a low crime rate that would not affect the laws of the land?

JF: Well, I've looked at several factors other than just laws, yuh know incidentally, I do recall the body that does, that produces reports ever so often that tells us about just as you say, the happiest countries with the lowest crime rate most favourable countries to live in and what they have found is that countries like Sweden, Norway, Holland, Switzerland, because of their homogenous nature are easier to govern, people follow rules easier or more easily than heterogeneous societies like ours so I do not know the studies that need to be done to look and see that, because of the homogeneity of their societies, compared to ours.

Additionally, they have long histories of war, warfare, killings and they seem to be settled now having learnt the value of life compared to us here who are still very young in our developmental stage. So there are questions that are I think, best answered by the scientists and not me right (laughs), about the shaping of yuh know things that they can put in place to reduce crime because we have laws that if yuh commit a particular crime, there are punishments and those countries have laws and something causes us not to adhere to those laws as easily as those other countries.

KLE: What would you consider to be the greatest problem facing the police at this time in terms of crime reduction?

JF: Trust.

KLE: Trust by?

JF: The population. The population does not trust us the way I think that they should and as such, they are not easily convinced to partner with us in that crime reduction drive.

KLE: Are you satisfied or dissatisfied with the development in the criminal justice system, after a sentence of death has been passed on a murderer?

JF: Could you rephrase that question, please?

KLE: Do you feel some sense of satisfaction or dissatisfaction in terms of the criminal justice where an accused person has been sentenced to death?

JF: I would feel a sense of satisfaction because our system is like any other system would be a probing of facts, if after probing all the facts, the court is, it has been proven that a particular person is responsible for the death of another and the court then administers the punishment that is mandated by law I am satisfied, whatever that punishment is, I am satisfied.

KLE: There are punishments that have been given to some accused persons that have not been carried out. Am I correct?

JF: Yes.

KLE: What are your views as it relates to those death sentences which have been passed on persons who have committed murders but yet, have not been carried out?

JF: That democracy is alive and well in Trinidad and Tobago.

KLE: And you are satisfied with the state of affairs as it relates to those death sentences that have not been carried out. Are you?

JF: Yes, based on the fact that persons are entitled to appeal because that is part of our democratic system and if it allows a person to appeal and it takes them however long that is beyond me and as I say if our system of law and order allows that then I have no qualms yuh know because that is our democratic system.

KLE: What about those persons who have not appealed their matters even though a death sentence has been passed on them but it has not been carried out, after so, after many years? What are your views?

JF: If a system like that occurs, then I think someone has fallen asleep on his or her job and should wake up and perform his or her function.

KLE: What do you think is most needed now to reduce the rate of violent crimes and murders in Trinidad and Tobago? You could look at violent crimes first and then we could look at murders separately.

JF: People in a society take their norms, their values, their morals from their leaders. I am a firm believer that when the leaders are good exemplars the rest of the society will try to fall in line. I believe that if we have double standards people make excuses to do wrong. The more good exemplars we have I think is the more we see the society with less crime, the more instances where persons who have been accused of committing white collar crime are investigated and if found guilty, if found to have been, if found culpable, charged and placed before the courts I think that might contribute to a much less violent society. Additionally, people need to be educated to understand that violence is not the only way or the best way to resolve the conflict. We need to teach people better inter-personal skills, how to communicate, how to empathize, how to resolve conflicts through communication as opposed to using violence.

KLE: And what do you think is needed now to reduce the rate of murder in Trinidad and Tobago?

JF: Upwards of 70% of the murders committed in this country are committed with the use of firearms and with the use of firearms in the hands of impressionable people I think what is most needed now, is a security blanket to prevent a lot of those firearms coming into the country because every day we are taking firearms off the street, every single day, we are taking firearms off the street and still people have access to firearms to kill other persons. We need to find a way to prevent those firearms coming into the country. I think that might help.

KLE: And how do we do that?

JF: We need to find ways to protect our porous borders. We need a sea wall not a literal wall but we need a sea wall. Our borders are too porous. They too open.

KLE: So are you saying Mr. Forde correct me if I am wrong that a lot of our firearms come via these porous borders?

JF: Well.

KLE: A lot of our illegal firearms—let me just qualify that.

JF: Well, based on information that I have been privy to from time to time, I strongly suggest a lot of our illegal firearms are coming through our seaports. I use the word seaport, not in the formal sense of a seaport that I use the word seaport and I link it to our porous borders.

KLE: What do you think then would be the role of the police as it relates to protecting our borders, porous borders?

JF: We will probably have to look at the re-establishment of a marine branch because remember we as the police, we are responsible for more or less land. It would be in exceptional cases we would go out to sea, but in the absence of a marine branch well let me put it this way, probably with the establishment of a marine branch then we can lend to the effort, once we talking sea we talking marine.

KLE: Is there anything else Mr. Forde that you would like to add as it relates to this topic or as it relates to the death penalty?

JF: The role of the police is to prevent crime also to detect crime and other infractions of the law. It has expanded but ah wouldn't go into the expanded part, but crime is not a police only activity, we need all these other sectors in the society coming on board. We need the other Ministries, the social services, the NGO's, the CBO's, we need all those bodies in a holistic effort working on one vision making Trinidad and Tobago a crime free society. It is a Utopian dream and I agree but, we work towards a crime free society. Until and unless all those sectors are working towards that one overarching objective or goal crime will continue to plague us.

The police alone cannot do it. We have all those other Ministries that are responsible for delivering service, as I said all those other NGO's or

CBO's, all have to be on board. Otherwise, 2 years from now, 3 years from now somebody else will come and conduct an interview with me about how to reduce crime and my views about crime and I may share the same information because I think, not because I am a police, but because I am a police on the inside, I know that the police, really doing yeoman service to this country. We don't always get it right, we make some mistakes and many of those mistakes are corrected as we go along, but I think the police doing yeoman service, but I believe that too many other agencies are falling down on the job and if we do not work hand in hand we would not arrest this crime situation.

KLE: If you had the authority to decide upon the punishment for someone who commits the offence of murder, what are your personal views in terms of what punishment would you inflict, if any?

JF: Well, firstly I will like to also have the opportunity to influence policy, that is formulation and I would want to see murders categorized so that we can give people terms of imprisonment by years and reserve the death penalty for probably the rare occasion when someone really commits a heinous crime. For example, like a mass murderer yuh know, I cannot in my good sense see a mass murderer being sentenced to 25 years or life imprisonment, so that, crimes of that nature, the most heinous of murders, we should have the death penalty reserved but it should not be used yuh know, arbitrarily. It should be used only when it is absolutely necessary.

Other than that, I am saying that persons who commit murders, they should be sentenced to years' imprisonment. The scientists in our society should be conducting sessions, they should be interviewing these murderers with a view of ascertaining if nurture or nature was involved, causing these persons to turn. That information can be fed back into the system so that we can look for the trouble signs and see when other persons, young persons coming up, if they are exhibiting that type of behaviour, we can intervene and prevent them from walking that road, because punishment alone, just straight punishment will not deter murderers.

The death penalty alone will not deter murderers. We have to be doing the studies, the scientists have to do studies, we have to be observing persons who are behaving in a deviant manner and see if they exhibit similar signs that can lead to them going down the same road so we can prevent that from happening and that is why I say the police alone cannot do it.

The police, researchers, it have persons who are specially trained to observe deviant persons, they need to also come on board.

KLE: I know you said punishment alone will not deter murderers? Right?

JF: Yes.

KLE: Why did you say that?

JF: Are we talking about the deterrent effect?

KLE: Yes.

JF: If a young person has a violent tendency because of whatever circumstance he, and I am using he, because it is mostly the he's who committing murders in our society, towards a brother he might have been exposed to and that can be spotted by an expert, a person who is specially trained to spot that. We will prevent a person who, from committing murders not just a murder, murders. I have spoken to persons who said that they were close to murderers.

They didn't want to admit that they committed murders and I recall a young man telling me once, when you kill a human being he say, it is a natural, he say yuh go home and yuh vomit, he say sometimes yuh defecate on yuh self but yuh holding it inside because yuh with yuh peers, he say it is not a nice feeling to kill another human being, he says but, there is a period of adjustment that takes place and yuh feel, yuh start to feel good about it and then there is a hunger and is like ah dog who has tasted blood, there is a hunger to go and commit again, he says and after the second or third killing it is easy to commit a murder after that.

That is a lost human being and we have to find ways to prevent that happening, so it is easy to say punish, hang like I say lethal injection whatsoever, but if nobody is doing the work to prevent murderers forming in society then I come back to what I said, punishment alone is a waste of time.

KLE: Whose job is it to prevent murders from being formed in society?

JF: All of us. All of us, the, the parents in the home have a responsibility to rear children who will be citizens that contribute to the well-being of the society, the schools have a responsibility, the churches, the other social organizations that children get into, the police officers, the stranger walking down the street who sees the young man behaving in a manner that is not expected of him has a responsibility to tell him something, all of us. If we allow ourselves to be by-standers and we live our lives by that syndrome then we can lay blame and we can tell the police solve more or we could tell the parents you are bad parents or we could tell the prisons you created this murderer but all of us have a stake in this.

KLE: Mr. Forde do you have any closing words?

JF: I want to thank you for giving me the opportunity to sit and share some of my thoughts with you. It is not easy to sit and speak with a level of clarity when you are hungry (laughs), but I think you have been a good host, so it was easy for me yuh know, to express my, myself. What I want to leave most is that the penalty for death, the penalty for murder, yes it is written in our books and we can execute people tomorrow, but a few planning for a country takes it beyond well, your existence on this earth.

It means that the powers that be, the policymakers have to find a way to get a message to every citizen that you are valuable, the person next to you is valuable and taking of a life is not the way to resolve your conflict and as such each and every one of us have a responsibility to make the society better and we can strive for a crime free country. I recall when I was in training 30 something years ago the words of my instructor are indelibly etched in my brain, he said if you shoot to hit the sky and you miss you sure you would hit the clouds, so if we aim for a crime free society it is not beyond us but we will get close to it. Thank you, ma'am, for taking time from your busy schedule to sit with an old man like me and hear me ramble (laughs).

KLE: Mr. Forde, I wish to thank you for availing yourself and to grant me this opportunity to interview you, it was indeed a wonderful interview. I enjoyed it tremendously and I wish the Trinidad and Tobago Police Service all the best and I hope we can go from strength to strength and find strategies that have been used by which we can treat with the crime problem we are currently experiencing or what we are to experience in the future. Thank you very much despite your famished state, I think you did really well and I am really grateful and wholeheartedly thank you not only on my own behalf but also on behalf of the author Dr. Wendell C. Wallace. Thank you very much.

JF: You are most welcome.

KLE: Thank you.

CONCLUSION

The interviewer felt the interview was informative and essentially corroborated with extant literature on the issue of the death penalty not being a deterrent (Ehrenfreund, 2014; Greenberg & Agozino, 2012). Although the interviewee felt that the death penalty does not deter, he suggested that following the last executions the crime rate and in particular the murder rate fell. The interviewee suggested that the death penalty was cruel and inhumane but still believed the death penalty should be used for the most heinous crimes; although as he suggested, it is not an effective deterrent. Then the question here is, why should the death penalty be retained if its purpose is not being fulfilled?

One of the major points of the interview was the need to categorize murders based on the circumstances under which it took place. Certainly, this view is in keeping with discussions at the local, regional, and international levels. In 2011, passage of the Capital Offences Bill tabled in Parliament, would have required an amendment to the Constitution of Trinidad and Tobago thus a pre-requisite was to obtain a two-thirds majority in the Senate and a three-fourths majority in the House of Representative which the government failed to secure and which would have seen the categorization of murders. Other critical issues raised were the involvement of young persons in heinous crimes, the ineffectiveness of other agencies, the country's porous borders, the prevalence in the use of firearms to commit murders and the dedication and commitment of police officers.

The interviewee was seemingly content with simply doing his job but not as passionate about the eventual outcome. Similarly, considering the interviewee is attached to the Homicide Bureau, his focus was primarily on murders although the interview was in relation to the death penalty, thus the interviewer felt it placed the interviewee at a significant disadvantage as critical issues as it relates to other offences for which execution is prescribed was not really ventilated. The interviewer felt that the interviewee did not elaborate on best practices from around the globe and admitted that he has not made real comparisons with other countries, including those with the lowest crime rates or murder rates.

The interviewer felt that if the Trinidad and Tobago Police Service is to reap positive rewards from their policing efforts they must adopt a "global posture," paying close attention and acting upon criminal events or activities around the world, particularly considering that today with the technological advances that have taken place and globalization, crime knows no border. Fortunately or unfortunately, despite repeated suggestions that a retributive system of justice upon which the criminal justice system is based is not serving the purpose for which it was designed, there seems to be no end in sight. Even if the policymakers were to replace such a system, Trinidad and Tobago is still ill-prepared as it would require significant adjustments to the legislative framework, policing style, and the justice system in its entirety.

The question which comes to mind from this interview is whether the actors in the criminal justice system are simply carrying out their duties and responsibilities without the confidence that their actions or activities will result in positive outcomes. If those charged with such a critical responsibility are sceptical about the system they are required to operationalize, how can it possibly work efficiently and effectively? Maybe, this study lays the foundation for furthering and broadening the discussion with the intention of finding feasible solutions.

REFERENCES

Allum, D., & Delzin, G. (2003). Report on the criminal justice system in Trinidad and Tobago. Para. 17; Bar Human Rights Committee. Retrieved from http://www.barhumanrights.org.uk/content/report-criminal-justice-system-trinidad-and-tobago.

Amnesty International. (2012). Death penalty in the English-speaking Caribbean: A human rights issue. Index AMR 05/001/2012. Amnesty International, International Secretariat, United Kingdom.

Clement, D. (2012). *Trinidad and Tobago human development Atlas 2012.* Port-of-Spain: Central Statistical Office.

Ehrenfreund, M. (2014). There's still no evidence that executions deter criminals. *The Washington Post.*

Greenberg, D. F., & Agozino, B. (2012). Executions, imprisonment and crime in Trinidad and Tobago. *British Journal of Criminology, 52,* 113–140.

International Covenant on Civil and Political Rights. (1969). Declarations, reservations, denunciations, withdrawals, B-32: American convention on human rights. *Pact of San Jose, Costa Rica*. Retrieved from http://cidh.oas.org/basicos/english/basic4.amer.conv.ratif.htm.

Parliament of the Republic of Trinidad and Tobago. (2011). The constitution (Amendment) (Capital Offences) Bill, 2011. First session of the 10th parliament: The constitution (Amendment) (Capital Offences) Bill, 2011. Retrieved from http://www.ttparliament.org/publications.php?mid=28&id=588.

The Constitution (Amendment) (Capital Offences) Bill 2011 Bill No. 2 of 2011; First Session of Tenth Parliament of Trinidad and Tobago.

Trinidad and Tobago Anti-Terrorism Act, Article 19(2) (b), Act 26 of 2005, September 13, 2005, updated to December 31, 2011.

Trinidad and Tobago Genocide Act, Article 3(1) (a), Act 1 of 1977, January 31, 1977.

Trinidad and Tobago Offences Against the Person Act, Article 4, Act 10 of 1925, April 3, 1925.

Trinidad and Tobago Treason Act, Article 2, Act 16 of 1842, July 22, 1844, updated to December 31, 2011.

United Nations General Assembly 67th Session, 60th Plenary Meeting. (2012). U.N. Document A/67/PV.60.

United Nations General Assembly Human Rights Council. (2011). Report of the working group on the universal periodic review: Trinidad and Tobago. United Nations Document A/HRC/19/7.

CHAPTER XII

CARIBBEAN POLICE LEADERS' VIEWS ON THE DEATH PENALTY, DETERRING CRIME, OBSTACLES TO EFFECTIVE POLICING, AND CRIME REDUCTION STRATEGIES

P olicing in the Caribbean is a divisive issue and so too is the death penalty. For many Caribbean residents, policing is viewed with scorn and derision; however, the yeoman and herculean mandate that Caribbean police officers are tasked with in the face of limited resources, is frightening. Added to this is the abysmal lack of contemporary policing tools (that is slowly being addressed), the over-reliance on the British Colonial Model of policing (traditional policing), which is the default position of most English-speaking police departments in the Caribbean and the general lack of co-operation and assistance by witnesses to crime. In spite of this, police officers throughout the region continue to perform their tasks diligently. Importantly, these police leaders possess a wealth of experience and knowledge that is important to harness. With this in mind, the manuscript is premised on the notion that research on policing should not be defined solely by academicians as policing professionals can offer contextual and practitioner knowledge. Instructively, emanating from the interviews with the Caribbean police leaders were thoughts and ideas as to barriers and challenges to effective policing, several strategies for reducing crime in the region, and importantly, views on the usage of the death penalty as a deterrent to homicides and violent crimes. These views are contained and discussed in the following paragraphs.

The Death Penalty

The very mention of the death penalty in the Caribbean invariably evokes passionate comments (Harrington, 2004). However, Birdsong (2005) points out that the death penalty remains on the statute books of almost every English-speaking Caribbean country via the "Savings Clause" which was inserted into their respective constitutions after being granted independence by Britain. It is in this context that the police leaders were questioned on their views as to what punishment they considered to be the most appropriate sentence for offenders who are convicted of homicide. On this question, the overwhelming response was the death penalty. This was followed by life imprisonment without parole.

Keeping in mind that Amnesty International (2012) argues that the death penalty as "cruel and inhumane punishment," the police leaders were asked to proffer their thoughts on whether they were in agreement with the pronouncement by Amnesty International (2012) that the death penalty constitutes cruel and inhumane punishment. Interestingly, four of the police leaders disagreed with the position advanced by Amnesty International (2012) that the death penalty constitutes cruel and inhumane punishment, three of the police leaders were supportive of the notion, and one police leader was non-committal on the issue. When asked whether the usage of the death penalty significantly reduced the number of homicides in their jurisdictions, three of the police leaders agreed that usage of the death penalty served to reduce homicides, three disagreed and two did not answer the question (citing lack of data to make a conclusive determination).

Importantly, the police leaders respondents were asked to identify from a list of four statements, the one statement that most closely represented their personal perspective on the death penalty. The statements that formed the list are as follows:

i. I support the death penalty and think it works well.

ii. I support the death penalty in certain circumstances.

iii. Philosophically, I support the death penalty, but I do not think it is an effective policing tool in practice.

iv. I oppose the death penalty.

The responses to this question serve to shed light on the personal perspectives of the police leaders and while it is not an adequate representation of the wider police leadership in the Caribbean, their views are of much importance as the respondents are police leaders in the region. Two of the police leaders were in full support of the death penalty and think that it works well, three of the police leaders support the death penalty in certain circumstances, and philosophically, two of the police leaders support the death penalty, but do not think it is an effective policing tool in practice. One police leader did not proffer a view on the death penalty. Importantly, but not surprisingly, none of the police leaders were fully opposed to the death penalty. This finding contradicts that of Dieter (1995) whose research found that a majority of the police chiefs in the United States were supportive of the death penalty, at least in the abstract.

Deterring Crime

It is important not only to solve crimes that are already committed but to deter convicted as well as potential offenders who may be minded to commit crimes. This is premised on the notion of specific and general deterrence (Mäkinen et al., 2003). With this in mind, the police leaders were questioned on what in their view is the most effective deterrent to the commission of homicides in their respective jurisdictions. The choices were: (1) the death penalty, (2) life imprisonment with the chance of parole, and (3) life imprisonment without the chance of parole. There was an even split of responses between choices one and three as 50% of the respondents favoured both the death penalty and life imprisonment without the chance of parole as the most effective deterrent to the commission of homicides.

The police leaders were also questioned on what in their estimation is the most effective deterrent to the commission of violent crimes (as distinct from the commission of homicides) in their respective jurisdictions. In the estimation of the police leader respondents, the death penalty was ranked as the most effective deterrent to the commission of violent crimes in the region. The second most effective deterrent to the commission of violent crimes in the region was the celerity, certainty, and swiftness of punishment for convicted offenders. This was followed by the implementation of harsher sentences, imprisonment for the rest of one's natural life, and long prison sentences with the chance of parole.

When asked whether the usage of the death penalty is the most important deterrent to the commission of homicides in the region, four of the police leaders were in agreement that the death penalty is the most important deterrent to the commission of homicides, three disagreed and one police leader did not proffer a response. This finding goes against that of Dieter (1995) who in his study on the death penalty as viewed police chiefs in the United States found that the police chiefs did not believe that the death penalty significantly reduced the number of homicides.

In response to the question on the usage of the death penalty as a specific deterrent (to offenders) to the commission of homicides, four of the police leaders were of the view that the threat of the death penalty serves to deter specific offenders, while three felt that the death penalty was not a specific deterrent. In a similar vein, the police leaders were questioned on the usage of the death penalty to send a message to would-be offenders (general deterrence) in the context of homicides. Four of the police leaders were of the view that the threat of the death penalty serves to deter in a general manner, while three felt that the death penalty was not a general deterrent to individuals contemplating the commission of homicides.

Obstacles to Effective Policing

Policing communities and the maintenance of law and order are of paramount importance to police officers in all jurisdictions. However, "policing is a difficult and complex task" (Cox, 2017, p. 3) and the implementation of crime prevention strategies is even more complex. With this in mind and noting the manuscript is solution oriented, the Caribbean police leaders were asked to identify the main obstacles to their success in trying to protect citizens and creating safer societies in their jurisdictions. The responses were wide and varied and encapsulated a plethora of obstacles and challenges that these police officers are confronted with on a daily basis and which often serve as mitigating (not justifying) factors in some instances.

Collectively, the main obstacles to successfully protecting citizens and creating safer societies in the Caribbean as espoused by the police leader respondents are listed below. These main obstacles (in decreasing order) are:

1. Easy access to firearms and poor law enforcement resources.

2. Overcrowded/overburdened court systems.

3. Slow court systems.

4. High unemployment rates in the region.

5. The prevalence of gangs/lack of respect for police officials.

In fact, 80% of police leaders listed the easy availability of firearms as a major problem in fighting crime and submitted the view that reducing the number of firearms would have a major impact on deterring crime in the Caribbean. Other obstacles to successfully protecting citizens and creating safer societies in the Caribbean included family problems, child abuse, and poor parenting.

Crime Reduction Strategies

An important aspect of the research was to seek out solutions from the battle hardened police leaders on the tactics that they would utilize to reduce the incidence of homicides in their jurisdictions. Based on the themes emanating from the discourse analysis conducted on the narratives of the Caribbean police leaders, increased police presence, visibility, and patrols were the number one strategy aimed at reducing homicides in the region. This was followed by enhanced border controls (due to the porous nature of borders of most Caribbean countries) and the implementation and usage of intelligence driven policing. The fourth most important strategy that the police leaders in the region envisioned as a tool for homicide reduction was the increased targeting and investigating of drug dealers and smugglers of arms and ammunition. The fifth most important strategy as elucidated by the police leaders as a tool of homicide reduction was education of and paying attention to juvenile offenders.

The police leaders were also asked to indicate their main choices of possible ways to reduce the incidence of violent crimes in the Caribbean. Consistent use of the death penalty was ranked as the number one choice of possible methods to reduce violent crime in the region, while increased social programmes aimed at the less fortunate in society was the second choice in terms of strategies to reduce violent crimes in the region. The third most popular choice of strategies is to reduce violent crimes in the region as espoused by the police leaders to increase the number of police officers on the street as a mean of deterring criminally minded individuals. Reducing the number of illegal guns in the respective islands (via enhanced border controls as alluded to in the paragraph above) was viewed as the fourth most important method of reducing violent crimes in the Caribbean as the leaders felt that the influx of guns (following drugs) into the region was a major cause of violence in the Caribbean. Improved police infrastructure and capacity was the fifth most popular choice of strategy aimed at the reduction of violence in the Caribbean. There was a consistent thread that ran throughout the interviews with the police leaders as they generally held the view that the police infrastructure and capacity in the region was not at its optimal level and that this somehow contributed to increasing levels of violence and criminality in the region.

CONCLUSION

This book on Caribbean police leaders' perspectives on the death penalty is novel in its approach. This position is premised on the notion that it appears to be the first manuscript emanating from the region that is exclusively devoted to shedding light on the views of regional (Caribbean) police leaders on a topic that evokes passionate comments—the death penalty. Instructively, there has been much research conducted on the death penalty, crime, and crime reduction strategies in the Caribbean; however, they were usually conducted by non-Caribbean researchers using a non-police sample as the proxy for their study. The current effort is "total local" in its ontology and authorship while aiming for a global readership.

This book is based on an examination of the discourses of eight ($N = 8$) police leaders in the Caribbean with an average of 28.9 years of policing experience and expertise. The authors aimed to attain an understanding of police leaders' views regarding the death penalty, deterring crime, challenges to effective policing, and crime prevention strategies in the Caribbean. Many of the leaders are University graduates holding undergraduate and postgraduate degrees in law, management, forensic science, policing, and other academic disciplines. In fact, of the eight police leaders who formed part of this study, only one did not hold a University degree. Importantly, the police leaders were all passionate about their jobs as protectors of life and liberty as well as enforcers of law and order. Collectively, their desire is to put their knowledge and experience on the front line to good use by doing whatever is in their power to reduce crime and deviance. Several of the police leaders support the death penalty to varying degrees, while others value its efficacy as a deterrent to serious crime.

For the majority of the police leaders who were interviewed, the death penalty seems to be a just, appropriate and legal sentence handed down to "vile, wicked, deviant, and recalcitrant" criminals who are bent on committing heinous crimes, including, but not limited to, murder, sexual assaults, robberies, and woundings without compassion to their often seriously traumatized victims. The police leaders opined that the criminal element then seek compassion from respective criminal justice systems (CJS) in the Caribbean, while they themselves failed to show any compassion to their victims. The police leaders espoused the view that due to the large numbers of protections and guarantees contained within the CJS (constitutional guarantees, DNA evidence, etc.) in the contemporary era, that it is highly unlikely that an innocent person will be sentenced to death. Further, they argue that while they understand the finality of death, the argument that an innocent person may be put to death does not resonate with them and that if the death penalty argument holds water, then an innocent man can similarly be convicted of rape. They, therefore, argue that if there is a problem with the CJS, then it should be fixed.

Without a doubt, police leaders throughout the Caribbean are deeply concerned about the crime problem, not only in their jurisdiction but due to the closeness of the region, the police leaders expressed their concern for the safety and security of residents and visitors in the entire Caribbean. While the police leaders are also concerned about the incoming tide of increased crime, they are also problem solvers and proffered several solutions to the challenges faced in their desire for effective and contemporary policing.

In sum, the Caribbean police leaders support a range of community programmes aimed at proactively fostering good values within Caribbean residents aimed at inculcating respect for the law. Instructively, then police leaders who were interviewed were equivocal in their position that the problems of crime and criminality cannot be solved by policing alone and proffer non-police programmes as possible solutions. These programmes include but are not limited to community policing, neighbourhood crime programmes, parental training and education, and a host of other engagement initiatives with community residents.

Several of the police leaders proffered the view that the creation of stronger family units, increased social capital in communities, proactive intervention on behalf of youth, punishing criminals swiftly and surely, controlling illegal drugs, enhanced border controls, and the creation of stronger economies with sufficient jobs and training are all necessary steps for the creation of safe societies and this will enhance the police's ability to reduce crime and deviance in the region. Many of the police leaders were supportive of the death penalty in principle but offered less theoretical support for it based on its lack of deterrent effect.

REFERENCES

Amnesty International. (2012). *Death penalty in the English-speaking Caribbean: A human rights issue.* United Kingdom: Amnesty International, International Secretariat.

Birdsong, L. E. (2005). The formation of the Caribbean court of justice: The sunset of British Colonial rule in the English speaking Caribbean. *The University of Miami Inter-American Law Review, 36*(2/3), 197–227.

Cox, S. M. (2017). Policing in the United States. In S. M. Fox, S. Marchionna, & B. D. Fitch (Eds.), *Introduction to policing* (3rd ed., pp. 1–15). Los Angeles: Sage Publications Inc.

Dieter, R. C. (1995). *On the front line: Law enforcement views on the death penalty.* United States of America: Death Penalty Information Center.

Harrington, J. (2004). The challenge to the mandatory death penalty in the Commonwealth Caribbean. *The American Journal of International Law, 98*(1), 126–140.

Mäkinen, T., Zaidel, D. M., Andersson, G., Biecheler-Fretel, M.B., Christ. R., Cauzard, J.P. et al. (2003). Traffic enforcement in Europe: Effects, measures, needs and future (Final report of ESCAPE). Espoo: VTT.

ABOUT THE AUTHORS

AINSWORTH SHAKES

Ainsworth Shakes is Deputy Superintendent of Police and the Chief Forensic Polygraphist for the Jamaica Constabulary Force (JCF) where he has spent the last 20 years in various areas of policing. Inspector Shakes currently leads a team of polygraph experts towards best practices in lie detection and has been instrumental in establishing law enforcement polygraph testing on the Jamaican landscape. His tenure in law enforcement has seen him working extensively with professionals in various areas of the criminal justice system locally, regionally, and internationally. As such, he is a member of the Canadian Association of Police Polygraphists and the British and European Polygraph Association.

At the local level, he is closely involved in community development and currently serves as the head of a local civic group that represents and articulates the views of stakeholders to the pertinent authorities. Inspector Shakes holds an MSc in Criminology and Criminal Justice from the University of Leicester and has been a guest lecturer at the Caribbean Regional Drug Law Enforcement Training Centre (REDTRAC) on a number of occasions. His quest is to further appreciate that which underscores deviance and to contribute to behavioural modification, thereby militating against high recidivism rates and facilitating effective methods of crime prevention. Inspector Shakes has a passion for articulating his views through the written word and enjoys stimulating discussions. He is also married and a father of two children.

ATLEE P. RODNEY

Atlee P. Rodney is a Deputy Commissioner of Police in the Royal Police Force of Antigua and Barbuda. He has been a police officer for over three and half decades. He is presently responsible for the administrative aspect of the Police Force which includes Human Resource and training. Over the years he has worked in several key areas of the Police Force. These included the Criminal Investigation Department (CID), the Narcotic Squad, the Special Service Unit (SSU), and the Prosecution Department.

He also served as the Chief Instructor at the Police Training Academy.

As a police officer, he has attended several training courses locally, regionally, and internationally on various subject matters including, Criminal Investigations, Senior Police Leadership, Project Management, Human Rights, Caribbean Security and Defence, and Disaster and Risk Management. In 2014, Mr. Rodney was seconded to the Regional Security System (RSS) Headquarters in Barbados where he served as the Staff Officer responsible for Operations and Plans. DCP Rodney has also served as a facilitator on several leadership RSS training courses.

DCP Rodney holds a Certificate in Public Administration from the Open Campus of the University of the West Indies and a Certificate in Public Relations from the Mona campus of the University of the West Indies. DCP Rodney also holds a Bachelor's Degree in Communication Science from the Universidad del Valle de Puebla in Mexico and a Diploma in Executive Development from the Cave Hill School of Business in Barbados.

KAREN LANCASTER-ELLIS

Mrs. Karen Lancaster-Ellis, President of the Association of Caribbean Caribbean Criminal Justice Practitioners (ACCJP), is the holder of a Bachelor of Arts Degree in Business Studies and a Master of Science Degree in Criminology and Criminal Justice. She is currently a Doctoral Student pursuing a PhD Degree in Criminology and Criminal Justice at the University of the West Indies, St. Augustine campus. Karen is an Adjunct Lecturer at a tertiary institution in Trinidad and Tobago, where she lectures in Police Management. She is also a part-time Tutor in Juvenile Delinquency at another tertiary institution in the island.

Karen is an acting Assistant Superintendent of Police in the Trinidad and Tobago Police Service (TTPS) at the Crime and Problem Analysis (CAPA) Branch. Her research interest lies in policing, punishment, corrections, organized crime, serious criminal offending, security planning, and white collar crime. Mrs. Lancaster-Ellis is the co-founder and first President of the Association of Caribbean Criminal Justice Practitioners (ACCJP) and the founder of the *Journal of Crime and Problem Analysis*. She has presented the findings of her research at several international conferences and her work is also published in several international Journals.

KELISHA A. FRANCIS

Kelisha A. Francis holds a Bachelor of Science Degree in Psychology and International Relations with First Class Honors and a Master of Science Degree in Criminology and Criminal Justice from the St. Augustine campus of The University of the West Indies. Additionally, she holds graduate membership from the British Psychological Society and is the co-author of a forthcoming publication entitled: *Living Dangerously in Trinidad and Tobago: An Assessment of the Cumulative, Comparative and Differential Risks Associated with Victims of Murders and Robberies in Trinidad and Tobago.*

KIM RAMSAY

Kim Ramsay is a clinical criminologist of 15 years standing. She was trained in Leicester in the UK in the field of clinical criminology. Miss Ramsay worked as a volunteer in the Leicester Probation Service while as a student with the Black Prisoner Support Project, which was a project aimed at supporting black prisoners from the Caribbean with issues they faced while incarcerated. On her return to Barbados, she worked as a Consultant with Her Majesty's Prison, Glendairy from 2003 to 2004 where she introduced a cognitive rehabilitation programme for inmates. She is presently employed at the Criminal Justice Research and Planning Unit as a Senior Research Officer, where she conducts research on crime and criminal justice. Some of her completed research include a self-report study on youth crime and delinquency, a study on homicides in Barbados over a 30-year period, recidivism of released prisoners from Glendairy, sentencing in Barbados, juvenile delinquency, and two public opinion surveys—one on crime and criminal justice issues in Barbados and the other on the Royal Barbados Police Force.

Miss Ramsay has been teaching Criminology at The University of the West Indies, Cave Hill campus for ~10 years. Her areas of interest are deviant subcultures, re-entry, prison research, and violence. Miss Ramsay has attended and participated in several international and regional conferences on Crime and Criminal Justice as part of her work at the Criminal Justice Research and Planning Unit (formerly National Task Force on Crime Prevention). Miss Ramsay's first book—*Barbados Most Wanted*—is forthcoming shortly.

MILISSA DUPRES-ROSERIE

Milissa Dupres-Roserie was born and raised in the small community of Desruisseaux located in the southern part of St. Lucia. She holds a Bachelor's of Science degree in Psychology with double minors in International Relations and Human Resource Management (First Class honours) and a Master's Degree in Criminology and Criminal Justice from the University of the West Indies, St. Augustine. Milissa is currently employed at the Bordelais Correctional Facility in St. Lucia. This has exposed her to many of the psychological and emotional challenges as well as social problems that youth face that influences the type of crime they commit. She believes in second chances for youth offenders. Therefore, her goal is to become a policymaker advocating for diverting of youth from the criminal justice system and the introduction of restorative justice in certain crimes committed by juveniles in St. Lucia. She is the founder of Kalon Girls Club which is an all-girls club for young girls between the ages of 5 and 13 which aims to assist girls with developing positive self-esteem, encourage holistic growth, and provide an avenue for recreation to offset negative peer pressure. In her spare time, she enjoys listening to music, reading, hanging out with friends, and exploring the beautiful island of St. Lucia.

MELLISSA IFILL

Dr. Mellissa Ifill is a lecturer in the Department of Social Studies at the University of Guyana. She has spent the past 18 years as a University lecturer in the Division of History and Department of Social Studies at the University of Guyana. Dr. Ifill is a former Vice President of the University of Guyana Senior Staff Association (UGSSA). In January 2016, she was appointed as chair of the Guyana Prison Service Board. In May 2018, she was re-appointed as chair of the Guyana Prison Service Board. Dr. Ifill's research interests include Democratic Governance, Ethnic Contestation, Citizen Security, Violence, and Crime—all with a focus on Guyana and the English-speaking Caribbean. She is Chairperson of the Guyana Prison Service Sentence Management Board and was the Project Manager for the U.S. State Department funded project "Engaging Communities in Guyana for Improved Implementation of Domestic Violence Laws" from April 2016 to June 2018.

PORTIA FRASER

Portia Fraser is the single mother of two daughters. She is the holder of a Bachelor's Degree in Business Management from the University of the West Indies, Open campus and is currently pursuing a Master's Degree in Project Management from the Global School of Project Management with the University of International Cooperation in Costa Rica. Professionally, Portia is a public servant presently attached to the Grenada Customs and Excise Department as a Senior Customs Officer, for the past 19 years. Her life's mantra is (1) "with God nothing is impossible," for the word impossible on a closer look says I'm possible, and (2) "if you fail to prepare, prepare to fail."

STEVE E. STEWART

Mr. Steve E. Stewart is an Attorney-at-Law, in St. Vincent and the Grenadines. Prior to becoming an Attorney-at-Law, he was employed as a trained teacher within the local school system, as a civil servant with the Public Service Commission Department and later served as Deputy Director and Director (Ag.) with the Public Sector Reform Unit in the Ministry of the Public Service in St. Vincent and the Grenadines. His last posting was with the Ministry of Labour where he had responsibility for all International Labour Organization matters. Mr. Stewart also served as National Coordinator of the St. Vincent & the Grenadines Labour Market Information System (SVG-LMIS). Mr. Stewart also worked as a part time tutor for more than 10 years with the University of the West Indies, Open Campus where he lectured on Public Sector Management, Organisational Behaviour and Environmental Relations at the undergraduate and Certificate levels. He also taught two modules of law with the St. Vincent branch of K. Beckles and Associates Law Tutors of Trinidad and Tobago.

Mr. Stewart is a published author as his article entitled "Facts Myths and Monsters: Understanding the Implementation of Public Sector Reform in St. Vincent and the Grenadines" has been published in Ann Marie Bissessar's edited book *Rethinking the Reform Question* (Cambridge Scholars Publishing, 2007). With an academic background in Public Sector Management at the graduate's level, and more recently, as a legal practitioner, Mr. Stewart has a keen interest in the development of public sector reform initiatives which include issues of criminal justice reform and penology.

SHERIDON M. HILL

Sheridon M. Hill is a member of the Association of Caribbean Caribbean Criminal Justice Practitioners (ACCJP), and an MPhil candidate in Criminology and Criminal Justice at the St. Augustine campus of The University of the West Indies. Sheridon is also a police officer and a qualified Attorney-at-Law. He currently serves as the Legal Officer for the Professional Standards Bureau of the Trinidad and Tobago Police Service. In 2005, he was seconded by the Government of Trinidad and Tobago to the Secretariat of the Inter-American Committee against Terrorism (CICTE) in the Organization of American States in Washington DC, United States, where he served as Program Manager Caribbean Affairs and later as Specialist and Consultant on Caribbean Relations in the Department of Public Security (DPS) until 2012.

He has served on several national committees on counter terrorism and information and intelligence sharing. Sheridon is the co-author of "The Private Security Industry in St. Lucia" in *Private Security Companies in the Caribbean*, UWI/Project Ploughshares (2013) and author of "The Rise of Gang Violence in the Caribbean" (2013) in *Gangs in the Caribbean* edited by Randy Seepersad and Ann Marie Bissessar, Cambridge Scholars Publishing. His latest publications include "An Emerging Regional Power: Trinidad and Tobago's Role and Influence on Caribbean Security" (2018) and "Drug Trafficking and Gang Violence in the Caribbean" (2018) (co-authored with Patrice Morris) in *Crime Violence and Security in the Caribbean*, edited by Dr. M. Raymond Izarali.

WENDELL C. WALLACE

Dr. Wendell C. Wallace, Vice President of the Association of Caribbean Caribbean Criminal Justice Practitioners (ACCJP), is a Lecturer in Criminology and Criminal Justice at the University of the West Indies, St. Augustine. He is the holder of an undergraduate degree in History and Human Resource Management, a Master of Science degree in Criminology and Criminal Justice (with Distinction), and a Doctorate in Criminology and Criminal Justice from the University of the West Indies, St. Augustine (the first student from all campuses of The UWI to attain a Doctorate in Criminology and Criminal Justice). He is also the holder of a Law degree from the University of London and a Postgraduate degree in Bar

Professional Training Course from Northumbria University, Newcastle, England.

Dr. Wallace also has professional qualifications in Alternative Dispute Resolution from the University of Windsor Law School, Canada as well as certificates in Caribbean Defense and Security from the National Defense University, Washington, DC. He is very passionate about the law and has been called to the Bar in both Trinidad and Tobago and England and Wales as a Barrister. As a student, he was awarded the prestigious title "Bar Professional Training Scholar" from the School of Law, Northumbria University, Newcastle, England and in 2014, his article "Addressing the Unmet Educational Needs of Children and Youth in Detention in Trinidad and Tobago" was awarded the Best Doctoral paper at the United States of America's Academy of Criminal Justice Sciences, Doctoral Student paper competition. Dr. Wallace is the recipient of the Frederic Milton Thrasher Award 2017 for Superior Accomplishments in Gang Research from the National Gang Crime Research Center (NGCRC) in the United States. His research interests include policing, gangs, violence, organized crime, school violence, and the tourism/crime relationship. He is an active member of the Accreditation Council of Trinidad and Tobago, the Honourable Society of Gray's Inn, London, the International Tourism Safety Association, the Caribbean Studies Association, and the Caribbean Child Research Conference Network.

www.ingramcontent.com/pod-product-compliance
Lightning Source LLC
Chambersburg PA
CBHW050648270326
41927CB00012B/2926